Together We Cannot Fail

FDR and the American Presidency in Years of Crisis

Terry Golway

Sourcebooks MediaFusion™
An Imprint of Sourcebooks, Inc.®
Naperville, Illinois

Photo and audio credit information can be found at the end of the book.

Published by Sourcebooks MediaFusion, an imprint of Sourcebooks, Inc.
P.O. Box 4410, Naperville, Illinois 60567-4410
(630) 961-3900
Fax: (630) 961-2168
www.sourcebooks.com

Library of Congress Cataloging-in-Publication Data

Golway, Terry
Together we cannot fail : FDR and the American Presidency in Years of Crisis / Terry Golway.
p. cm.
Accompanying CD contains corresponding speeches and addresses given by Franklin D. Roosevelt during his presidency.
Includes bibliographical references and index.
1. Roosevelt, Franklin D. (Franklin Delano), 1882-1945—Oratory. 2. Roosevelt, Franklin D. (Franklin Delano), 1882-1945—Oratory—Sources. 3. Roosevelt, Franklin D. (Franklin Delano), 1882-1945—Political and social views. 4. Roosevelt, Franklin D. (Franklin Delano), 1882-1945—Political and social views—Sources. 5. New Deal, 1933-1939. 6. New Deal, 1933-1939—Sources. 7. World War, 1939-1945—United States. 8. World War, 1939-1945—United States—Sources. 9. United States—Politics and government—1933-1945. 10. United States—Politics and government—1933-1945—Sources. I. Title.
E806.G64 2009
973.917092—dc22

2009007153

Printed and bound in the United States of America
BG 10 9 8 7 6 5 4 3 2 1

For Peter Kaplan

Contents

On the CD vii

Franklin Delano Roosevelt, 1882–1945 1

Part One: A New Deal, 1933–1936

Introduction 13

Chapter 1: Fear Itself . . . . [*Track 1*] 17

Chapter 2: The Beginning of a Conversation . . . . [*Track 2*] 27

Chapter 3: "The Country Was Dying by Inches" . . . [*Track 3*] 35

Chapter 4: "I Still Believe in Ideals" . . . . [*Track 4*] 43

Chapter 5: A Feeling of Security . . . . [*Track 5*] 51

Chapter 6: "A Rendezvous with Destiny" . . . . [*Track 6*] 59

Chapter 7: "I Welcome Their Hatred" . . . . [*Track 7*] 69

Part Two: Recovery, Recession, and War, 1937–1940

Introduction 79

Chapter 8: A Third of the Nation . . . . [*Track 8*] 83

Chapter 9: Packing the Court . . . . [*Track 9*] 91

Chapter 10: Distant Drums . . . . [*Track 10*] 101

Chapter 11: A Roosevelt Recession . . . . [*Track 11*] 109

Chapter 12: Purging the Democratic Party . . . . [*Track 12*] 119

Chapter 13: War . . . . [*Track 13*] 129

Chapter 14: A Stab in the Back . . . . [*Track 14*] 137

Chapter 15: Breaking with Tradition . . . . [*Track 15*] 145

Chapter 16: The Arsenal of Democracy . . . . [*Track 16*] 155

Part Three: Freedom's Champion, 1941–1945

Introduction 165
Chapter 17: The Four Freedoms. . . . . [*Track 17*] 169
Chapter 18: Lend-Lease . . . . [*Track 18*] 177
Chapter 19: Closer to the Edge. . . . . [*Track 19*] 185
Chapter 20: Day of Infamy . . . . [*Track 20*] 195
Chapter 21: Fear, Again. . . . . [*Track 21*] 203
Chapter 22: The Folks Back Home . . . . [*Track 22*] 213
Chapter 23: The Sands of North Africa . . . . [*Track 23*] 221
Chapter 24: The G.I. Bill . . . . [*Track 24*] 229
Chapter 25: Managing the Alliance. . . . . [*Track 25*] 237
Chapter 26: "An Unusually Bellicose Speech" . . . . . . [*Track 26*] 247
Chapter 27: A Prayer on D-Day . . . . [*Track 27*] 257
Chapter 28: Fala. . . . . [*Track 28*] 265
Chapter 29: "We Cannot Live Alone" . . . . [*Track 29*] 273
Chapter 30: Final Words. . . . . [*Track 30*] 279

Notes. 287
Bibliography 295
Index 297
Credits 307
About Sourcebooks MediaFusion 308
Acknowledgments. 309
About the Author 310

On the CD

The audio on the accompanying compact disc has been selected by the author to enrich your enjoyment of this book, to allow you to experience the words of Franklin Roosevelt in his own voice. These selections represent some of the most remarkable moments of his presidency and offer a window to the mind of the man. At the start of each chapter in the book, you will find an icon and track number denoting the corresponding speech on the CD. We encourage you to use, and we hope you enjoy, this mixed-media presentation of the life of Franklin D. Roosevelt.

1: First Inaugural Address • *March 4, 1933*

2: First Fireside Chat • *March 12, 1933*

3: Fireside Chat • *May 7, 1933*

4: Fireside Chat • *September 30, 1934*

5: Fireside Chat • *April 28, 1935*

6: Speech at the Democratic National Convention • *June 27, 1936*

7: Preelection Speech in Madison Square Garden • *October 31, 1936*

8: Second Inaugural Address • *January 20, 1937*

9: Fireside Chat • *March 9, 1937*

10: The Quarantine Speech • *October 5, 1937*

11: Fireside Chat • *April 14, 1938*

12: Fireside Chat • *June 24, 1938*

13: Fireside Chat • *September 3, 1939*

14: Speech in Charlottesville, VA • *June 10, 1940*

15: Speech at the Democratic National Convention • *July 19, 1940*

16: Fireside Chat • *December 29, 1940*

17: State of the Union Address • *January 6, 1941*

18: Speech to the White House Correspondents Association • *March 15, 1941*

19: Fireside Chat • *September 11, 1941*

20: Speech to Congress • *December 8, 1941*

21: Fireside Chat • *February 23, 1942*

22: Fireside Chat • *September 7, 1942*

23: State of the Union Address • *January 7, 1943*

24: Fireside Chat • *July 28, 1943*

25: Fireside Chat • *December 24, 1943*

26: State of the Union Address • *January 11, 1944*

27: Fireside Chat • *June 6, 1944*

28: Campaign Speech • *September 23, 1944*

29: Fourth Inaugural Address • *January 20, 1945*

30: Speech to Congress • *March 1, 1945*

Franklin Roosevelt in 1895, the year he turned 13.
He enrolled in Groton the following year.

Franklin Delano Roosevelt, 1882–1945

He was born into two prominent families, the only child of James Roosevelt and his second wife, the formidable Sara Delano. They were American aristocrats for whom the late nineteenth century was indeed a Gilded Age. Franklin Delano Roosevelt weighed ten pounds when he arrived into the world on January 30, 1882, a large child whose journey through the birth canal took twenty-six hours. Two months went by before his doting parents agreed on a name. Sara was determined to name her new son after her father, Warren Delano. But James Roosevelt wished to name the boy Isaac, in honor of *his* father. The disagreement was settled only when Sara's brother lost a baby son named Warren. As Roosevelt biographer Jean Edward Smith noted, Sara decided it would be inappropriate to name her son Warren following the tragic death of her nephew. She suggested a compromise: why not call the baby Franklin, after a favorite uncle? James Roosevelt agreed, and so the baby boy was christened Franklin Delano Roosevelt on March 20, 1882, in Hyde Park, the Hudson Valley town that the Roosevelts called home.

The Roosevelts were an old New York family of Dutch and English ancestry, which traced its prosperity and its prominence in America to a Dutch immigrant named Claes van Rosenvelt, who arrived in the colony of New Amsterdam in the middle of the seventeenth century. Successive generations built on the family's initial good fortune, so that by the time of Franklin's birth, the Roosevelts were well invested in railroads, global trade (including business in China), and real estate. Some contemporaries noted that the family, for all its affluence and connections, was not particularly accomplished. But surely nobody would say the Roosevelts were imprudent, for the family fortune survived the severe economic storms that swept away others before and after the American Civil War.

The Delanos were Hudson Valley patricians as well. Three Delano ancestors signed the Mayflower Compact in 1620, one of the founding documents in U.S. history. Warren Delano, Sara's father, added to the family fortune as a young businessman in China before the Civil War. He returned to the United States in 1842, met and married Catherine Lyman, and returned to China for several years. Children arrived with startling regularity. Sara, born in 1854, was the couple's seventh child on their way to eleven. The ever-expanding Delano brood was reared near the Hudson River port town of Newburgh, just south of the Roosevelt homestead in Hyde Park.

The match between twenty-six-year-old Sara Delano and fifty-two-year-old James Roosevelt pleased the bride's parents, for they had disapproved of their daughter's most recent suitor, a young, unproven architect named Stanford White. James Roosevelt was mature and wealthy—a member of the club. His wife had died in 1876 after twenty-three years of marriage, leaving him with a twenty-two-year-old son, James Roosevelt Jr. The elder James Roosevelt was enthralled by Sara Delano, beautiful and yet, given the times, somewhat old for a single woman. While she yearned for the man her father rejected, Stanford White, she seemed to welcome the attention of the older man who met with her father's approval. James Roosevelt and Sara Delano were married in 1880.

Sara was an especially doting mother, and James had the time and inclination to be a full partner in Franklin's upbringing. Young Franklin grew into a confident, optimistic young man. His family's combined wealth—the Delanos were much richer than the Roosevelts—allowed him to lead the life of a gentleman squire in training. He learned to sail in the Hudson River, he spent summers in Europe, he was tutored in foreign languages, and he developed interests, like stamp collecting and conservation, which would remain with him for the rest of his life. James Roosevelt was friendly with President Grover Cleveland, a New York Democrat, and on at least one occasion young Franklin met the president in the White House. "My little man," the president told the young boy, "I am making a strange wish for you. It is that you may never be president of the United States."[1]

At the age of fourteen, Franklin enrolled in Groton, a new boarding school for boys in Massachusetts. The school's founder and headmaster was an intellectually formidable Anglican minister named Endicott Peabody. He wished to create an adolescent version of Harvard University—a place where the sons of America's industrial titans would be inculcated in Yankee values, Protestant morals, and American manliness. Sports, including the new craze on campus, football, were emphasized as part of a boy's development. Groton students were aspiring gentlemen, but they also were expected to be tough and disciplined.

Roosevelt never forgot the lessons he learned from Peabody, including his admonition to hold on to the ideals of youth even in old age. He emphasized the possibilities of politics as a means to serve the nation and the common good. "If some Groton boys do not enter political life and do something for our land, it won't be because they have not been urged," Peabody said.[2] Roosevelt took Peabody's exhortations very seriously, but Peabody was not his only role model. A cousin of his, Theodore Roosevelt, was making a name for himself in the last decade of the nineteenth century. A Republican reformer, Cousin Teddy ran for mayor of New York in 1886 at the age of twenty-eight (he lost in a three-way race) and was elected governor a decade later.

Franklin followed in his cousin's footsteps when he enrolled at Harvard University in 1900. His academic career was solid although not spectacular. His most conspicuous success, and it was no small achievement, was his election as president of the university's daily newspaper, the *Crimson*. As president, Roosevelt was the paper's top editor, a distinction he relished. He wrote editorials, oversaw the paper's production, and worked with other student journalists. Later on in life, he proudly referred to himself as an old newspaperman—perhaps not coincidentally, he developed a famous rapport with the reporters who covered him during his presidency.

During his first year at Harvard, his father died of a heart attack and his cousin Teddy was elected vice president. James Roosevelt's death in December 1900 strengthened the bond between Sara and her son—they traveled together through Europe the following summer, consoling each other. While they were sailing home in September, they learned that President William McKinley had died of an assassin's bullet. Theodore Roosevelt was now the nation's chief executive. When Cousin Teddy ran for a full term of his own in 1904, Franklin eagerly cast his first presidential ballot for him.

Franklin Roosevelt earned a bachelor's degree in history in three years, but he stayed on at Harvard for a fourth year because of his commitment to the *Crimson*. He entered Columbia Law School in September 1904, while he was courting the niece of President Roosevelt—and his own distant cousin—Anna Eleanor Roosevelt. Two years younger than Franklin, Anna, better known as Eleanor, was the daughter of an alcoholic, philandering father, Elliott Roosevelt, and Anna Hall. Eleanor's mother died of diphtheria when Eleanor was just eight years old. Her younger brother died six months later of the same disease, and her father, unstable and perpetually drunk, died two years later. Eleanor moved in with her maternal grandmother and later attended a boarding school in England, where she was known as a serious, earnest student.

Eleanor and Franklin became engaged in late 1904 and were married on March 17, 1905. President Roosevelt, less than two weeks removed from his inauguration following the 1904 election, escorted the bride up the aisle. Alice Roosevelt, the president's daughter, was the maid of honor. The Rev. Endicott Peabody, headmaster of Groton, performed the wedding ceremony.

Sara Roosevelt built a townhouse for the young couple on Manhattan's Upper East Side. The new groom continued his studies at Columbia Law, passed the bar exam while still in school, and immediately began practicing. He never finished the required program at Columbia, and so did not receive his degree.

Eleanor and Franklin welcomed their first child, Anna, in 1906. Five more followed, but one, Franklin Jr., died in 1910 during a rash of infant deaths related to spoiled milk. Another son, born in 1914, would also bear the name Franklin Roosevelt Jr.

Eleanor and Franklin lived well, thanks to their trust-fund income and his work as a lawyer. But Franklin found the law tedious, hardly what he had in mind when he thought about Dr. Peabody's injunction to serve his fellow men and women. In 1910, Roosevelt ran for the New York State Senate on the Democratic ticket and won handily. His political career had begun.

He was not a particularly distinguished legislator. Like many self-styled reformers—and Roosevelt considered himself exactly that, in the mold of his cousin Teddy—he took every opportunity to denounce his fellow Democrats who ran Tammany Hall, New York City's dominant political machine. That position didn't win him many friends among city Democrats, including Tammany's boss, Charles Francis Murphy, and two of his young protégés, Assemblyman Alfred E. Smith (a future governor and presidential candidate) and State Senator Robert Wagner (a future U.S. senator and ardent New Dealer). The professional politicians from Manhattan saw Roosevelt as a wealthy lightweight who need not be taken seriously.

Roosevelt did have one asset that was hard to ignore—his famous last name. Cousin Teddy left the presidency in March 1909, but he was very much a presence in his home state. Franklin Roosevelt was the beneficiary of the state's fond memories of their unforgettable former governor, and Franklin sought to fashion himself as a reformer in his cousin's mold. Teddy busted business trusts; Franklin sought to bust the political machine's monopoly on power. He helped lead an upstate Democratic rebellion against Boss Murphy's choice for U.S. senator in 1911—state legislatures appointed U.S. senators until 1913—but Murphy simply changed candidates. Roosevelt saw this as a victory, but shrewder observers noted that Murphy got his way in the end.

A year later, Roosevelt outmaneuvered Murphy and Tammany when he led an insurgency on behalf of Woodrow Wilson's presidential campaign. The New York machine favored House Speaker Champ Clark, but Roosevelt and other reformers backed Wilson, the eventual nominee. When Wilson won the presidency, Franklin Roosevelt was well positioned for a job with the new administration. He had his eyes on becoming assistant secretary of the navy, a position his cousin Teddy once held. "All my life I have loved ships and have been a student of the Navy," Roosevelt wrote at the time.[3] The offer, the dream job, came through in March 1913, just before Wilson was inaugurated. Franklin Roosevelt quit the state senate and moved to Washington.

Roosevelt served at the Navy Department for the duration of Wilson's two terms, and so was a key part of America's mobilization after the United States entered World War I. Early on in his tenure, he became romantically involved with his wife's social secretary, Lucy Mercer, a member of an old Washington family that had lost most of its wealth. Lucy spent a great deal of her time minding the Roosevelt children, to their great delight. She was outgoing and playful, a far cry from their more serious, distant mother. Eleanor learned of the relationship in 1918, when Franklin returned to New York after a tour of Europe's battlefields. Franklin became seriously ill during the journey from Europe and was taken directly to a hospital after landing. It was left to Eleanor to unpack her husband's luggage; as she did so, she found intimate letters from her secretary to her husband.

There is some question about whether Eleanor offered to leave Franklin so that he might marry Lucy. But there is little question that Roosevelt's mother, Sara, and his chief political advisor, Louis Howe, argued against divorce. Franklin promised that he would stop seeing Lucy—a promise he kept until 1941, but then broke—and Eleanor agreed to remain in the marriage. Divorce in 1918 would have put an end to Franklin Roosevelt's political career.

While their married life was never the same, Eleanor and Franklin developed a mutual respect for each other's work and ideals. Eleanor Roosevelt went on to redefine the role of a First Lady through her activism, her support for unpopular causes like civil rights, and her staunch advocacy of progressive politics. Her husband would grow to depend on her advice and her observations.

In 1920, with the Mercer affair resolved quietly, the Democratic Party nominated Franklin Roosevelt for vice president on a ticket led by Ohio governor James Cox. The ticket was doomed, for the public was in the mood for change. Two terms of Woodrow Wilson, ending in the debacle over Wilson's plan for a League of Nations, led voters to choose the Republican nominee, Ohio senator Warren Harding.

Roosevelt performed well on the campaign trail despite the disaster, and returned to New York to consider his political future.

In early August 1921, Franklin Roosevelt joined his family at their summer cottage on Campobello Island off the coast of Maine. After a frantic week of recreation, Roosevelt began to feel ill. His temperature was high, but he had no symptoms of a common cold or any other familiar illness. His legs felt weak, and before long, he could not stand up. He was paralyzed.

Doctors were summoned to the island, and they made a frightening diagnosis. Roosevelt, they said, had contracted infantile paralysis, or polio. His life would never be the same.

As she came to terms with her son's condition, Sara Roosevelt saw little in Franklin's future but a long, peaceful retirement. He could, she thought, take over management of the family estate in the Hudson Valley and lead the sort of quiet life for which an invalid was best suited. Eleanor Roosevelt and Louis Howe had a very different idea: they believed Franklin still could pursue a career in politics, still could live the sort of life Dr. Peabody recommended so many years ago at Groton. It was a vision Franklin happened to share. It was a vision he was determined to realize, regardless of the rigors he faced and the obstacles he would have to overcome.

With determination and grit, Roosevelt learned what he called the "art" of "walking on crutches."[4] He "doggedly worked" on his rehabilitation, according to biographer Frank Freidel.[5] He was convinced that he would one day walk again, but while that remained an impossible dream, he taught himself to "walk" by strapping his useless legs into heavy braces, swinging his hips, and leaning on a cane or on somebody's arm. And, all the while, he followed politics.

Incredibly, on June 26, 1924, Franklin Roosevelt appeared as a featured speaker at the Democratic National Convention in New York's Madison Square Garden. New York governor Alfred E. Smith, one of two leading candidates for the party's presidential nomination, asked Roosevelt to place his name in nomination. Roosevelt agreed, setting the stage for his first appearance since being stricken.

Behind the scenes, far from the eyes of the thousands of delegates and reporters, he was wheeled to a spot near the main podium. He was helped to his feet, his legs encased in braces, a crutch partially hidden under his right arm, his left arm leaning on his son, James. Then he emerged on the convention's stage, "walking" several steps by swinging his hips and leaning heavily on his son's arms. And he was smiling, a great, happy smile that took eyes away from his withered legs. It was as courageous a performance as any in American political history. Roosevelt's brow was soaked in sweat once he reached the podium and gripped it with both hands to steady himself. And still he smiled. The warring delegates hushed in shared admiration.

Roosevelt sought to broaden Smith's appeal beyond the northeast, no small task. Smith was a Catholic, a city dweller, and an opponent of Prohibition at a time when the party was Southern Protestant, rural, and dry. Roosevelt addressed not only the party's urban delegates, but also those who came from "the plains and hills of the West, from the slopes of the Pacific and from the homes and fields of the Southland." He argued that they would find in Al Smith of the Lower East Side a man who understood their problems, even if his working class, ethnic New York accent sounded foreign, even if his immigrant roots might make him exotic. Smith, he said, "had the rare power to express the great fundamental truths and ideals in homely language carrying conviction to the multitude."

Then, as he officially placed Smith's name in nomination, he read the lines that made his speech famous: "He is the 'Happy Warrior' of the political battlefield," he said, his voice rising as the cheers from his fellow New Yorkers began to rise from the gallery. "Alfred E. Smith!"

Four years later, Franklin Roosevelt was nominated to replace Smith as governor of New York after Smith won the 1928 presidential nomination. Smith, the first Catholic to lead a major party's national ticket, lost in a landslide that almost led to Roosevelt's defeat as well. After nearly a decade of prosperity and peace under Republican administrations, even New York voters were not eager for change in the White House, despite their affection for Smith.

As governor, Roosevelt built on Smith's formidable legacy of social reform, although he did so without some of Smith's key advisors, like Robert Moses and Belle Moskowitz, who were instrumental in implementing Smith's policies in the 1920s. But he brought into office a talented group of his own advisors, including Howe, Edward J. Flynn, the boss of Bronx County, and Raymond Moley, a political science professor at Barnard College, while retaining some of Smith's people, like Frances Perkins.

Given the magic of his name and the prominent office he held—for to be governor of New York in the first half of the twentieth century was to be considered presidential material—it seemed just a matter of time before Roosevelt sought higher office. His landslide reelection in 1930 made him a national figure and a presumed presidential candidate in 1932.

By the time Roosevelt won his second two-year term, New York and the nation were beginning to suffer the effects of a stock market crash in 1929. The Great Depression shadowed the land in 1930 and only became bigger and bleaker during the ensuing months. President Herbert Hoover, who soundly defeated Al Smith in 1928, had the look of a lame duck as he tried to come to terms with the economic catastrophe around him.

As Hoover's reelection prospects dimmed, confident Democrats looked forward to their first presidential victory since Woodrow Wilson's reelection in 1916. But Franklin Roosevelt was not the only Democrat who saw himself as Hoover's successor. Another popular Democrat believed the party owed him a second chance—Al Smith.

Smith had a devoted base of Catholic voters, many of them Irish, and the support of Tammany Hall, which resented Roosevelt's decision to investigate corruption charges against New York City mayor James Walker, a Tammany man. But by 1932, Franklin Roosevelt was a much shrewder, more complicated politician than he was in 1911, when he reflexively condemned urban political bosses and machines. While Tammany did not support him, other urban bosses did, including Ed Flynn of the Bronx, James Farley of New York, and other Irish Catholic leaders who saw Roosevelt as a winner and Smith as yesterday's candidate. At a stormy, tense, and historic convention in Chicago, Roosevelt won the nomination on the fourth ballot. He immediately flew from New York to Chicago to accept the nomination in person, something no candidate had ever done before. The flight was bumpy and late, but when Roosevelt arrived in the early evening on July 2, 1932, a band broke into a rendition of "Happy Days Are Here Again," and Roosevelt delivered a speech in which he pledged a "New Deal" for the American people.

The following November, he and running mate John Garner of Texas won a smashing victory over Hoover, taking 57 percent of the vote to Hoover's 39 percent, and 472 electoral votes to Hoover's 59.

Franklin Roosevelt would go on to win three more terms, and serve for more than twelve years before dying in office on April 12, 1945, in Warm Springs, Georgia. In poor health for months, Franklin Roosevelt died while sitting for a portrait. With him was Lucy Mercer Rutherfurd, his onetime mistress and his frequent companion once again.

He entered office in the midst of a worldwide economic catastrophe, and dared to speak of hope. He taunted his fellow American elites, and shaped his words to appeal to ordinary Americans. Through the medium of radio, he carried on a conversation with the American people that no president has been able to repeat. His husky voice and his patrician accent reassured the nation that all was not lost, as long as they did not allow their fear to overcome their natural American optimism.

When the nation's attention moved from hard times at home to war abroad, Roosevelt's message remained the same: fear, not poverty, not fascism, was America's greatest enemy. All people, he said, deserved to be free from fear.

Fearless he was, when so many around him believed that polio meant an end to his ambitions, when so many believed that the nation was doomed during the Depression, when the nation's Pacific Fleet was sent to the bottom of Pearl Harbor. His voice, his words, bolstered the nation's spirits. And for decades after his death, Americans who gathered by the radio to hear their president speak would think of him not just as a great leader, but as a friend—a friend who wouldn't let them give in to their fears.

PART ONE:
A New Deal, 1933–1936

Introduction

Franklin Roosevelt's election as president in 1932 was a foregone conclusion once he obtained his party's nomination against his onetime friend and colleague, Alfred E. Smith. Incumbent president Herbert Hoover was a political pariah destined to be remembered as a man overtaken and overwhelmed by the nation's worst economic catastrophe, the Great Depression. Roosevelt's victory was not so much an affirmation of the Democratic Party platform as it was a resounding rejection of Hoover's performance since the stock market crash of 1929.

The new administration, however, had to wait until March to take office, because a new constitutional amendment changing Inauguration Day from March 4 to January 20 did not take effect until 1937. During the long interregnum, Hoover sought to co-opt the president-elect by asking him to commit to a balanced budget while rejecting calls for massive public works spending. Roosevelt refused to do so.

As the new president took office, the unemployment rate was nearly 25 percent. In some cities, half of all workers were jobless. Hospitals were recording deaths due to starvation. Hundreds of banks had failed; the life savings of millions had disappeared.

Roosevelt, faced with a peacetime calamity like no other in the nation's history, wasted no time acclimating to his new position. He immediately ordered a bank holiday to shore up the nation's financial system. Then, over the next one hundred days, the new president proposed a series of relief measures, including federal aid to the unemployed and assistance to farmers, which greatly expanded the reach of federal power.

Later in his first term, Roosevelt replicated his initial success with another package of reforms designed to provide long-term solutions to economic instability. The National Labor Relations Act, the Social Security Act, and other measures were the foundation of a new economic and political order that emphasized government's role in providing a measure of collective economic security in a nation that prized individual effort.

Roosevelt's first term ensured his place in American history. But it was only the beginning of his legacy.

An enthusiastic campaigner, Roosevelt connected with voters with folksy stump speeches and a broad smile.

CHAPTER I

Fear Itself

First Inaugural Address

March 4, 1933

TRACK I

ALTHOUGH HE HAD BEEN GOVERNOR OF NEW YORK FOR ONLY THREE YEARS, Franklin Roosevelt had his eyes fixed firmly on the White House as the election year of 1932 began. Politicians and commentators had been speculating about his ambitions for more than two years; in fact, on the day after Roosevelt won a smashing reelection as governor in 1930, humorist Will Rogers wrote, "The Democrats nominated their president yesterday, Franklin D. Roosevelt."

A week after the announcement, on January 30, the governor's inner circle was invited to Hyde Park to celebrate Roosevelt's fiftieth birthday. Edward J. Flynn, the Democratic boss of Bronx County and secretary of the state—a job that gave him authority over the electoral process in New York—was among those in attendance. As a memento of the occasion, he received a place card from Roosevelt with a poem written in his honor:

The Secretary of the State
(Our Constitution doth relate)
Must certify our people's voice
As who for President's their choice
Oh! Flynn I hope you will remember
I'm your friend—come next November.[1]

Roosevelt, of course, was counting on a great many friends come November. The key was getting there. Roosevelt was not the only Democrat with presidential ambitions, for it was becoming clear that the party's nominee very likely would become the next president of the United States. After losing three consecutive presidential campaigns and seven of the last nine, Democrats understood that victory was, at last, within their grasp.

That confidence, albeit born of suffering and despair, was something entirely new for a generation of Democrats that came to power in the first quarter of the twentieth century. Even Woodrow Wilson's victories in 1912 and 1916 were hardly ringing endorsements of Democratic policies. Wilson owed his first win to the bitter split between two Republican presidents, incumbent William Howard Taft and his predecessor, Theodore Roosevelt. In a four-way race with the Republican Taft, the Progressive Roosevelt, and the Socialist Eugene V. Debs, Wilson won just 42 percent of the vote. His reelection in 1916 was similarly unimpressive: he defeated Charles Evan Hughes by just twenty-three votes in the Electoral College. California put Wilson over the top, but he won the state by fewer than four thousand votes.

The presidential campaign of 1932 figured to be a very different story. Democratic victories in the off-year races for Congress in 1930 indicated that stunned and angry Americans would demand drastic changes to meet an economic calamity that Hoover seemed incapable of resolving. With that in mind, Roosevelt's friend and aide Louis Howe kept up an extensive correspondence with Democratic activists around the country, creating a huge network of potential supporters. And as the effort began in earnest, Roosevelt assigned James Farley, secretary of New York's Democratic State Committee, to travel the country and meet personally with key Democratic leaders in an effort to win their support. Farley was a brilliant choice, for he was gregarious and charming, an ideal political salesman and an absolute Roosevelt loyalist.

The work of Howe and Farley was critical in an era in which party leaders, not primary voters, played a decisive role in determining presidential nominees. That is not to say the leaders were a monolith capable of simply imposing their will on the party's rank and file. The Democratic convention of 1924 demonstrated the deep divisions that could exist among party bosses with competing agendas. Nevertheless, as Roosevelt knew, support from leaders representing a cross-section of the country was invaluable heading into a presidential convention.

Roosevelt's fledgling candidacy faced one obstacle that neither Howe's letters nor Farley's meetings could easily overcome. The obstacle's name was Alfred E. Smith.

Al Smith knew what Roosevelt's people knew, indeed, what so many other Americans knew as well: the candidate chosen by the 1932 Democratic National Convention very likely would defeat Hoover in the fall. Smith believed the party owed him for his valiant but doomed campaign in 1928, when prosperity, Prohibition, and prejudice combined to thwart his dream of becoming the nation's first Catholic president.

As the early maneuvering got underway, Smith told Flynn that he was not interested in the presidency. But, to Flynn's surprise, Smith had a change of heart. On February 8, 1932, as Roosevelt's men were wooing fellow Democrats, and newspapers were openly discussing Roosevelt's as yet unannounced candidacy, Smith released a statement saying that if "the Democratic National Convention...should decide that it wants me to lead, I will make the fight."[2] Soon afterwards, after Roosevelt delivered a radio address in which he spoke of the plight of the "forgotten man," Smith delivered an angry speech implicitly accusing his friend and successor of trying to "stir up" the "poor against the rich." This, he said, "is not time for demagogues."[3]

The stage, then, was set for a titanic battle between two New York governors who worked with each other and supported each other through the 1920s. Smith, bitter over his defeat in 1928 and especially his failure to carry his home state, had a difficult time reconciling himself to Roosevelt's rise to prominence and the ease with which he became a national figure. Roosevelt encountered none of the class prejudice Smith faced among the party's intellectual leaders. In 1928, the *Nation*, a reliably Democratic periodical, engaged in a soul-searching debate about whether or not liberals should vote for Smith—the editors were not especially enthusiastic, and left it to readers to decide for themselves whether to cast their ballot for Smith or for Norman Thomas, the Socialist Party candidate with elite, Progressive sensibilities. There would be no such hand-wringing over Roosevelt's prospective candidacy.

While Smith had a tendency to underestimate Roosevelt, FDR did not make a similar mistake when it came to Smith. In the battle for support of key urban Democrats, FDR knew that Smith, a proud child of Manhattan's Lower East Side, had a decided advantage. "Al Smith knows these city people better," Roosevelt conceded. "He can move them. I can't."[4]

He was relying, then, on city people like Flynn and Farley to achieve what he could not. And they had their work cut out for them. Although Roosevelt won the New Hampshire primary in March and party caucuses in the west and rural plains, Smith handily defeated FDR in the Massachusetts primary in late April. Smith then won Rhode Island and Connecticut while California went to a dark horse from Texas, John Garner.

But that was the public campaign. Behind the scenes, Roosevelt's deputies worked on local party officials and decision-makers—and it was hardly an accident that among the campaign's chief implementers were Flynn and Farley, who were, like Smith, Irish Catholic. While both of them, along with Boston mayor James Michael Curley, liked and admired Smith, they also were haunted by the defeat of 1928. The country, it seemed to them, was not prepared to elect a Catholic, and they were not inclined to support a noble but doomed cause. Quietly but effectively, Roosevelt's forces piled up commitments by the hundreds.

Lurking in the background was the jaunty figure of New York City's Jazz Age, Mayor Jimmy Walker, the successful son of Irish-Catholic immigrants. A onetime colleague of Roosevelt's in the New York State Senate, Walker was a charismatic but not especially dutiful public official whose heart and taste seemed more suitable to show business and the 1920s than the Depression and 1932. In fact, before he became a politician, he wrote the lyrics to a song that remains well-known even today: "Will You Love Me in September (As You Do in May)?"

A state investigation led by Judge Samuel Seabury was looking into corruption in the Walker administration, which was aligned with Tammany Hall. The machine, which had promoted progressive reformers like Al Smith, Robert Wagner, and Ed Flynn, reverted to its dark side after the death of legendary boss Charles F. Murphy in 1924, immersing itself in rackets, kickbacks, and other illegal activities during Walker's watch. Seabury's investigation was a political nightmare in the making for Roosevelt. A huge scandal in his home state might doom his candidacy, but if he went along with calls to remove Walker from office, as he was empowered to do, he risked offending his party's Irish-Catholic base, including big-city bosses. As the convention neared, Seabury sent Roosevelt a copy of his case against Walker, including accusations of outright corruption by the mayor himself. Roosevelt sent Seabury's report to Walker, demanding a response. The mayor replied coolly that Roosevelt would have to wait until the convention was over.

As the Democratic convention opened in Chicago on June 27, 1932, Roosevelt lacked the 768 votes needed for the nomination, but his total of about six hundred delegates gave him a huge edge over Smith, who had less than a hundred. A sign of Roosevelt's strength came early on, when his choice for the convention's permanent chairman, Senator Frank Walsh of Montana, won the spot after hours of back-room maneuvers over rules and procedures.

After the nominating speeches, the delegates began the long process of roll-call ballots. Roosevelt won 666 on the first ballot, short of the required two-thirds majority. Two more ballots followed, with similar results. Roosevelt's momentum, it seemed, had stalled; talk began to center on possible compromise candidates. Roosevelt's forces feared that their allies in the South were about to break ranks, so Flynn, monitoring the proceedings from a hotel room, ordered Louisiana governor Huey Long to have a candid chat with his colleagues from Mississippi and Louisiana. According to Flynn's account, Long told senators from those two states that if they strayed from the Roosevelt line, "I'll break you."[5] They did not stray, and Roosevelt won the nomination on the fourth ballot, with Texas providing the clinching votes. After Texas voted, a band in the hall began playing "Happy Days Are Here Again."

The following day, July 2, Franklin Roosevelt boarded a plane and flew to Chicago to accept the nomination in person. No candidate had ever done so before, but Roosevelt was determined to show voters that he was prepared to bring about change. Months earlier, in his "Forgotten Man" address, he said that "the country demands bold, persistent experimentation."[6] His dramatic appearance in the convention hall was in keeping with those demands.

To the cheering delegates, who soon would return to suffering cities, towns, and farms, Roosevelt offered a promise. "I pledge you, I pledge myself, to a new deal for the American people.…Give me your help, not to win votes alone, but to win in this crusade to restore America to its own people."[7] Those were words that the Al Smith of 1932 could not have delivered. It was one thing to promise a new deal, one thing to promise a return to prosperity—it was quite another to promise to "restore America to its own people." The phrase had more than an edge of class antagonism; that a patrician from the Hudson Valley delivered it made the phrase all the more intriguing.

Roosevelt was triumphant. He was the Democratic Party's presidential nominee in a year when a Democratic victory seemed almost certain. But he also was governor of New York. And wearing that hat, Roosevelt began to take care of his unfinished business with Mayor Walker. He personally presided over a public grilling of the mayor in August. Walker resigned on September 1.

The last real obstacle to Roosevelt's election had passed. A nation that at times seemed moving towards revolution was not about to return Herbert Hoover to the White House. During the summer, the U.S. Army, under the personal command of Chief of Staff Douglas MacArthur, used tear gas to remove an informal army of veterans encamped on the National Mall and demanding bonuses promised them after World War I. The sight of soldiers using violence on civilian protesters was frightening, because it seemed to offer a glimpse of the nation's future.

On Election Day, Franklin Roosevelt won 23 million popular votes and 472 votes in the Electoral College, compared with Hoover's 16 million and 59 electoral votes. The nation rallied to the promise of a new deal.

Roosevelt was about to become the last president inaugurated in March, rather than January. (The Twentieth Amendment changed the date of the new term from March 4 to January 20.) During the long four months between Roosevelt's victory and the start of the new administration, the nation's economy worsened. Farmers in the plains states were burning their corn as fuel during the winter. Bread lines snaked through entire neighborhoods in the nation's urban centers. In February, with his inauguration a month away, Roosevelt traveled to Miami to give a speech. Afterwards, as the president-elect sat in an open car, a man named Guiseppe Zangara fired five shots from a park bench about ten yards away. Chicago mayor Anton Cermak, who was chatting with the president-elect when the assailant opened fire, crumpled to the ground, wounded in the stomach. Despite his own disability, Roosevelt calmly helped pull the bleeding Cermak into the car and comforted him during a frenzied trip to a nearby hospital, but the mayor died several weeks later. Zangara was convicted of murder and executed.

Roosevelt returned north, to Hyde Park, to begin work on his inaugural address. On the evening of February 27, as he sat near a roaring fireplace that helped take the winter chill out of his bones, the president-elect drafted a version of the speech in longhand on a yellow legal pad. It began with a stiff, formal opening line: "I am certain that my fellow Americans expect that on my induction to the Presidency I will address them with a candor and a decision which the present situation of our nation impels."

The longhand draft was typed and revised as late as March 3, the day before Roosevelt took office. That morning, a cold, gray day, Roosevelt added a phrase in the typewritten copy, describing Inauguration Day "a day of consecration." Roosevelt's last-minute tinkering with the speech was not unusual, according to speechwriter Samuel Rosenman. It was, he wrote, "typical of what the President could do with a speech—even in the great rush and excitement of those days before his first inauguration."

The speech's most memorable line is in the speech's first paragraph, part of a longer sentence that has been chopped down to the famous sound bite. After assuring the anxious nation that it would "endure as it has endured, will revive and will prosper," Roosevelt said: "So, first of all, let me assert my firm belief that the only thing we have to fear is fear itself—nameless, unreasoning, unjustified terror which paralyzes needed efforts to convert retreat to advance." Roosevelt delivered the line perfectly, pausing between the words "fear is" and "fear itself."

Rosenman, one of FDR's best-known speechwriters, later confessed that he had no idea where Roosevelt came up with the line, and never asked him. He noted, however, that the line sounded something like a phrase composed by Henry David Thoreau, who observed that "nothing is so much to be feared as fear." Eleanor Roosevelt said that a friend of hers gave Roosevelt a Thoreau collection shortly before the inauguration, and she noticed the book in the president-elect's hotel suite. Rosenman thought this a likely explanation.

What is extraordinary about the rest of the speech are its jagged edges. Roosevelt took office at a time of crisis, but his inaugural address was not entirely a unifying document. Fingers were pointed; blame was assigned. The economic catastrophe was not the result of a natural disaster, like a plague of locusts, but the result of the "stubbornness" and "incompetence" of the "rulers of the exchange of mankind's goods."

"Practices of the unscrupulous money changers stand indicted in the court of public opinion, rejected by the hearts and minds of men," he said to his immediate audience and to the millions who listened on radio. "They know only the rules of a generation of self-seekers. They have no vision, and when there is no vision the people perish.

"The money changers have fled from their high seats in the temple of our civilization. We may now restore that temple to the ancient truths. The measure of the restoration lies in the extent to which we apply social values more noble than mere monetary profit."

The restoration process would include a change in the nation's values, he said. Americans had to be reminded that happiness "lies not in the mere possession of money; it lies in the joy of achievement, in the thrill of creative effort." The suggestion that money could not buy happiness might have rung hollow with listeners who had neither money nor happiness, but Roosevelt wished to make a point rooted in the moral instruction he received from his mentor Dr. Peabody at Groton. "These dark days," he said, "will be worth all they cost us if they teach us that our true destiny is not to be ministered unto but to minister to ourselves and our fellow men."

Roosevelt set out the parameters of his agenda, using phrases and summoning images that will sound familiar to Americans in the first decade of the twenty-first century. He promised to take action to prevent "the tragedy of the growing loss through foreclosure of our small homes and our farms." There must be, he said, "strict supervision of all banking and credits and investments."

To bring about the changes he proposed, Roosevelt said he would use all powers given him under the Constitution—and perhaps even more. He was, he said, prepared to "recommend" measures to assist the "stricken nation." But if Congress refused to act, Roosevelt said he would ask for "broad executive power to wage a war against the emergency, as great as the power that would be given to me if we were in fact invaded by a foreign foe."

Delivered in a harsher tone, these words could have sounded like a demagogue's diatribe. But in Roosevelt's patrician tones, the demand for greater power sounded like action, and the indictment of the old order sounded like justice.

Radio allowed Roosevelt to communicate with Americans on an unprecedented scale. The new medium brought the president's voice into living rooms across the nation.

CHAPTER 2

The Beginning of a Conversation

First Fireside Chat

March 12, 1933

TRACK 2

Even before the late-winter sun rose on March 5, 1933—a Sunday, and the first full day of the Roosevelt administration—lights were ablaze in the West Wing of the White House and upstairs, in the residential quarters. The new president and his team were awake and at work while the rest of the nation slept.

It was not an especially restful sleep. The president's air of calm confidence and his comforting words of the previous day may have soothed the nation's anxiety, but an immediate crisis required more than just words. In the weeks leading to Inauguration Day, the nation's banking system teetered on collapse. Four thousand banks throughout the country closed their doors in January and February, a financial catastrophe for millions of small depositors who were left with little or nothing. The closings led, inevitably, to a run on banks that remained open as panic-stricken Americans tried to withdraw their savings before they, too, lost all they had. In small towns and great cities from east to west, grim lines formed outside banks and stretched around corners as fearful depositors waited to withdraw their cash. As historian William E. Leuchtenburg observed, it "seemed safer to put your life's savings in the attic than to trust the greatest financial institutions in the country."[1]

The crisis boiled over in Michigan in mid-February when the state's governor, William Comstock, took the extraordinary measure of ordering the state's banks to close for eight days in a desperate attempt to give the institutions a chance to regroup. Nearly a million depositors lost access to about $1.5 billion in savings.

The action in Michigan prompted more state-ordered closings around the country. Adding to the sense of panic, the nation's gold supplies were hurriedly making their way across the Atlantic to Europe as speculators anticipated that Roosevelt might take the United States off the gold standard, as the British did in September 1931. The gold standard was a symbol of the old financial order, represented by Herbert Hoover, which insisted that a nation possess enough gold to back the value of its paper money. Hoover and his like-minded colleagues saw the gold standard as a tool of global economic stability, an assurance against widespread inflation. As the banking crisis deepened in late February, Hoover sent Roosevelt a long letter urging him to maintain the gold standard. For Hoover, the catastrophe of early 1933 surely seemed like the end of the world, or at least the end of a world he trusted, understood, and symbolized. Journalist Agnes Meyer—whose daughter Katharine would one day become publisher of the *Washington Post*—noted in her diary that the Hoover administration was ending "to the sound of crashing banks...the tragic end of a tragic story."[2]

During the final days of the Hoover administration, the nation's banking system "was in a state of either chaos or paralysis," according to Roosevelt biographer Frank Freidel.[3] Banks in thirty-eight states were shut down by order of the nation's governors. The Stock Exchange in New York, the Boards of Trade in Chicago and Kansas City, and several commodities exchanges suspended operations. Millions of dollars in gold continued to flow out of the United States, bound for Europe.

The new administration inherited a crisis of monumental proportions. And so the lights inside the White House were turned on early on Sunday morning, March 5. Later that afternoon, after the new president met with a group he called the "brains trust"—soon to be popularly rechristened the "brain trust"—he issued an order imposing a national bank holiday effective immediately.

Most governors already had closed banks in their respective states, but Roosevelt's order not only closed the remainder, but also suspended all transactions involving the nation's shrinking supply of gold. In addition, Roosevelt ordered a special session of Congress to convene on March 9 to deal with the banking emergency.

Lawmakers arriving on Capitol Hill on the appointed day found a quickly drafted bill awaiting disposition. The Emergency Banking Act of 1933 was drawn up in a matter of days and submitted to Congress at one o'clock in the afternoon of March 9. The bill was read aloud in the House; there were no other copies available.

If the nation's bankers feared that Roosevelt might act on the "money changers" rhetoric of his inaugural address, they soon learned that they had, in fact, nothing to fear, at least on that front. Roosevelt did not propose a government takeover of the nation's banks. Instead, he sent over a bill drafted, in the main, by the late Hoover Administration. The bill called for government assistance to banks that reopened after the holiday was over, set up procedures for reopening of banks that were on solid financial ground, ratified the new president's control of the nation's gold supply, and established a framework that would allow failing banks to reorganize. While the bill was a conservative document at its heart, it gave the federal government broad new regulatory powers. For example, banks wishing to reopen needed the secretary of the treasury's approval, and the Treasury Department was empowered to demand that private citizens who owned gold turn over their supply to the government in exchange for currency.

The House approved the measure unanimously without having read or studied it. The Senate then gave its approval over the objections of seven senators. Roosevelt signed the bill just after eight thirty that night, a little more than six hours after it was introduced in the House.

The flurry of activity, some of it arcane, required a public explanation. During his years as governor of New York, Roosevelt used the new mass medium of radio to great effect. Now, with more urgent decisions to make that would affect the entire nation, Roosevelt decided to address the entire nation as he once did his fellow New Yorkers. "To the great mass of American citizens," wrote presidential aide Samuel Rosenman, the bank holiday and the emergency banking bill were "as understandable as the theory of relativity or nuclear fission."[4] Roosevelt decided to explain to the nation what he did, and why he did it.

And so the notion of a "fireside chat" was born.

Radio provided Franklin Roosevelt with the opportunity to deliver his message without the filter of the print media. Of course, politicians always had the opportunity to speak directly to voters, but only from an orator's platform, in front of crowds that measured in the thousands—and usually more like the hundreds. But Franklin Roosevelt was able to address audiences measured in the tens of millions.

The medium and the messenger were well matched, adding to the power of the message itself. Among Franklin Roosevelt's many gifts was a voice suited for radio and a demeanor that seemed to invite the intimacy of strangers. Through the many fireside chats that followed the first, Roosevelt became a guest in the homes of everyday Americans. Actually, he became more than a guest. This squire from the Hudson Valley, with his privileged lifestyle and aristocratic accent, became a friend to America's suffering men, women, and children. Thanks to radio and his own personality, Roosevelt engaged in what seemed like a conversation with the American people, even if the limitations of the infant medium did not allow for the instant feedback of the call-in, town-hall-style meetings of the late twentieth century.

As Roosevelt prepared to address the country for the second time as president, he asked the Treasury Department to draft a speech explaining the bank holiday and the measure he introduced shortly thereafter to begin the process of reopening sound banks. The department, according to Rosenman, returned a document that Roosevelt quickly rejected. It was, Rosenman recalled, far too "scholarly" for a mass audience. The president himself wrote a new draft, mercifully free of jargon and academic prose.

The speech was scheduled for ten thirty Washington time on the night of March 12, a Sunday. Several microphones were set up on a desk in Roosevelt's office, along with a pitcher of water and a glass. About thirty folding chairs were set up facing the president, reserved for special guests who would watch Roosevelt deliver his speech.

Roosevelt, holding a cigarette, was wheeled into the room shortly before airtime, and the room grew quiet. Sixty million people across the country were tuned in as an announcer introduced "the president of the United States." Roosevelt began with no discursive introduction, no generalized comment about the country's condition. Suggesting the urgency of the problem, he got to the heart of the issue in his opening sentence: "I want to talk for a few minutes with the people of the United States about banking—with the comparatively few who understand the mechanics of banking—but more particularly with the overwhelming majority who use banks for the making of deposits and the drawing of checks." Instantly, most realized that the president was talking to them, that their concerns were his concerns.

Before he explained his actions, he offered his listeners a tutorial. "First of all, let me state the simple fact that when you deposit money in a bank the bank does not put the money into a safe deposit vault," he said. "It invests your money...the bank puts your money to work to keep the wheels of industry and of agriculture turning around." But in recent weeks, he added, public confidence in the banks was shattered, leading to a run that even the largest banks could not sustain. They simply didn't have the cash on hand, Roosevelt said. So he ordered a halt on withdrawals to give banks the breathing room they needed. "The bank holiday, while resulting in many cases in great inconvenience, is affording us the opportunity to supply the currency necessary to meet the situation. No sound bank is a dollar worse off than it was when it closed its doors last Monday." Even struggling banks, he added, were no worse for the holiday. For a bewildered and frightened nation, these were comforting words, spoken by none other than the president of the United States.

With emergency legislation in hand and a week's respite coming to a close, Roosevelt announced the banks in twelve cities would reopen the following morning because they had been "found to be all right" by the Treasury Department. Other reopenings would follow, some sooner, some later. But Americans, he said, shouldn't fear for their banks if they did not reopen quickly. "Let me make it clear to you that if your bank does not open the first day, you are by no means justified in believing that it will not open," he said in a tone that softened the scolding message of his words. "A bank that opens on one of the subsequent days is in exactly the same status as the bank that opens tomorrow."

In office only a week, still a stranger to many Americans, Roosevelt began building his bond with those who would come to regard him as a long-lost friend by anticipating their thoughts and their everyday anxieties. He understood, he said, that "when the banks resume, a very few people who have not recovered from their fear may again begin withdrawals." In other words, there might be yet another run on the banks. If so, he said, "the banks will take care of all needs." Those "few Americans" who still were fearful no doubt heaved a sigh of relief.

Although Roosevelt's first fireside chat was designed to comfort, to reassure, and to project confidence, he could not resist the urge to again identify villains. His inaugural address chastised the "money changers." To his radio audience, Roosevelt said that some of "our bankers had shown themselves either incompetent or dishonest in their handling of the people's funds. They had used the money entrusted to them in speculations and unwise loans." Wild, unregulated capitalism was to blame for the nation's plight.

And now an activist government would set things right. "It was the government's job to straighten out this situation and do it as quickly as possible—and the job is being performed."

The following morning, banks began opening throughout the country. A trend began to develop: more people lined up to make deposits than to make withdrawals.

Presidential advisor Raymond Moley, a member of the brain trust, noted, "Capitalism was saved in eight days."

The nation's jobless rate was nearly 25 percent during the depths of the Great Depression. Idle men and vacant storefronts were a common sight in American cities and towns.

CHAPTER 3

"The Country Was Dying by Inches"

Fireside Chat

May 7, 1933

TRACK 3

Not since Abraham Lincoln took office in March 1861, had a new president faced so momentous a crisis as Franklin Roosevelt did in 1933. And no new administration, before or since, achieved so much so quickly as Roosevelt managed to do during a hundred-day span that has become the standard by which new presidents are measured.

Beginning just hours after taking the oath of office and continuing through the spring, Roosevelt accomplished more than meeting the nation's economic crisis. He and his advisors rewrote the nation's social contract, established a more aggressive role for public intervention in the private marketplace, and set in motion a series of reforms that restored the public's confidence and faith in its government.

The spring of 1933 quickly became known as the Hundred Days, a three-month period during which Roosevelt swept away the malaise and helplessness of the Hoover years, proposed initiatives ranging from the Civilian Conservation Corps to the Tennessee Valley Authority, and began a conversation with the American people that would last until his death in 1945.

The economic calamity and the people's mandate offered Roosevelt an opportunity to transform the presidency itself. He saw the office as "predominantly a place of moral leadership," a view shared by other strong presidents, including Theodore Roosevelt, Woodrow Wilson and Abraham Lincoln.[1] But those leaders were exceptions to a more general view that regarded the president as an administrator rather than exhorter-in-chief. The succession of colorless presidents during the antebellum years, the Gilded Age, and the 1920s spoke to the chief executive's role as a manager and facilitator rather than as spokesman for shared values and a national ideology.

The calamity of the early 1930s, however, was unmanageable, at least by the standards of the old order that Hoover and his immediate predecessors represented. Restoring prosperity and confidence required the talents not of an administrator, but of a leader willing to challenge discredited platitudes with experimentation and innovation.

Roosevelt's emergency banking bill, passed sight unseen during a special session of Congress on March 9, was the beginning of an unprecedented flurry of activity in the White House. Roosevelt originally thought the special session would last only so long as it took to get the banking bill passed. Sensing an opportunity to accomplish a good deal more, however, he kept Congress in town and active far beyond his original deadline. He sent another new bill to Capitol Hill on March 10, this one designed to cut the pensions of veterans by $400 million and the salaries of federal workers by $100 million.

Given the popular association of Roosevelt with more expansive, and more expensive, government, his first economic message to Congress might seem surprisingly conservative and politically dangerous. Veterans, after all, helped create the impression that the country was close to revolution when they marched on Washington in the spring of 1932 demanding that the government make good on promised bonuses for their service during World War I. Nevertheless, however much Roosevelt railed at the nation's "money changers," he was no wild-eyed populist. Privately he regarded some of Hoover's spending as extravagant and unjustified. In recent years, Roosevelt noted, "liberal governments have been wrecked on the rocks of loose fiscal policy."[2] Indeed, Germany's Weimar Republic, designed to transform that nation from an autocracy to a liberal democracy, had run aground, buffeted by the tempests of rampant inflation. Public bitterness led to the appointment, in January 1933, of Adolf Hitler as the country's chancellor.

Economic recovery, Roosevelt believed, required prudent fiscal policy as well as strong leadership. FDR biographer Frank Freidel noted that the spending cuts were "not a minor aberration...[but] an integral part of Roosevelt's overall New Deal."[3] Though he promised new solutions and advocated new approaches, he also believed in restraint, not extravagance, and was no less committed to a balanced budget, in theory, than was Hoover. His first economic message reflected those concerns.

But when the bill made its way to the floor of the House and Senate, many of Roosevelt's fellow Democrats were appalled. The man who excoriated the nation's financial community and spoke up for the "forgotten man" had proposed an economic measure of which Hoover surely would have approved, and one that the money changers certainly did approve. Democratic congressmen condemned the measure as a boon to what one representative called the "big powerful banking racketeers."[4]

Roosevelt, however, had a mandate from the public and the bully pulpit of the presidency in his favor. Congress was not about to act as precipitously as it did on March 9, when the banking bill passed without having been read. But deliberations on the spending cutback were not protracted: the spending cuts passed on March 11 over the objections of ninety Democratic House members.

It was clear now that Roosevelt had the upper hand in his relations with Congress. And so the pace of activity stepped up as the administration sought to take advantage of momentum gained after only a week in office. On Monday, March 13, a day after FDR's first fireside chat, the president asked Congress to speed up the impending end of Prohibition by passing legislation to allow production of beer with an alcohol content of 3.2 percent. The end of the nation's dry run was coming to a close in any case, for Congress voted to repeal Prohibition weeks before Roosevelt's inauguration. State legislatures, whose approval also was necessary, were considering and expected to overwhelmingly approve a constitutional amendment overturning the Eighteenth Amendment's ban on liquor.

In the meantime, as debate over the Twenty-first Amendment played out in state capitals, Roosevelt wished to make good on promises to open taps that had never really been closed during the dozen years of Prohibition. But the culture war that had raged for so long over alcohol—and its connections to cities, immigrants, and Catholics—did not lend itself to a neat and peaceful conclusion. Roosevelt's proposal led to impassioned debate in Congress as the dwindling number of dry stalwarts fought a rearguard action, hoping to kill the bill in one last, desperate show of force against demon rum, or in this case, its malty cousin.

The wets, knowing that they had public opinion on their side, rallied when the drys sought to delay a vote on Roosevelt's proposal. Some shouted "We want beer" on the floor of the House—they probably were not the first members of Congress with such desires, but they certainly were the first, and the last, to articulate them during a debate.

The beer bill, with an add-on that allowed for the sale of wine with a similar alcohol content, passed Congress within days, and Roosevelt signed the bill into law on March 22.

After the wets defeated the drys in Congress, the floodgates opened. Roosevelt's White House deluged Congress with proposals ranging from a new farm bill to an unemployment relief program that would give birth to the Civilian Conservation Corps, a program that would become one of the New Deal's great legacies. A bill to create the Tennessee Valley Authority, which would bring parts of the rural South into the twentieth century, landed on Capitol Hill in mid-April. Around the same time, FDR proposed an aid package for farmers struggling to pay their mortgages.

Congress did not respond as it had to Roosevelt's first few messages. The farm bill, championed by Secretary of Agriculture Henry Wallace, led to prolonged debate in the Senate over demands from western farmers to cheapen currency through inflation. Roosevelt saw a battle he was unwilling to fight, and so in mid-April he decided, almost matter-of-factly, to take the country off the gold standard. This blow to the old economic order shocked those who saw the gold standard as pillar of economic order. Financier Bernard Baruch believed Roosevelt caved into what he called "mob rule."[5]

Roosevelt's actions allowed his administration to take more direct control over monetary policy through currency manipulation. Farm prices began to rise, precisely the intent of the farmers' advocates in

Congress, but continued discontent in the Midwest and other farming regions led, in mid-May, to passage of the Agricultural Adjustment Act, offering price supports for farmers.

On May 7, in the middle of Washington's frenzied spring, President Roosevelt returned to the nation's living rooms with his second fireside chat. His first chat was meant to explain a specific action—passage of the banking bill. This time, Roosevelt's themes were more general, although he wished to rally public opinion behind several specific proposals, including creation of the TVA. But he also sought to reassure his listeners that Washington's unprecedented assertion of power was no threat to individual liberty and economic freedom.

Before going on the air, Roosevelt hashed out the text of his chat with speechwriter Raymond Moley, who raised an objection to a phrase in the speech, in which Roosevelt referred to government intervention in farming, industry, and transportation as a partnership, not a seizure of control. "You realize, then, that you're taking an enormous step away from the philosophy of equalitarianism and laissez-faire?" Moley asked.[6]

Roosevelt, according to Moley's account, "looked graver than he had been at any moment since the night before his inauguration." Finally, he said, "If that philosophy hadn't proved to be bankrupt, Herbert Hoover would be sitting here now. I never felt surer of anything in my life than I do of the soundness of this passage."

Determined to deliver a message of partnership—not outright control, and certainly not laissez-faire—Roosevelt addressed the nation on May 7. He explained that he wished to give the nation "my report" on the first two months of his administration. The rush of activity and the pace of change in Washington allowed Roosevelt to assert that his administration already had made a difference after just eight weeks. "Two months ago, we were facing serious problems," he said. "The country was dying by inches. It was dying because trade and commerce had declined to dangerously low levels; prices for basic commodities were such as to destroy the value of the assets of national institutions such as banks...That situation in that crisis did not call for any complicated consideration of economic panaceas or fancy plans. We were faced by a condition and not a theory."

In his journey from a self-styled reformer from the Hudson Valley to chief executive of a wounded nation, Roosevelt learned the trade of politics in part through his dealings with the ultimate pragmatists who inhabited the public payrolls of New York. And pragmatism, not ideology, was to be his guiding light in this crisis. Conditions, not dogma, would dictate his actions. Theory did not interest him, nor did ideology. During one of the frequent press conferences that became a hallmark of his governing style, Roosevelt was asked to describe his philosophy. He seemed genuinely puzzled.

"Philosophy?" he asked, wondering what his inquisitor might mean. "Philosophy? I am a Christian and a Democrat—that's all."[7]

But if he were a pragmatist, it did not follow that he lacked a central, moral core. He told his audience that upon taking office, he had two choices to make, two paths on which he might set out to cure the nation's ills. One would have required him to stand by while foreclosures and bankruptcies mounted, creating a buyer's market for new investors looking for bargains. That course, he said, would have led to "extraordinary hardships" in a nation where hardship already was common.

The only other option, he said, was a "prompt program" of reforms to be implemented through special powers given by Congress to the president. New regulatory and fiscal powers were incorporated in both the banking and economic bills, and there would be more such delegation of power to the president in the future.

At a time when dictators were in power in the Soviet Union, Germany, and Italy, Roosevelt understood that his requests for additional power would be seen in a troubling global context. Those concerns, he insisted, were overstated. "The members of Congress realized that the methods of normal times had to be replaced in the emergency by measures which were suited to the serious and pressing requirements of the moment," he said. "There was no actual surrender of power, Congress still retained its constitutional authority and no one has the slightest desire to change the balance of powers."

After he delivered his homage to partnerships between industry and government, Roosevelt obligingly provided an example of what he meant. "Take the cotton goods industry," he said. "It is probably true that ninety percent of the cotton manufacturers would agree to eliminate starvation wages, would agree to stop long hours of employment [and] would agree to stop child labor...But what good is such an agreement if the other ten percent of cotton manufacturers pay starvation wages, require long hours [and] employ children in their mills..." he asked. "The unfair ten percent could produce goods so cheaply that the fair ninety percent would be compelled to meet the unfair conditions."

A referee, then, was needed, to ensure that the unfair were punished and the fair rewarded. "Here is where government comes in," he said. "Government ought to have the right and will have the right...to prevent, with the assistance of the overwhelming majority of that industry, unfair practice and to enforce this agreement with the authority of government."

This kind of intervention in the private economy was not without precedent—the Wilson administration engaged in economic planning and rigorous regulation during World War I, and Roosevelt's predecessor as governor of New York, Al Smith, presided over an expansion of social welfare and regulatory policies. But because of the scope of the New Deal's ambitions and the transfer of responsibility to the president's office, Roosevelt felt compelled to explain that his "policies are wholly within purposes for which our American Constitutional government was established 150 years ago." He conceded that he would "make mistakes of procedure," but, quoting the words of Theodore Roosevelt, he said he hoped to be right "seventy-five percent of the time."

He closed his second chat by thanking his listeners, on behalf of himself and his colleagues in government, for being patient. In the days that followed, in what would become a pattern for the Roosevelt years, the White House received sacks of mail from Americans responding to the president's address. Many of the correspondents told the president about their personal stories and troubles in the course of encouraging him. They told him what they might tell a close friend. One farmer from Oklahoma noted that his parents were dead and he was trying to make a life for himself. "I have just heard that splendid talk over the radio," the farmer, Walter C. Tabor, said. "It sure did come in good and clear. 'We are for you.'"

There would be many such letters before the Hundred Days ran its course.

The National Recovery Administration formed a partnership between government regulators and businesses large and small. Here, a restaurant displays an NRA eagle, showing that it is part of Roosevelt's recovery effort.

CHAPTER 4

"I Still Believe in Ideals"

Fireside Chat

September 30, 1934

TRACK 4

Franklin Roosevelt's response to the crisis of spring 1933 eased the sense of emergency and the nation's fears that either a revolution or a complete national collapse was just around the corner. Two of FDR's signature innovations, the Agricultural Adjustment Administration (AAA) and the National Recovery Administration (NRA), helped revive the farm economy and established a code of conduct governing the practices of the business community, respectively. Another new agency, the Public Works Administration (PWA), embarked on thousands of new construction projects, from bridges to sewage treatment plants to hospitals. In its first three years of existence, from 1933 to 1935, the PWA pumped $3.3 billion in federal money into local economies—the equivalent of more than $30 billion in the early twenty-first century.

Many of FDR's initiatives—inevitably known by their acronyms, such as the NRA and AAA—were designed to create jobs for the nation's army of unemployed. As historian William E. Leuchtenburg noted in his study of the New Deal, mass unemployment was especially brutal in a modern economy. "To be unemployed in an industrial society is the equivalent of banishment and excommunication," Leuchtenburg wrote. "A job established a man's identity—not only what other men thought of him but how he viewed himself; the loss of his job shattered his self-esteem and severed one of his most important ties to other men."[1] As Leuchtenburg noted, the ranks of the jobless included both blue-collar and white-collar workers from all sectors of the economy.

Many of these workers wanted not relief, but jobs, as author T. H. Watkins observed in his study of the Depression, *The Hungry Years*. Watkins found that relief administrators inevitably heard complaints from the jobless that they resented what they saw as handouts. "I don't want no God-damn relief orders," one worker told a relief administrator named Lorena Hickok, a friend of Eleanor Roosevelt. "I want work, I tell you! Work! Work! I got to have a job."[2]

Roosevelt understood these anxieties, for they spoke to his own view of government's role in offering relief rather than opportunities. Public relief programs, he would tell Congress in 1935, were a "narcotic, a subtle destroyer of the human spirit..."[3] Roosevelt's skepticism about relief, however, did not prevent his administration from pouring hundreds of millions into relief programs. By the end of 1934, when some 20 million Americans were receiving some form of public assistance, the federal government had spent $2 billion—about $20 billion today—on relief programs since FDR's inauguration.

The Federal Emergency Relief Administration, created during the Hundred Days, emphasized not relief in the form of public assistance but in jobs. Roosevelt chose Harry Hopkins, a friend and advisor from his Albany days, to preside over FERA. Hopkins was a social worker by profession and an implementer par excellence by inclination. A chain-smoking bundle of nerves and energy, he enjoyed FDR's complete confidence, even as he began spending federal money by the tens of millions in an effort to provide not relief, as the name of his agency suggested, but work.

During the winter of 1933–34, Hopkins expanded his burgeoning federal empire through the creation of an agency called the Civil Works Administration, which hired unemployed workers to build public works projects around the country. In the span of just a few weeks, the CWA hired more than 4 million people who were sent to work building roads, recreational facilities, government buildings, and other projects. Some fifty-two thousand CWA workers found jobs in New York City's parks and recreation system.

Hopkins also expanded the concept of public works hiring to include white-collar workers, such as teachers, writers, and artists, who put their talents to work in classrooms and in local centers for the arts. About fifty thousand teachers were placed on the CWA's payroll, allowing local governments to restaff schools decimated by layoffs.

But the CWA lasted only as long as winter did. As much as Roosevelt wanted to provide jobs, not relief, he also was philosophically committed to ideals like a balanced budget and a fiscally prudent government. The CWA had cost $825 million, about $10 billion today, in less than a year. It helped millions get through the cold weather, Roosevelt noted, but with the arrival of spring, its job was done. "Nobody is going to starve during the warm weather," he said.[4] By April, CWA's 4 million workers were back on the street, looking for another job, although FERA itself continued to spend liberally to fund construction projects, nursery schools, literacy programs, and other programs.

Franklin Roosevelt famously described himself as a juggler—"I never let my right hand know what my left does," he said in 1942. In these early years of the New Deal, his left hand and his right hand did seem to be working independently of each other. Just two months after he shut down the CWA over concerns about cost and about creating a class of workers that would remain dependent on public employment, FDR created a committee within his Cabinet to study social insurance. It was the beginning of a process that would lead to the introduction and passage of Social Security, the largest federal entitlement program of its time.

A year into his term, with midterm congressional elections due in November, Roosevelt sought to steer a middle ground by cobbling together a program that would not alienate the nation's business community entirely, but one that would provide a measure of relief, and hope, for the millions who were out of work. He signed the Securities Exchange Act of 1934, which created the Securities Exchange Commission to regulate portions of the financial community, over the bitter objections of business leaders, one of whom contended that the New York Stock Exchange was "a perfect institution."[5] Such claims, made while millions were out of work in the aftermath of the Exchange's collapse, only served to help the populist side of FDR's program.

On the other hand, Roosevelt met frequently with the business community, which welcomed the opportunity to, in essence, regulate itself through the National Recovery Administration. Under the leadership of Hugh Johnson, the NRA implemented a series of codes that set minimum wages, regulated the length of workweeks, and sought to establish fair business practices. But the codes were written and implemented by business leaders working with and for the NRA.

Roosevelt's approach was too cautious for critics on the left and too radical for those on the right. Former president Herbert Hoover complained that Roosevelt was moving the country towards "gigantic socialism" through "the most stupendous invasion" of liberty "since the days of Colonial America."[6] Business leaders and dissident Democrats, including FDR's friend and predecessor as New York governor, Al Smith, formed an organization called the American Liberty League to organize opposition to the New Deal. The Liberty League charged that Roosevelt's program of government intervention and regulation was more radical than the programs being put in place in Benito Mussolini's Italy, Joseph Stalin's Soviet Union, and Adolf Hitler's Third Reich.

Meanwhile, in Louisiana, the man who helped Roosevelt win the 1932 presidential nomination over Smith, Senator Huey Long, embarked on his own campaign of reform. In a clear and deliberate challenge to Roosevelt, Long formed a national political organization called "Share Our Wealth," which dispatched mailings to more than 7 million everyday citizens and political activists throughout the nation. Long's hyperpopulist program called for the confiscation of large fortunes and its redistribution to Americans of lesser means. He promised pensions and scholarships and a more ambitious program of public works. Long's ambitions were made loud and clear—as with everything else he did—in the title of a book published in 1935: *My First Days in the White House*.

Long attracted converts who were disappointed that Roosevelt did not act on his "money changers" rhetoric. One of Long's supporters wrote that the nation needed "men with guts to go farther to the left."[7]

To the north, in Illinois, a Roman Catholic priest named Charles Coughlin used his wildly popular radio program to criticize Roosevelt after having rallied support for FDR as a candidate and during his first year in office. Coughlin's attacks mounted through the fall, leading to the founding of the National Union for Social Justice, a leftish-sounding organization whose patron soon descended into anti-Semitism and hysterical anti-New Deal harangues.

As Americans prepared to go to the polls to pass the first judgment on Roosevelt and the New Deal, the president announced a major change at the National Recovery Administration. Johnson, the agency's administrator, resigned, giving Roosevelt an opportunity to reorganize and re-energize the agency. On September 30, five days after accepting Johnson's resignation, Roosevelt addressed the country for another Sunday night fireside chat. His topic was the relationship between government and capitalism, a relationship that was at the heart of criticism from the left and the right during his first two years in office.

Mediating that relationship was the NRA, and Roosevelt devoted a long portion of his chat to an explanation of how the NRA worked and what it had achieved during its two years under Johnson. Ninety percent of the country's workers, Roosevelt noted, were employed in "trades and industries" that "have adopted codes of fair competition...Under these codes, in the industries covered, child labor has been eliminated. The work day and the work week have been shortened. Minimum wages have been established and other wages adjust...The emergency purpose of the NRA was to put men to work and since its creation more than four million persons have been re-employed, in great part through the cooperation of American business..."

That model of cooperation among capital, labor, and government was grounded in Roosevelt's experience during the war years of the Wilson Administration, when Washington created a War Industries Board to encourage a collaborative, rather than an authoritarian, relationship with the private sector in the face of a national emergency. Roosevelt, having heard his name linked to the dictatorships of Mussolini, Hitler, and Stalin, was careful to note that the NRA functioned as it did because of the cooperation of business leaders. They were, in fact, the authors and enforcers of the codes that governed businesses that participated in the NRA, identifiable by the blue-eagle NRA stickers in their windows.

The NRA, he said, had successfully "passed through" its "formative period." Now, after a reorganization made possible by Johnson's departure, the agency would move forward to modify and revise its codes and establish itself not as an emergency measure but as "party of the permanent machinery of government." Before it did so, however, some pointed questions had to be asked. And the answers had to come from big business, whose representatives, Roosevelt noted, demanded "what has been called self-government in industry."

A "question arises as to whether in fixing minimum wages on the basis of an hourly or weekly wage we have reached into the heart of the problem which is to provide such annual earnings for the lowest paid worker as will meet his minimum needs," he said, suggesting an answer by merely raising the question. "We also question the wisdom of extending code requirements suited to the great industrial centers and to large employers, to the great number of small employers in the smaller communities." With this language, Roosevelt sought to address criticism that the NRA and its codes unfairly favored large businesses that had produced the regulations in question. The president made it clear that he was not entirely satisfied with the result.

Labor did not emerge from the president's report unscathed. Strikes, he said, had set back the recovery effort, and he intended to make a personal effort to meet with capital and labor in an effort to achieve industrial peace.

Though he closed down the CWA earlier in the year, the lack of dramatic progress in job creation and economic growth during the summer of 1934 tested his patience. A return to prosperity would come from jobs, not relief. So he defended "our expenditures for Public Works" as an important "means for recovery."

"Demoralization caused by vast unemployment is our greatest extravagance," he said. "Morally, it is the greatest menace to our social order. Some people try to tell me that we must make up our minds that for the future we shall permanently have millions of unemployed just as other countries had had them for over a decade." This, he said, was unacceptable. "I stand or fall by my refusal to accept as a necessary condition of our future a permanent army of unemployed."

That refusal would entail boldness, risk-taking, and experimentation. There were some who were "cowed" by those choices, he conceded, but luckily, nearly "all Americans are sensible and calm people." Recovery, he said, could be accomplished while avoiding "on the one hand the theory that business should and must be taken over into an all-embracing Government" and on the other "the equally untenable theory that it is an interference with liberty to offer reasonable help when private enterprise is in need of help."

Through the successes and disappointments of his first two years in office, Roosevelt said, "I still believe in ideals. I am not for a return to that definition of Liberty under which for many years a free people were being gradually regimented into the service for a privileged few."

Five weeks later, Americans went to the polls and gave Roosevelt an important mid-term victory. Democrats won thirteen more seats in the House of Representatives, and with nine more Senators, they reduced Republicans to less than a third of the upper chamber.

The way was clear for bolder action.

Jobless workers register for unemployment benefits in the nation's capital after passage of the Social Security Bill.

CHAPTER 5

A Feeling of Security

Fireside Chat

April 28, 1935

TRACK 5

THE MIDTERM ELECTIONS OF 1934 ONLY ADDED TO THE MANDATE FRANKLIN Roosevelt received in 1932. Democrats picked up a dozen seats in the House of Representatives, giving them 322 and leaving the Republicans with just 103. In the Senate, Democrats added nine seats, widening the chasm between the two parties in the upper chamber. With those victories, the Democrats controlled sixty-nine of the ninety-six seats in the new Senate. The *New York Times* proclaimed the Democratic/New Deal triumph to be "the most overwhelming victory in the history of American politics."[1]

Although Roosevelt expected Democrats to suffer at the polls in November, if only because that was the usual pattern, he was planning an ambitious agenda for the new year and the new Congress even before Election Day. The party's strong showing emboldened both the White House and the Democratic leadership of Capitol Hill. "Boys, this is our hour," Harry Hopkins told his staff after the election. "We've got to get everything we want—a works program, Social Security, wages and hours, everything—now or never."[2]

Many new members of Congress, elected on a wave of populist sentiment, were inclined to agree. They arrived in Washington determined to keep pushing the country to the left, a course that the president himself was not especially prepared to follow. Roosevelt was a master of the art of the possible, not the herald of a radical new economic order. Three weeks after the midterm election, in a letter to Colonel Edward House, an advisor who had served as Woodrow Wilson's top aide. Roosevelt displayed his traditional, conservative side in discussing plans for the coming year. "What I am seeking is the abolition of relief altogether," he wrote. "I cannot say so out loud yet but I hope to be able to substitute work for relief."[3]

For Roosevelt, relief remained a program of last resort, an unpalatable although clearly necessary measure designed for short-term emergencies. He continued to regard outright payments to the jobless as destructive over the long term.[4] Equally destructive, he said, were unproductive, make-work jobs that ultimately did little to bring about a true economic recovery. "I am not willing that the vitality of our people be further sapped by the giving of cash, of market baskets, or a few hours of weekly work cutting grass, raking leaves or picking up papers in the public parks," he told Congress in his annual State of the Union message in January 1935. "We must preserve not only the bodies of the unemployed from destruction but also their self-respect, their self-reliance and courage and determination."

Roosevelt knew that he could not simply eliminate the programs he despised without proposing an alternative. The nation's spirits might be better than they were in 1932, and voters might be pleased by the results of the New Deal thus far, but times remained difficult at best for millions of Americans. Eleven million people—nearly 22 percent of the work force—were unemployed, and total national income was 50 percent less than it was before the crash in 1929.

Roosevelt had in mind a sweeping new jobs program designed to take the place of emergency relief. He proposed the elimination of all federal relief agencies, to be replaced by a comprehensive national jobs program that would provide work for an estimated 3.5 million people. He estimated that the program would cost about $4 billion (about $60 billion today) in new federal spending, along with another $880 million (more than $12 billion today) already in the federal budget for relief programs.

The sweeping nature and cost of the program were historic. So was the renewed assertion of federal power. Only the federal government, Roosevelt told Congress, had "sufficient power and credit to meet this situation."[5] But the bill did more than expand federal authority—it extended the authority of the president. Congress merely authorized the money. The president would decide how it would be spent.

Fiscal conservatives in Congress were astonished when they learned how much the program would cost. If only they had been privy to some of the initial discussions of the jobs program, known formally as the Emergency Relief Appropriation Act. Months earlier, in the late summer of 1934, Harry Hopkins put together a proposal that would have cost $5 billion a year for five years. During the ensuing months, Roosevelt scaled back Hopkins's plan several times until deciding on a one-year, $4 billion appropriation. Roosevelt's caution was in keeping with his steadfast unwillingness—despite his occasional bursts of inflammatory rhetoric—to side with those who sought radical change. He consistently preferred to fix, rather than replace, what was broken. One fervent New Dealer, Rexford Tugwell, an economics professor and assistant secretary of agriculture, complained that the president refused to lead the country "into a new world." Tugwell left the administration after one term.[6]

Roosevelt may not have been radical enough for Tugwell or for other progressives who dismayed of the president's leadership in early 1935, but his jobs bill was the most expensive piece of legislation ever brought before Congress. The question was not whether it would pass—with Democrats dominating Capitol Hill, Republican critics could do nothing to stop it—but who would administer the billions of dollars and millions of jobs. Two of FDR's key domestic advisors, Harry Hopkins and Interior Secretary Harold Ickes, saw themselves as the rightful stewards of the new program. And neither was especially fond of the other.

Ickes was a combative Republican from Illinois who was invited to join FDR's Cabinet as a gesture towards the progressive wing of the GOP. Eloquent and fearless, Ickes was a strong supporter of civil rights for African Americans at a time when many white politicians turned a blind eye to Jim Crow in the South and de facto segregation in Northern cities like Chicago. As FDR's choice to run the Public Works Administration in 1933, Ickes seemed a natural leader for the new jobs program, but for one problem: FDR believed his interior secretary moved too slowly as he tried to keep precious federal money out of the hands of corrupt political operatives. Even Treasury Secretary Henry Morgenthau, perhaps the most fiscally conservative member of the cabinet, complained that Ickes was so worried about graft that he "spent money through a medicine dropper."[7]

Given his role with the PWA, Ickes not surprisingly envisioned the new program as an opportunity to build large-scale public works projects. Hopkins, however, saw it as a chance to put millions of people to work, quickly. He had done it once before, when, as head of the Civil Works Administration during the winter of 1933–34, he hired nearly 4 million people in a matter of weeks. While Roosevelt rejected the CWA as a model—he had scant regard for the make-work jobs the agency provided—he certainly admired the way in which Hopkins moved with great speed and efficiency to create something out of nothing. FDR decided to put Hopkins in charge because, he said, "Harry gets things done."[8]

Congress approved the massive (but not massive enough for critics on the left) appropriation on April 8, 1935. A month later, Roosevelt created a new agency to coordinate the hiring of millions of unemployed Americans and the work they would perform: it was called the Works Progress Administration. Under Hopkins's creative leadership, the WPA not only built thousands of hospitals, schools, and other civic institutions, but created programs for writers and artists who produced oral histories, state travel guides, theatrical productions, and folk art. Of the many so-called alphabet agencies created during the Depression, the WPA remains among the best-known and most fondly remembered.

The second item on Roosevelt's agenda for 1935 also produced a long-term legacy: Social Security. His support for old-age pensions and financial payments to the disabled and to dependent children symbolized the philosophical changes embedded in the chaotic experiment known as the New Deal. Social Security, a federally administered system of social insurance, explicitly rejected traditional American notions of self-reliance and rugged individualism. In its dry, legalistic language, the Social Security Act of 1935 argued that Americans had a collective responsibility for the aged, for mothers and children with no other means of support, and for the unemployed.

Labor Secretary Frances Perkins, the first woman Cabinet member in U.S. history, was the guiding force behind the Social Security Act. She and fellow members of the president's Committee on Economic Security cobbled together a proposal that contained several disappointing compromises and exceptions, including a provision that left out farm workers and domestics along with other workers from the Social Security umbrella. The bill also demanded that employees pay into the system, which meant a tax increase for already struggling workers. Economists believed it was foolish to impose a new tax when the nation's economy was mired in depression, but Roosevelt had his reasons. Not only did employee contributions square with his more conservative side—the side of him which abhorred government giveaways—but they also provided another kind of insurance. "We put those payroll deductions there so as to give the contributors a legal, moral and political right to collect their pensions and their unemployment benefits," he said.[9] "With those taxes in there, no damn politician can ever scrap my social security program."

Scrapped during the debates among members of the Perkins committee was a proposal for national health insurance. Roosevelt and other aides were unwilling to fight that political battle in 1935, again to the dismay of liberals who complained that the president was siding with conservatives rather than pressing ahead with radical reforms. Roosevelt, however, chose the pragmatic over the ideological: it was, he believed, better to get what was gettable, rather than fight the nation's doctors over what they saw as socialized medicine. Still, even without health insurance, the Social Security Act was a transformative piece of legislation, as its critics recognized. New Jersey senator Harry Moore complained that Social Security would "take all the romance out of life," an assertion that, if nothing else, suggested that the senator had an uncertain connection to everyday reality in 1935.[10] For the New Deal's critics and opponents on the right, programs like Social Security denied the poor and others a chance to pull themselves up by their own bootstraps. Moore sarcastically suggested that the nation hire nurses to "protect [children] from every experience that life affords." For the jobless, for the aged, for the nation's dependent children, life had provided plenty of experience since 1929. Roosevelt and his supporters wished, indeed, to protect them from some of life's harsher experiences.

After an absence of more than three months from the nation's living rooms, Roosevelt scheduled another fireside chat, his seventh, on the evening of April 28, 1935. He sought to answer critics who believed he was going too far or not far enough in rewriting the nation's social compact. But he also wished to speak directly to the people about his plans for their economic security, both short-term and long-term.

He opened with a defense of his program, which even then was under attack—as it has been ever since—for its seemingly scatter-shot approach to the nation's vast problems. "The Administration and the Congress are not proceeding in any haphazard fashion in this task of government," he declared. "Each of our steps has a definite relationship to every other step." Roosevelt, drawing on his love of the sea, compared his program to the construction of a ship. "At different points on the coast where I often visit they build great seagoing ships," he said. "When one of these ships is under construction and the steel frames have been set in the keel, it is difficult for a person who does not know ships to tell how it will finally look when it is sailing the high seas." Not to worry, though. He knew exactly how it would look. He was a sailor, after all.

After reassuring the public that, in essence, he knew what he was doing, FDR introduced the two major points of his springtime agenda, Social Security and the WPA. He portrayed them as part of a piece, part of the larger project of creating a more secure society. "We must begin now to make provision for the future," he said. It was a bold assertion at a time when most Americans did not have the luxury of thinking beyond the next paycheck, if they were lucky enough to have one, or the next meal, if they were hungry and jobless.

Old-age pensions, he said, would "help those who have reached the age of retirement to give up their jobs and thus give to the younger generation greater opportunities for work and to give to all a feeling of security as they look toward old age." Federal pensions, then, were not just about old-age security or social justice. They also were a means by which the government could create jobs for the young by encouraging retirement of the old.

The Social Security bill, which Congress would debate through the summer, also contained a provision for unemployment insurance, which FDR described as a means to "cushion the shock of economic distress." Critics argued that the cushion would only encourage the jobless to take a nap. "With unemployment insurance no one will work," asserted the head of General Motors, Alfred Sloan. Roosevelt, in his fireside chat, contended that the program would act as a "guard" against "dependence on public relief" and, in a nod to businessmen like Sloan, would help the jobless sustain their "purchasing power."

Important though Social Security was, Roosevelt acknowledged that the problems it sought to solve lay in the future. The more pressing business was job creation. He explained that he was "losing no time in getting the government's cast work relief program underway." He explained in detail how the WPA would work, emphasizing that the projects it would undertake would be "useful," would eventually produce revenue for the Treasury, and would create jobs for those on relief.

The keynote of his chat came after his technical explanation of the legislation. He turned away from details and spoke explicitly about the changes programs like Social Security, unemployment insurance, and the WPA represented. In a passage in which he spoke directly to his listeners, encouraging their participation in a "great national crusade" against "enforced idleness," Roosevelt addressed the concerns of those who might see his jobs program as just another boondoggle, vaster than any Washington had yet produced.

"There are chiselers in every walk of life; there are those in every industry who are guilty of unfair practices; every profession has its black sheep, but long experience in government has taught me that the exceptional instances of wrong-doing in government are probably less numerous than in almost every other line of endeavor...I call upon my fellow citizens everywhere to cooperate with me in making this the most efficient and cleanest example of public enterprise the world has ever seen. It is time to provide a smashing answer for those cynical men who say that a democracy cannot be honest and efficient. If you will help, this can be done."

His arguments may have swayed skeptics in his audience. But there were other skeptics who were unimpressed by his arguments about his New Deal. They happened to be on the U.S. Supreme Court.

Franklin Roosevelt and Al Smith were political allies in the 1920s. But Smith broke with Roosevelt in 1935 and campaigned for doomed Republican presidential nominee Alf Landon in 1936.

CHAPTER 6

"A Rendezvous with Destiny"

Speech at the Democratic National Convention

June 27, 1936

TRACK 6

TO THE CHAGRIN AND INDIGNATION OF SOME LIBERAL DEMOCRATS, FRANKLIN Roosevelt seemed less than eager to confront big business in the spring of 1935. Instead, in the spirit of the Progressive president he so admired, Woodrow Wilson, Roosevelt sought to find a way to include business leaders as part of a public-private partnership. He presided over the ouster of agrarian reformers from the Agricultural Adjustment Administration, he backed off a program to build public housing projects, and he seemed less than enthusiastic about New York senator Robert Wagner's National Labor Relations Act, which sought to enhance the powers of labor unions. Critics on the left even found fault with his massive work-relief program, which led to the creation of the WPA. They argued that it fell far short of offering work for all who needed a job.

At the same time, however, the business community began to argue that Roosevelt's reforms and proposals were preventing the nation from achieving genuine recovery. The national Chamber of Commerce criticized the New Deal in May, just after he introduced the Social Security Act. As Congress began to debate Social Security, Roosevelt found himself fending off assaults from the left and right.

Matters were about to get worse. On May 27, 1935, Roosevelt received a jolt from the judiciary branch when the Supreme Court ruled that the National Industrial Relations Act, which gave birth to the National Recovery Administration—the centerpiece of FDR's recovery program—was unconstitutional. At issue were NRA codes governing workers' hours and wages, as well as the definition of interstate commerce. The A.L.A. Schechter Poultry Company, which sold live poultry from its plant in Brooklyn, had been charged with violating NRA codes and with selling diseased chickens—thus, the Supreme Court case became known as the "sick chicken case."

The Court ruled that Congress, by passing the NIRA, improperly delegated its legislative authority to the executive branch, and that the sick chickens did not constitute interstate commerce since they were sold within the boundaries of New York State—although the vast majority of the live poultry arrived at the Schechter plant from outside New York. The Court ruling was unambiguous and unanimous—even noted liberals Louis Brandeis and Benjamin Cardozo agreed with the finding.

Roosevelt was furious. "The implications of this decision are much more important than any decision probably since the Dred Scott case," he said. The Court's ruling meant that the "Federal Government has no right" to "take any part in trying to better" the nation's economic and social problems. The people, he said, would not stand for such a regressive interpretation of what he called a "horse-and-buggy" definition of interstate commerce.[1]

The Schechter decision came on the heels of weeks of soul-searching in the White House. Criticism from the business sector suggested that Roosevelt's policy of accommodation wasn't working. Presidential advisor Felix Frankfurter wrote of the futility of believing that business would support Roosevelt in the 1936 campaign. Now was the time for confrontation, Frankfurter said.

After Schechter, Roosevelt concluded that advisors like Frankfurter were right. The decision was a major defeat for the president, but if critics on the right believed it would force the president to retrench, they were mistaken. Instead, Roosevelt introduced a new flurry of proposals and goals that set the stage for one of the most memorable legislative sessions in American history—the Second Hundred Days, as they were called. Social Security, the jobs bill, Senator Wagner's National Labor Relations Act, new tax legislation, and an assortment of other reform bills were dispatched to Capitol Hill. FDR took special pleasure in the tax bill, which called for a stiff increase in taxes on the wealthy. Saying he wished to encourage a "wider distribution of wealth," Roosevelt asserted that it was government's "duty" to "restrict" high incomes "by very high taxes."[2] How high? FDR's bill increased the top tax rate from 59 percent to 75 percent, and imposed a new corporate income tax ranging from a little more than 10 percent to as high as nearly 17 percent.

Roosevelt put a whip to Congress, keeping members in session through the humid Washington summer and insisting that nobody would leave town until his agenda was passed. Roosevelt proved tougher than his critics on Capitol Hill, employing all the powers of persuasion in his considerable arsenal to rally support while his opponents withered in the mid-summer heat.

Roosevelt won every battle that summer. Critics like Huey Long and Father Coughlin found themselves without a rhetorical leg to stand on. Long had become a national figure by demanding that the nation share its wealth. But Roosevelt stole Long's thunder, indeed, his very message, with his tax bill and his sharpened, class-based rhetoric. In the fall, after the Second Hundred Days were over, Roosevelt told an audience in Georgia that he knew that "gentlemen in well-warmed and well-stocked clubs" opposed his plan to spend billions on work relief. They preferred to keep the poor on the dole, Roosevelt said, because it was less expensive. The president denounced such critics for having "too little contact" with "the true America."[3] Americans wanted work, FDR said, and he was prepared to give it to them, regardless of the anxieties of wealthy business leaders.

When Roosevelt spoke in Georgia in November 1935, there was no reply from his onetime ally in Louisiana. Huey Long's voice was silenced in September, when an assassin gunned him down on the steps of the state capitol in Baton Rouge.

Roosevelt opened the election year of 1936 with more sharp words, this time in his annual State of the Union message. Urged on by his friend and advisor Louis Howe, Roosevelt reveled in the accomplishments of the previous summer, asserting with great satisfaction that he and his fellow Democrats had "earned the hatred of entrenched greed."[4] The speech set the tone for the upcoming campaign season, which, the president told his advisors, would focus on just one issue: the performance of Franklin Delano Roosevelt. "There is just one issue in this campaign," FDR said. "It is myself, and the people must be either for me or against me."[5]

Some of Roosevelt's fellow Democrats were eager to make the case against him. In fact, in a worrisome display of disunity, the party's two previous presidential nominees, Alfred E. Smith and John W. Davis, were among those determined to stop the president's reelection. Smith, bitter over his loss to FDR at the Democratic National Convention in 1932, traveled to Washington in late January 1936 to deliver a vicious attack on the New Deal and its author at a meeting of the Liberty League in the Mayflower Hotel. Smith compared the New Deal with socialism and equated its proponents with "Karl Marx, or Lenin, or any of the rest of that bunch."[6]

It was, by any definition, a sad and tragic performance. Al Smith's tenure as governor of New York paved the way for many New Deal reforms. But Smith's envy and anger got the better of him, allowing Republicans and the business community to point out that they were not alone in believing that the New Deal was nothing more than socialism dressed up as reform. Smith's attacks, along with the opposition of Davis and other Democrats in the Liberty League, gave Roosevelt's allies reason for anxiety as they considered their prospects in 1936.

The banks of the Potomac River were decked out in the bright colors of spring as Roosevelt and two advisors, Sam Rosenman and a Republican convert named Stanley High, set sail aboard the presidential yacht in late May. The topic at hand was Roosevelt's reelection campaign, a campaign that would be missing the talents of Louis Howe, who died in April after a long illness. Franklin and Eleanor mourned the loss of a trusted confidant who often carried messages between the president and the first lady when times were tense. Howe, as he lay near death, took stock of what his death might mean for the man he had served so well for so long. "Franklin is on his own now," he said.[7]

He was not so lonely, of course, and the task ahead of him was not so daunting at it was in 1933. The country was in far better shape than it was three years earlier. But Rosenman was not confident as he and High and their wives joined the president aboard the USS *Potomac* over the Decoration Day (now known as Memorial Day) holiday weekend. Rosenman, who helped write Roosevelt's inaugural address and then returned to private life, believed that "prospects for reelection did not seem quite that bright." He was concerned about Democratic defections, about accusations that the New Deal had taken the country too far to the left, and that big business would do all it could to unseat FDR.[8] When he expressed those concerns to the president, however, Roosevelt simply smiled. "Lots of things can happen before November," the president said.[9]

Rosenman got the president's point, but he remained concerned about the influence of the nation's press. He figured about 85 percent of the nation's newspapers opposed Roosevelt and would enthusiastically support the Republican Party's eventual nominee despite the country's improving economy. Still, with national income, industrial production, and stock prices all higher than they were in 1933, Roosevelt's confidence was understandable. A *Fortune* magazine poll showed that more than half of those questioned believed the Depression was over.

The Republicans met in Cleveland on June 10 to choose a nominee to face Roosevelt in the fall. Kansas governor Alfred Landon, a moderate with a streak of independence, emerged with the nomination. He was a competent, decent public official with a good record and a bland personality. Roosevelt's aides were delighted with the Republicans' choice.

More troubling was the emergence of a third-party challenge that had the support of Father Coughlin, the late Huey Long's supporters, and another well-known critic of the New Deal, Dr. Francis Everett Townsend. The new Union Party nominated a congressman from North Dakota named William Lemke just days after Landon accepted the Republican nomination. As the Democrats assembled in Philadelphia on June 23, they faced opposition from the right and the left. While potentially troubling, the two-front battle merely reflected the larger struggle Roosevelt fought during most of his first term.

After an uneventful few days during which Democrats found nothing to dispute, the party faithful assembled in Franklin Field in Philadelphia on June 27 to hear their president's acceptance speech. The stadium held more than a hundred thousand people, and it was jammed. Roosevelt arrived by car at around ten o'clock to deliver a speech that would be broadcast throughout the county by radio.

Such occasions were never routine, of course, given the president's disability and his insistence on performing as if he really could command his legs to carry him forward. He strode slowly from the car toward the podium, leaning on the arm of his son James, smiling as flashbulbs illuminated his face and all those teeth. In an instant, however, the façade collapsed. One of the president's leg braces came loose, causing FDR to lose his balance. The pages of his acceptance speech went flying, and the president himself nearly tumbled to the ground. According to biographer Jean Edward Smith, Roosevelt had been moving towards the elderly poet, Edwin Markham, when the brace came undone. Embarrassed and furious, Roosevelt told his aides to "clean me up" and to "keep your feet off those damned sheets," meaning the pages of his speech.[10] Roosevelt later described his near fall as "the most frightful five minutes of my life." Markham, watching the president's helplessness, was moved to tears. Most of the audience was unaware of what happened.

As Roosevelt reached the podium, the stadium exploded in cheers, allowing him time to catch his breath and to shuffle through the pages of his speech to make sure they were in the right order. The text itself was the product of two teams of writers, Rosenman and High working on one version, and two other aides, Thomas Corcoran and Raymond Moley, working on another. Both teams worked independently of one another—for a while, neither team knew about the other team's work—and the final version was a combination of the two drafts.

The result was a speech that contained the militant language that Roosevelt had been using since the Schechter decision—that was the work of Rosenman and High—along with several humble passages aimed at FDR's critics, which Corcoran and Moley wrote.

He began on a grace note, thanking not only his fellow Democrats but "those of other parties" in Congress and in state capitals who "participated unselfishly...to achieve recovery and destroy abuses." But, he quickly added, he was unable to "tell you that all is well with the world." Although Americans had wiped out "political tyranny" in the very city in which he spoke, a new king of tyranny was at work in the land. New tyrants—Roosevelt called them "economic royalists"—had built a system in which there was "no place" for ordinary working Americans. "And as a result the average man once more confronts the problem that faced the Minute Men."

Roosevelt placed the New Deal squarely in the tradition of the American Revolution, a struggle for equality and for liberty. "Liberty requires opportunity to make a living—a living decent according to the standard of the time, a living which gives man not only enough to live by, but something to live for." Here, then, was an expansive notion of liberty, born of the trials of the Depression. Americans had political liberties, but those were not enough. The right to make a decent living was as precious as the right to choose one's leaders.

He continued to use a phrase that was certain to infuriate his opponents. "These economic royalists," he said, "complain that we seek to overthrow the institutions of America. What they really complain of is that we seek to take away their power...In their blindness they forget what the flag and the Constitution stand for."

In such a struggle, ordinary Americans had no choice but to turn to the one entity that could defeat the forces of "economic tyranny." And that was "the organized power of Government."

Roosevelt's speech was extraordinarily divisive. He described other Americans—the wealthy and privileged—as "the resolute enemy." "For more than three years we have fought them," he said, inviting his audience to think of themselves as soldiers aligned against the "economic royalists."

He conceded, perhaps in a subtle reference to the Schechter case, that governments "can err, Presidents do make mistakes, but the immortal Dante tells us that divine justice weighs the sins of the cold-blooded and the sins of the warm-hearted in different scales." His mistakes, then, were errors of the heart.

Despite those mistakes, the nation would continue to move forward toward a goal he could see in the distant horizon. “There is,” he said, “a mysterious cycle in human events. To some generations much is given. Of other generations much is expected.

“This generation of Americans,” he thundered, “has a rendezvous with destiny.” The nation was destined to fight a “war against want and destitution and economic demoralization,” but the task did not stop there.

“It is more than that; it is a war for the survival of democracy. We are fighting to save a great and precious form of government for ourselves and for the world. I accept the commission you have tendered me. I join with you.

“I am enlisted for the duration of the war.”

With that, a hundred thousand Americans leaped to their feet to salute their president, a man who had put aside five frightening minutes to define a struggle in which they all would play a part.

The Tennessee Valley Authority provided jobs and transformed the South during the 1930s. Here, work progresses on the Douglas Dam, a TVA project on the French Bread River.

CHAPTER 7

"I Welcome Their Hatred"

Preelection Speech in Madison Square Garden

October 31, 1936

TRACK 7

PERHAPS BECAUSE HE SAW HIMSELF AS THE SOLE ISSUE IN THE 1936 CAMPAIGN, Franklin Roosevelt campaigned for reelection as if he were in a tight contest with a formidable foe. As biographer Jean Edward Smith noted, once the campaign began in earnest after Labor Day, Roosevelt delivered more than two hundred speeches during a sixty-day railroad trip across the country. The journey was all the more grueling, Smith observed, because Roosevelt insisted that his train never travel faster than 30 miles an hour. The slower speed made it easier for him to move about the train, according to Smith, but he also enjoyed watching the scenery—the mountains, plains, towns, and cities visible from the windows of his car. FDR wasn't interested in speeding from speech to speech. He wanted to absorb the stories written in the American countryside, stories about people far removed from the Hudson Valley, from New York City, from the corridors of power in Washington, DC.

He understood and appreciated that his life experience was far removed from the average American's. He was president; he was wealthy; he was from New York. The people he saw from his window—some staring back at him, others ignoring the commotion altogether as they harvested their crops or went about their chores—were not the people he socialized with, haggled with, dealt with, on a daily basis. And he was aware of that, even if some of his aides occasionally forgot. When James Farley, chairman of the Democratic National Committee, described Alf Landon's Kansas as a "typical prairie state," Roosevelt took him to task. According to Smith's biography, Roosevelt told Farley: "Never use the word 'typical'" when referring to a state like Kansas. The word, he said, was "meat for the opposition" because it came from a New Yorker.[1]

Aside from the dustup over Farley's insensitive remark, Roosevelt's reelection campaign was relatively flawless. Landon never gained any traction even though, as Rosenman predicted, he had the support of many editorial pages. The Republicans had little problem raising money, especially from wealthy donors infuriated by Roosevelt's soak-the-rich tax hike. In fact, with $14 million (more than $200 million today) to spend, the Landon campaign was better funded than Roosevelt's, which raised about $9 million (or about $130 million today).

While the Republicans were unable to take advantage of their financial edge, they did sharpen their attacks on FDR as the campaign unfolded. Some Republicans suggested that FDR was on the verge of becoming a dictator, a serious charge at a time when Germany, Italy, and the Soviet Union were in the hands of tyrants. Father Coughlin, attempting to prop up his faltering Union Party, became unhinged when he spoke of Roosevelt, which was often. He called Roosevelt a liar, he engaged in anti-Semitic attacks on FDR's Jewish advisors, and he accused the president of being an "anti-God."

The relentless attacks and their bitter tone angered Roosevelt, although he did his best to ignore them in public. His anger began to boil over, however, when some of the country's large employers included something extra in the pay envelopes of their workers—not additional pay, but political leaflets attacking the new Social Security program. "The propaganda was intended to create the impression that employees alone were going to pay for their unemployment and old-age insurance and would not reap corresponding benefits," Rosenman recalled.[2] In fact, to the chagrin of some in the business community, employer contributions to Social Security were double that of workers. The circulars also hinted that the money collected for social insurance might actually be used for other purposes.

As the campaign neared its final days, Roosevelt decided to answer his critics in kind. His ire was not aimed at Landon, who conducted a fairly innocuous campaign and who, as a moderate Republican, was not necessarily opposed to every aspect of the New Deal program. Roosevelt and Landon were quite civil in speaking of one another, and when their paths crossed at a conference during the campaign, they greeted each other warmly. "Governor, however this comes out, we'll see more of each other," Roosevelt told Landon. He also had a piece of advice for his adversary: "And Governor, don't work too hard."[3]

Roosevelt was not so kindly disposed to those acting on Landon's behalf, particularly those in the business community who, he believed, were trying to spread fear among workers—fear, the very emotion he sought to banish during his first term. The president lashed out at the business community during a speech in Wilkes-Barre, Pennsylvania, in the heart of the commonwealth's old coal belt. "No employer has a right to put his political preferences in the pay envelope," Roosevelt said. "That is coercion even if he tells the whole truth..."[4]

Two days later, on October 31, Roosevelt was due to speak in New York's Madison Square Garden at a get-out-the-vote rally in his home state. The president assigned four speechwriters—Sam Rosenman, Thomas Corcoran, Benjamin Cohen, and Stanley High—to produce a document that would give voice to his anger while reminding voters of the achievements of his first term. FDR told his writers to take the gloves off, and so they did, crafting a speech that portrayed his critics as idle in the face of catastrophe and selfish in the face of suffering. Rosenman later recalled that the speechwriting team and FDR himself spent more time drafting the Garden speech than any other during the campaign. Rosenman believed the final result was the best speech of the '36 campaign.[5]

New York's Democrats turned out en masse to salute one of their own at the Garden rally. Presiding over the affair were Senator Robert F. Wagner, hero of the labor unions that were a vital part of Roosevelt's popular coalition, and Governor Herbert Lehman, Roosevelt's handpicked successor as the state's chief executive. Those who streamed into the Garden worshipped Roosevelt as the man who delivered them from despair, even though the city's economy, like the nation's itself, was far from prosperous.

Roosevelt, beaming as his fellow Democrats shook the arena's rafters with their cheers and stomping, began with a reprise of 1932, reminding his audience of those dark days and all that was at stake in that year's presidential election. "In 1932 the issue was the restoration of American democracy, and the American people were in a mood to win. They did win." Those two sentences might sound like generic campaign rhetoric today, but there was no mistaking the message. Roosevelt framed his triumph in 1932 not as a rejection of a failed economic policy, not as a collective yearning for a more aggressive response to widespread unemployment and want, but as nothing less than a victory for democracy. He and his supporters, then, stood not simply for economic change, but for democracy itself. His critics, by extension, were undemocratic; they opposed the restoration of democracy and, in fact, were responsible for its decline. They were, after all, "economic royalists," as the president described his critics earlier in the year.

Warming up to the topic, and giving a hint of harsher rhetoric to come, Roosevelt said there was no reason to reprise the details of "the program which this Administration has been hammering out on the anvils of experience." He was, after all, among friends who had been his partners in struggling for change. "Tonight," he said, speaking directly to his listeners, "I call the roll—the roll of honor of those who stood with us in 1932 and still stand with us today." That list would not include Democrats like Al Smith and John Davis, prominent Democratic businessmen who joined the Liberty League, and rhetorical bomb-throwers like Father Coughlin. They stood with Roosevelt in 1932, but they were among the missing as Roosevelt recited from his roll of honor.

Written on that roll, he said, "are the names of millions who never had a chance—men at starvation wages, women in sweatshops, children at looms." The word picture offered a glimpse of a Dickensian America, a place where men, women, and even children sold their labor for desperation wages. "Written on it," he continued, "are the names of those who despaired, young men and young women for whom opportunity had become will o' the wisp...Written there in large letters are the names of countless other Americans of all parties and all faiths, Americans who had eyes to see and hearts to understand, whose consciences were burdened because too many of their fellows were burdened, who looked on these things four years ago and said, 'This can be changed. We will change it.'"

Roosevelt's roll of honor was broad and expansive, no mere roster of partisan loyalists. It included—in large letters—those who crossed party lines to support him in 1932, and would do so again, because they saw suffering and wished to end it.

What of those left off the roll of honor? Roosevelt launched into his assault with a barrage of words and images that he held in reserve until the campaign's last moment. The anger that had been building up for weeks finally exploded in a torrent of abuse.

"For twelve years this Nation was afflicted with hear-nothing, see-nothing, do-nothing government," he said, expanding his targets of opportunity to include not just the Hoover administration and the Depression, but the Roaring Twenties and the presidencies of Calvin Coolidge and Warren Harding as well. "The nation looked to government but government looked away." Roosevelt then deployed biblical language to frame the prosperity of the 1920s as false and hollow, leading almost inevitably to destiny's retribution. "Nine mocking years with the golden calf," he said, referring to the long-forgotten Jazz Age, "and three years of the scourge! Nine crazy years at the ticker and three long years in the breadlines! Nine mad years of mirage and three long years of despair! Powerful influences strive today to restore that kind of government with its doctrine that that government is best which is most indifferent."

Roosevelt's description of the 1920s is telling. The decade surely was memorable. The nation was at peace. Cultural figures like Charles Lindbergh, Babe Ruth, tennis champion Helen Wills, actress Mary Pickford, actor Charlie Chaplin, and golfer Bobby Jones kept the nation entertained, and distracted. Men and women who were young and prosperous during the Roaring Twenties enjoyed themselves as few Americans ever had.

They might have been expected to look back at those years with bittersweet nostalgia. But the crash and the Depression taught them lessons that would remain with them for the rest of their days. They did not object when FDR described the twenties as a "golden calf" and a "mirage." With their votes in 1932, they had passed judgment on the ethos and excesses of the Jazz Age.

After hooking his listeners with the bait of class warfare, Roosevelt prepared to reel them in with a scorching assault on the New Deal's enemies. He avoided party labels, as well he might, for he brought Republicans into his administration from the very beginning, and implicitly acknowledged the support of Republican voters in the opening of this very speech. But he was about to issue some of the most divisive words of his presidency.

He and his supporters, he said, "had to struggle with the old enemies of peace—business and financial monopoly, speculation, reckless banking, class antagonism, sectionalism, war profiteering." It was an astonishing litany: The New Deal's foes were not merely obstacles to economic reform. They were the enemies of peace. They profited from war. They were reckless. They were greedy. "They had begun to consider the Government of the United States as a mere appendage to their own affairs," he continued. "We know now that Government by organized money is just as dangerous as Government by organized mob."

He was not nearly done, but his listeners were in a frenzy. "Never before in all our history have these forces been so united against one candidate as they stand today," Roosevelt said, setting up his punch line. "They are unanimous in their hate for me," he said, pausing for effect, "and I welcome their hatred."

The crowd roared. They welcomed their hatred as well. But Roosevelt was not finished. He had waited long enough to reply to the pay-envelope propaganda campaign; now, he gave full vent to his anger. Those who hated him, he said, were "desperate" because he had the "pass-key" to the White House—and they didn't. "Only desperate men with their backs to the wall would descend so far below the level of decent citizenship as to foster the current pay-envelope campaign against America's working people," he said.

"Only reckless men, heedless of consequences, would risk the disruption of the hope for a new peace between worker and employer by returning to the tactics of the labor spy.

"Here is an amazing paradox! The very employers and politicians and publishers who talk most loudly of class antagonism and the destruction of the American system now undermine that system by this attempt to coerce the votes of the wage earners of this country."

The Garden faithful went wild as FDR replied in kind to his critics. But a seemingly innocuous phrase captured as much attention as his slashing condemnation of those who hated him. "I should like to have it said of my first administration that in it the forces of selfishness and of lust for power met their match," he told the crowd. "I should like to have it said of my second administration that in it these forces met their master."

The display of absolute confidence was notable—three days before Election Day, FDR was speaking about his second term as if it were already assured. But one word at the end of the passage caught the ear of critics. The word was "master."

Speechwriter Sam Rosenman, who helped draft this speech, later wrote that "the wires began to hum, the columnists began to should, the editorial writers began to scream, and the Republican orators began to orate." Roosevelt's description of himself as a "master" showed that he was intent on becoming a dictator. Critics charged that the president had confirmed their assertions that he was intent on seizing absolute power—the comparison with the dictators of Europe was both implicit, and explicit. Rosenman recalled that in the campaign's final hours, some Democrats asked Roosevelt to retract or clarify his assertion. He refused to do so, convinced that the charges were desperate and ridiculous.

The American people agreed. On November 3, 1936, Franklin Roosevelt was reelected in an historic landslide. He took nearly 61 percent of the popular vote, winning 27.7 million votes to Landon's 16.6 million. He won every state except for Maine and Vermont, piling up 523 votes in the Electoral College to Landon's eight.

With a sweeping mandate in hand, Roosevelt was ready to confront those he saw as obstacles to change.

PART TWO:
Recovery, Recession, and War, 1937–1940

LINE FOR
1¢ RESTAURANT
20 MEALS FOR $1
DONATIONS INVITED
HELP FEED THE HUNGRY
$1 WILL FEED 20
1¢ RESTAURANT
107 W 43rd ST.
D.S.

Introduction

As Franklin Roosevelt took the oath of office for the second time in 1937, he was determined to take advantage of the huge mandate voters gave him in his race against Alf Landon. What followed was a textbook example of presidential overreach as Roosevelt misjudged the nation's sentiments and his own ability to sell a so-called "court reform" package that was, in fact, an effort to pack the Supreme Court with supporters of his program.

The plan to appoint a new Supreme Court justice for each one over age seventy failed miserably, handing Roosevelt a bitter defeat at a time when he seemed politically invulnerable. It led to another blunder, this one an attempt to purge the Democratic Party of critics and opponents. The purge, carried out by presidential aides who were more fluent in policy than in politics, failed miserably.

On a more substantive level, an unexpected recession in 1937 brought economic growth to a screeching halt and led Roosevelt and some aides to adopt a more conservative course. Roosevelt, determined to eliminate deficit spending, cut the federal budget to bring it nearly into balance for fiscal year 1938. The measure failed to restore economic growth. In fact, the stock market crashed again in early 1938. With congressional elections looming and voters grumbling about a "Roosevelt recession," the president ramped up federal spending again to stimulate the economy. He proposed and Congress quickly approved a stimulus package of more than $3 billion in new spending.

As the president attempted once again to pull the nation out of hard times, events overseas began to intrude. Dictators in Germany and Italy were dazzling their nations with talk of expansion and war, while militarists in Japan dispatched troops to China. As Roosevelt's second term—his final term, according to tradition—progressed, events around the globe took a more sinister turn as Germany swallowed up Austria and Czechoslovakia, Italy invaded Ethiopia, and the Japanese and Chinese engaged in a full-scale war. Voices in America demanded that the United States remain aloof from a world out of control.

Roosevelt, however, believed the nation had a stake in halting and rolling back the forces of aggression in Europe and Asia. On September 1, 1939, Germany invaded Poland, and Britain and France declared war on Germany several days later. Roosevelt promised that American troops would not be sent overseas, but he also believed that Britain and France were fighting not only for their own freedom, but America's.

In a break with precedent, Franklin Roosevelt ran for a third term in 1940. He did so as an overt ally of embattled Britain, which faced the prospect of invasion after the French surrendered to Germany in the spring.

On Election Day, voters gave Roosevelt another four-year term, hoping he might guide them to safety in a frightening and dangerous world. But not long after the election, Roosevelt made it clear that America would have a role to play in the war: the country, he said, would be an "arsenal of democracy."

Even as the nation's fortunes improved under the New Deal, unemployment remained high and soup kitchens continued to be a fixture in American life.

CHAPTER 8

A Third of the Nation

Second Inaugural Address

January 20, 1937

TRACK 8

According to speechwriter Sam Rosenman, Franklin Roosevelt devoted more time and effort on his second inaugural address than on any other speech during his presidency. Rosenman wrote that the president spent hours making "corrections, inserts, substitutions and deletions" on various drafts.[1] The president's year of editing the Harvard *Crimson* no doubt gave him the confidence to critique his writers' prose in search of the right language for the messages he wished to deliver. Roosevelt, Rosenman remembered, "had a marked ability to contract a long sentence into a shorter and more effective one."[2] That was the mark of any good newspaper editor.

The president's historic landslide over Alf Landon in November prompted his allies to dream big. The *New Republic*, a leading journal of liberal opinion, saw the president's victory as "the greatest revolution in our political history."[3] Many New Deal supporters believed that a second Roosevelt term could build on reforms designed to alleviate the economic crisis, to create a new economic order with an expanded and permanent place for government in the private economy. Those hopes were based on the New Deal's undeniable successes during FDR's first term. The nation's private corporations showed a profit of

$5 billion in 1936, compared with collective losses of $2 billion four years earlier.[4] The nation's gross national product grew by about 14 percent in 1936, a far cry from the 15 percent decrease in GNP in 1932. The crisis, it seemed, had passed. Washington could now think beyond the nation's immediate problems to a more comprehensive program of change.

Roosevelt, however, understood that while the economy was healing, it was by no means recovered. Short-term solutions, improvisation, and flexibility remained paramount as the administration grappled with an unemployment rate of nearly 17 percent. Perhaps most important, the Supreme Court was proving to be a formidable barrier to change and would surely prevent the ambitious reforms that many liberals were anticipating.

While the president and his speechwriters worked on the second inaugural, Roosevelt was thinking about a political revolution, but perhaps not the sort that the editors of the *New Republic* envisioned. Like many of his social class, Roosevelt was keenly interested in British politics. In private conversations with aides, the president compared his plight to that of a Liberal Party government nearly thirty years earlier. FDR was fuzzy on the facts—he believed a confrontation between the House of Commons and the House of Lords grew out of attempts to give the Irish home rule. In fact, it was much more analogous to his own situation.

Beginning in 1908, the House of Lords, filled with aging members of the opposition Conservative Party, used its powers to block Prime Minister Herbert Asquith's sweeping reforms, which included old-age pensions and budgets designed to redistribute wealth from Britain's landed class to its workers. Asquith, leader of the Liberal Party, fired back by introducing a bill designed to strip the Lords of its powers over legislation passed in the Commons, especially budget bills. When the Lords tried to stop this bill as well, Asquith, working with King George V, prompted a constitutional crisis by proposing the creation of 250 new members of the Lords, all of them Liberals loyal to his program. The Conservative majority in the Lords surrendered rather than agree to a Liberal takeover, allowing Asquith's reforms to pass. The House of Lords was removed as an obstacle to reform in Britain.

Roosevelt scholar William E. Leuchtenburg said that the British precedent "captivated" Roosevelt, inspiring him to begin to think about diluting the influence of the Court's conservative majority with new justices who would support his reforms.[5] With his overwhelming mandate from the people, Roosevelt believed he had the power to provoke a confrontation just as Asquith did a generation earlier.

The final draft of Roosevelt's second inaugural hinted at his annoyance with the Court. But that was hardly the only message FDR wished to send as he embarked on a second term. He wanted to speak directly to those who believed hard times were over, that reduced rates of unemployment meant an end to mass suffering, that the time had come to look ahead rather than deal with the problems of the present. Roosevelt sought to remind the country that many fellow citizens remained in dire straits, still unable to make ends meet.

As he and his aides pored over drafts of the inaugural address, Roosevelt took pen in hand and scribbled several phrases that conveyed the themes he wished to strike as he began his second term. Implicit in Roosevelt's own words was a criticism of the Court and of critics who believed that the New Deal had gone far enough, that there was no further need for change. "Shall we pause now and turn our back upon the road that lies ahead?" he wrote. "Shall we call this the promised land?" Clearly, he did not believe most of his listeners were content with the status quo. They reelected him not simply because of his performance in the past. They reelected him so that he might continue the New Deal's work.

He continued to write, making an argument on behalf of those who still were suffering. Rosenman described what it was like when the president was moved to try his own hand at speechwriting. Roosevelt, he wrote, "would suddenly lay down his pen, lean back in his large swivel armchair, throw his head back, and look up at the ceiling intently."[6] He was quiet for three or four minutes, his aides waiting to hear the great man's thoughts. Finally, he would either start writing or would dictate passages to his secretary, Grace Tully.

On this occasion, the phrases he chose became the best-remembered passage of the speech. In simple language, he evoked the injustices he saw: millions without education, millions without recreation, millions denied the chance for a decent life. "I see one-third of a nation ill-housed, ill-clad, ill-nourished," he wrote.

He read the passages aloud to his speechwriters. "He was very pleased," recalled Rosenman, "so was his audience."[7]

Inauguration Day 1937 was the first to be held in January rather than March. The Twentieth Amendment to the U.S. Constitution, ratified not long after FDR's first inauguration, set the date earlier to speed up presidential transitions and allow an incoming president to take control more quickly.

While the change did allow for a quicker, more efficient transition, Roosevelt and the thousands who gathered for his second inaugural may have wondered about the wisdom of the new date. January 20, 1937, was cold and dreary, a midwinter's day. More than forty thousand people huddled under umbrellas to witness the swearing-in. The president and his party must have looked out at the audience with envy, for the podium and platform on the Capitol's east side had no covering at all. Everybody was drenched; rainwater dripped down the side of Roosevelt's face as he delivered his speech.

It was a surprisingly partisan speech that spared little in its description of the New Deal's critics. Not so surprisingly, Roosevelt reminded his listeners of the nation's plight four years earlier, and the progress the nation had made since. The nation, he said, had tried to meet the economic catastrophe "without the aid of government," only to be left "baffled and bewildered." The genius of the New Deal, he argued, was that it understood that "we must find practical controls over blind economic forces and blindly selfish men." As he demonstrated in his preelection speech in New York, Roosevelt increasingly was willing to take rhetorical potshots at business leaders and other economic elites, to the delight of his base of supporters.

He hinted, however, that there were other obstacles to change besides the desires of "blindly selfish men." During the course of what seemed like a boilerplate tribute to the Constitution in a year that marked the 150th anniversary of its passage, he noted that the founders sought to create a government that would "promote the general welfare and secure the blessings of liberty to the American people." That remained the goal of government, he said. But that goal could not be achieved through "the absence of power." Rather, it required the use of power by those chosen by the people in "honest and free elections."

"The Constitution of 1787," he intoned, "did not make our democracy impotent." On that dreary, wet afternoon, Roosevelt's words may not have struck his drenched listeners as particularly memorable. But, as they would soon learn, they offered a hint about his evolving plans to change the Supreme Court so that his administration would no longer feel helpless in the face of continued economic and social suffering.

He then drew on the questions he wrote himself for this occasion, asking his listeners if they believed the effort of the last four years was sufficient. "Have we found our happy valley?" he asked. He then provided the answer he wrote himself:

"I see a great nation, upon a great continent, blessed with a great wealth of natural resources...But here is the challenge to our democracy: In this nation I see tens of millions of its citizens—a substantial part of its whole population—who at this very moment are denied the greater part of what the very lowest standards of today call the necessities of life.

"I see millions of families trying to live on incomes so meager that the pall of family disaster hangs over them day by day.

"I see millions whose daily lives in city and on farm continue under conditions labeled indecent by a so-called polite society half a century ago...

"I see one-third of a nation ill-housed, ill-clad, ill-nourished."

He did not seek to paint a picture of despair, he said. Rather, he saw in the imagery he presented a picture of hope, because the nation was determined to make sure that the ill-housed, ill-clad, ill-nourished were given the help they needed. "The test of our progress," he said, "is not whether we add more to the abundance of those who have much; it is whether we provide enough for those who have too little."

The speech framed the government's continued commitment to the poor as a moral obligation worthy of a great nation that understood the lessons of the past. "Old truths have been relearned; untruths have been unlearned," he said. "We have always known that heedless self-interest was bad morals; we know now that it is bad economics." Roosevelt focused more on the former than the latter, framing his program and his views in a moral setting. The language was familiar to him, for the Progressives he admired, like his cousin Teddy Roosevelt and his former boss Woodrow Wilson, saw politics and government as a morality play. He declared: "Out of the collapse of a prosperity whose builders boasted their practicality has come the conviction that in the long run economic morality pays." His program sought to achieve "the establishment of a morally better world."

Roosevelt said he was confident that Americans would demand an end to "the cancers of injustice." Doing so would require collective action, for while Americans were "individualists" in their "personal ambitions," he said, they understood that in the struggle for economic and political progress, "we all go up, or else we all go down, as one people."

But there were nine people who had the power to block economic and political progress. They were on the platform, as wet and cold as everybody else. The nine justices of the Supreme Court didn't realize it, but Franklin Roosevelt was about to declare war. On them.

President Roosevelt, emboldened by his landslide reelection, believed he had public support for his attempt to reform the Supreme Court. But even a fireside chat about the proposal failed to change the nation's negative opinion.

CHAPTER 9

Packing the Court

Fireside Chat

March 9, 1937

TRACK 9

WHAT TO DO WITH THE SUPREME COURT?

The question was not new. Roosevelt started asking it in early 1935, even before the Schechter sick chicken case, when he asked his attorney general, Homer Cummings, to look into the possibility of appointing additional justices to the bench just as Ulysses Grant had done during a similar confrontation with the Court in 1870. As he began his new term, after the justices struck down a half dozen pieces of New Deal legislation during his first four years in office, Roosevelt was determined to find a way of getting a friendlier reception for his program in the nation's highest court.

Few of the president's aides were aware that Cummings was working on a plan to restructure the Court so that FDR would have a built-in majority. Ironically, the Cummings plan had an administrative precedent—during the Wilson Administration, Attorney General James McReynolds proposed adding a new justice to the Court for every member over seventy with more than a decade of experience. McReynolds's plan went nowhere, but now he was on the Court himself, and was among the justices FDR regarded as an obstacle to change.

Roosevelt's inaugural address offered a hint of his dissatisfaction with the Court and his determination to do something about the impasse between the executive and judicial branches. He received a report from Cummings in late January in which the attorney general outlined a bill to reorganize the entire federal judiciary, setting the retirement age at seventy and allowing the president to appoint a new justice for every one over the retirement age. Roosevelt was delighted: Cummings's proposal, he said, was "the answer to a maiden's prayer."[1]

Emboldened by his historic mandate, worried that a hostile Court would continue to thwart his agenda for another four years, FDR set out to remake the judicial branch in his own image. He was unwilling to simply wait for the older members of the Court to retire or to die with their robes on. Picking on McReynolds, the unwitting inspiration of the plan FDR seized upon, the president said that the elderly justice and irritating foe of the New Deal "will still be on the bench when he is a hundred and five years old."[2]

Continuing to keep his own counsel, Roosevelt asked his attorney general and solicitor general, Stanley Reed, to put the proposal into legislative language. The bill had to be crafted so that the president could present it, with a straight face, as a nonpartisan measure aimed at improving the efficiency of the federal court system.

In late January, Roosevelt expanded the small circle that knew what he had in mind. Speechwriter Samuel Rosenman was summoned to the White House for an impromptu luncheon with the president on January 30, 1937. Attorney General Cummings, Solicitor General Reed, and lawyer and presidential advisor Donald Richberg joined Rosenman and Roosevelt for what appeared to be an inconsequential, meandering meal in the Oval Office. The president said the lunch reminded him of a story about a warship disguised as a merchant vessel during World War I. When a German submarine confronted the ship on the high seas, its captain meekly allowed the sub to approach it in preparation for boarding. But when the sub grew close, Roosevelt said, the innocent merchant vessel was transformed into a warship, a false side wall collapsing to reveal an array of guns. Roosevelt, Richberg, Cummings, and Reed burst into knowing laughter. Rosenman wondered what in the world the story had to do with their lunch. He soon found out.

Once the plates were put away and the Oval Office door was closed, Roosevelt revealed the purpose of the luncheon meeting. Cummings, he said, had presented him with a letter and a draft of a proposed message to Congress. The president read them aloud. They contained several recommendations to reform and reorganize the federal judiciary system. The burden on the nation's federal judges was oppressive, the draft message stated, resulting in inefficiencies and a backlog in the federal court system. To remedy this intolerable situation, the Cummings document proposed that the president be given the power to appoint an additional judge for every judge over the age of seventy in the federal judiciary system—including the Supreme Court.

Rosenman quickly realized that he was the only one of the five men in the room who didn't have a clue that this proposal was in the works. He also realized that the president was enamored with the idea of emphasizing the workload on current federal judges, rather than a more straightforward appeal to the public for support in adding younger judges to the bench. "The whole plan appealed to Roosevelt as a subtle device for getting what he wanted without being charged with 'packing' the Court because of disagreement with the trend of its decisions," Rosenman later wrote. Roosevelt may have seen the plan as subtle, but not everybody did, Rosenman included. "It was hard to understand how he [FDR] expected to make people believe that he was suddenly interested primarily in delayed justice rather than in ending a tortured interpretation of the Constitution, but the cleverness, the too much cleverness, appealed to him."[3]

It fell to Rosenman, the only man in the room who was not privy to the proposal before the meeting, to revise the plan's language before it was sent to Congress. Roosevelt told him privately that the proposal, as drafted by Cummings, "leaves me cold."[4]

"We will have to rewrite it," he told Rosenman. "I wish you would try to get up another draft."

Roosevelt knew that however clever the language, however subtle the message, the proposal was bound to create an enormous controversy. That certainty presented him with a diplomatic problem: the entire Supreme Court was due for dinner at the White House on February 2. Common decency dictated that the president could not reveal his plan before the dinner. But the justices were due to hear arguments on a number of New Deal issues on February 8, and Roosevelt wanted the proposal made public before they began their deliberations. The president decided to go public with the plan in the days between the two events.

So, on the evening of February 2, Roosevelt prepared to welcome his antagonists to the White House for an annual event known as the Judiciary Dinner. Before the guests arrived, Roosevelt assembled several aides in the first-floor dining room for cocktails, a daily routine in the White House before dinner. The president himself was in charge, mixing and matching various concoctions without the assistance of any measuring equipment. Gin, vermouth, and sometimes rum flowed in great quantities, with the president serving as an overly solicitous bartender. "How about another little sippy?" he'd ask an aide whose glass seemed too dry.[5]

On this occasion, the liquor no doubt helped the president and his aides prepare for an extraordinary night at the White House. The atmosphere was more serious, the conversation more muted, than was usually the case during these sessions. The very men who were about to come under Roosevelt's fire were assembling in the East Room while Roosevelt and his top aides drank a toast, apparently without irony, to the Supreme Court. But FDR grumbled that he was not looking forward to the evening, insisting several times that it was time to do something about the Court.

As show time approached, Eleanor Roosevelt joined the less-than-festive festivities. She scolded the president about his appearance, saying that his trousers were showing signs of wear. Roosevelt, with a knowing wink, replied that he didn't have the money to buy a new suit.

The drinks were put away, and the president and his party moved to the East Room, where seven of the nine justices, along with nearly a hundred other guests, were gathered for dinner. Justice Louis Brandeis was among the missing, as he always was—he made a point of not participating in Washington's social life. Justice Harlan Stone also was absent because of an illness.

As the other justices mingled with White House aides who knew what the president was planning, some of the president's men could barely stand the tension. Attorney General Cummings, author of the still-secret scheme, grabbed Rosenman and told him he wished the proposal had already been publicized. "I feel too much like a conspirator."[6]

If the attorney general was sweating a bit, the president was perfectly at ease, smoking, sipping brandy, and chatting pleasantly with Chief Justice Charles Evans Hughes. Both men were former governors of New York, and they addressed each other as "Governor." There was not a hint of tension between the head of the executive branch and the chief of the judicial branch.

Roosevelt thoroughly enjoyed himself. Rosenman, who watched him carefully, concluded that FDR was at ease with his decision and glad to be doing something about the problem.

The dinner was a success. Three days later, Roosevelt's guests found out that their host was not nearly as convivial as they thought.

If Roosevelt managed to hide his emotions over dinner, he was less inhibited about expressing his anxiety in the hours leading up to publication of his plan. He asked Rosenman to stay at the White House rather than return to New York until the proposal was sent to Congress on February 5. He told White House staff to come to work at six thirty in the morning to make copies of the message to avoid any leaks. He quickly scheduled a morning meeting to inform his Cabinet of his decision, and then sent the proposal to Capitol Hill at noon.

Reaction was swift, and emotional. If Roosevelt thought he was being subtle, or clever, he soon learned that nobody was taken in by his declared desire to lessen the work load for federal judges. His obvious assault on older justices didn't sit well even with some New Dealers, who noted that the oldest man on the Court was Louis Brandeis, an eighty-year-old ally of the president.

Part of the problem was the proposal's secrecy. Roosevelt consulted only a handful of aides—and no members of Congress—as the proposal was being formulated. Allies in Congress were taken by surprise, and as a general rule, members of Congress do not like surprises, especially when they're controversial. William Bankhead, Speaker of the House of Representatives, was at a loss when he heard of Roosevelt's plan. He asked a colleague, Representative Lindsay Warren: "Lindsay, wouldn't you have thought that the President would have told his own party leaders what he was going to do?"[7] Perhaps, but that was not FDR's style. Most of his Cabinet was kept in the dark as well.

Opposition came from the left, the center, and the right. The chairman of the House Judiciary Committee, Hatton Summers, announced his opposition, a key defection. The *Nation*, a liberal journal, noted that the proposal could lead a segregationist president to pack the Court with opponents of civil rights. Some Democrats pointed out that expanding the number of judges was no guarantee that the new appointees would vote as the president wished.

Franklin Roosevelt had a first-class public-relations catastrophe on his hands. He decided to take his case directly to the voters, the people who handed him such a huge landslide in November. "The people are with me," he said.[8] But he adjusted his message—rather than continue to assert that he was interested in the judges' caseload, he began making the case that the Court was an obstacle to necessary reforms and so required a reform of its own.

He began his appeal on March 4 with a campaign-style speech to a group of fellow Democrats. He used a memorable word picture, which he dictated himself, to describe the three branches of government and the way in which one of those branches—the judiciary—refused to pull its weight. "If three well-matched horses are put to the task of plowing up a field where the going is heavy," he said, "and the team of three pull as one, the field will be plowed. If one horse lies down in the traces or plunges off in another direction, the field will not be plowed."[9]

The imagery was imaginative, but the result was not what Roosevelt expected. He was losing the public relations battle to foes who sensed a sudden vulnerability in the White House, and from friends who simply believed the president was wrong. FDR decided to make his case to the nation as a whole, using the medium that had served him so well in the past. On Sunday, March 9, Roosevelt delivered the first fireside chat of his second term. His sole topic was the battle over the judiciary.

He reminded his audience of the difficult times they had been through, and the progress they had made together. Government action, he said, helped to "prevent and to cure the abuses and the inequalities which had thrown the system out of joint." But now, he said, the nation was "at a crisis in our ability to proceed with that protection."

In times of crisis, nations pulled together, and an informed citizenry took its obligations seriously. Roosevelt told his listeners of his hope that "you have re-read the Constitution of the United States in these past few weeks. Like the Bible, it ought to be read again and again."

Roosevelt set himself up not as a dictator who sought to remove dissidents and critics from an independent judiciary, but as the protector of the nation's founding document. The Constitution was endangered not by his actions, but by those of the justices. "We have, therefore, reached the point as a nation when we must take action to save the Constitution from the Court and the Court from itself," he said. "We want a Supreme Court which will do justice under the Constitution and not over it."

Roosevelt reviewed the proposal that by now was so familiar to his audience. By adding a federal judge for every one over the age of seventy, he said, he would bring in "a steady and continuing stream of new and younger blood." These younger judges would have "personal experience and contact with modern facts and circumstances under which average men have to live and work.

"This plan," he said, "will save our national Constitution from hardening of the judicial arteries."

He knew, and his listeners knew, that critics were suggesting that for all his arguments about the Constitution and the importance of the judicial branch, ultimately he simply wished to override the Court's objections to New Deal reforms. He sought to blunt that criticism by tackling it head on. "Those opposing this plan have sought to arouse prejudice and fear by crying that I am seeking to 'pack' the Supreme Court and that a baneful precedent will be established," he said. "What do they mean by the words, 'packing the Court'? Let me answer this question with a bluntness that will end all honest misunderstandings of my purposes.

"If by that phrase 'packing the Court' it is charged that I wish to place on the bench spineless puppets who would disregard the law and would decide specific cases as I wished them to be decided, I make this answer: that no president fit for his office would appoint, and no Senate of honorable men fit of their office would confirm, that kind of appointees to the Supreme Court."

His plan, he insisted, "is not attack on the Court; it seeks to restore the Court to its rightful and historic place in our Constitutional government..." Those who insisted otherwise, he said, were the very same people who sought "to frighten workers" during the debate over Social Security. "The workers were not fooled by that propaganda then. The people of America will not be fooled by such propaganda now."

Unfortunately for the president, his description of the opposition was not remotely true. While anti-New Dealers certainly opposed the Court plan, so did many otherwise enthusiastic supporters of FDR's agenda. They included one of Roosevelt's earliest supporters in 1932, Senator Burton Wheeler of Montana. He denounced the plan as "not liberal" and was among its leading opponents in the Senate.[10]

As the debate raged on Capitol Hill and across the country, the Court itself was preparing a response in the form of two eagerly awaited decisions. On March 29, the Court declared a state minimum-wage law to be constitutional. The key vote in the 5–4 decision came from Justice Owen J. Roberts, who had voted against other New Deal reforms. A few weeks later, on April 12, the Court upheld the National Labor Relations Act, or Wagner Act, by a 5–4 vote. Roberts again voted for the majority. Suddenly, FDR's plan to remove the Court as an obstacle to change seemed moot. Commentators, speaking of Justice Roberts's apparent change of heart, wryly noted that a switch in time had saved nine.

The White House had won the war, but Roosevelt insisted on continuing the battle, even after another foe on the Court, Justice Willis Van Devanter, announced his retirement in May, and the Court upheld the Social Security Act on May 24. Roosevelt continued to press for his bill, keeping Congress in session through the summer, further alienating friend and foe alike. A key ally, Senate Majority Leader Joseph Robinson of Arkansas, died of a heart attack as he worked desperately to achieve some sort of face-saving compromise for Roosevelt. The president chose not to attend Robinson's funeral, leading to further criticism in the Senate. On July 22, the president's proposal was defeated in the Senate by an overwhelming vote, only twenty in favor, and seventy against.

The Court fight was bungled from beginning to end. Franklin Roosevelt suddenly appeared vulnerable, and the mandate of 1936 seemed a long time ago.

The rise of Adolf Hitler in Germany and Benito Mussolini in Italy prompted Roosevelt to challenge America's isolationists in the late 1930s.

CHAPTER 10

Distant Drums

The Quarantine Speech

October 5, 1937

TRACK 10

WHILE THE UNITED STATES LOOKED INWARD THROUGH THE 1930S, WHILE THE Roosevelt administration rewrote the nation's social compact to include a larger role for government in the management of domestic affairs, ominous events were taking place overseas. Adolf Hitler became chancellor of Germany in January 1933, just a few weeks before Roosevelt took the oath of office for his first term as president. Benito Mussolini already was entrenched as Italy's duce, or supreme leader, and was promising to bring about a new Roman empire. Militarists in control of Japan's government launched an invasion of Manchuria in 1931, leading to armed conflict with China. Civil war broke out in Spain in 1936 when rebel forces supported by Germany and Italy challenged a leftist government supported by the Soviet Union.

Less than two decades had passed since the end of the Great War, when the fields of Europe were soaked with the blood of a lost generation, when the world learned that the mechanization that produced breathtaking innovations in production could also produce enormous slaughter. Modern weapons of war meant that conflict would be fought on a scale never before seen, and that civilians as well as soldiers could be made targets of opportunity.

Great Britain and France, bled dry in the war and subject to the same harsh economic winds that toppled the prosperity of the Roaring Twenties, followed events in Germany and Italy with increasing anxiety. Although both nations had significant military assets—Britain's Royal Navy was the largest in the world, and France's army was formidable—their political leaders feared the consequences of confrontation. The last war had been catastrophic; the next one figured to be unimaginably worse. Air power, primitive during the Great War, now was capable of bringing war from the Continent to the cities and villages of England. Paris, one of the great achievements of human civilization, could be turned into ash by enemy airplanes loaded with bombs.

Ghosts haunted the sleep of decision-makers in both nations, the ghosts of a generation wiped out while fighting for a few feet of land, the ghosts of 1.5 million soldiers killed during the Battle of the Somme in 1916, the ghosts of twenty thousand young British soldiers killed in a single day, July 1, 1916.

Franklin Roosevelt was haunted, too. As assistant secretary of the navy in the Wilson Administration, Roosevelt crossed the Atlantic in the summer of 1918 to pay a firsthand visit to the battlefields of France. It was a mission he didn't have to take, but he was eager to see the war firsthand. And so he did, touring what was left of places like Belleau Wood, where American soldiers and marines attacked and defeated German forces near Paris just weeks before Roosevelt's arrival. Roosevelt's sense of excitement soon gave way to the sobering reality of the western front: corpses half-buried, the remains of letters to loved ones scattered amid the battle's debris; houses roofless and in ruins, men walking through the fields as if in a daze. Roosevelt never forgot those scenes of devastation and horror. The young assistant secretary who was so eager to see war close up returned to Washington a wiser and perhaps sadder man. He supported Woodrow Wilson's dream of resolving international disputes in a League of Nations, telling an audience in 1919 that "the United States would commit a grievous wrong to itself and to all mankind if it were even to attempt to go backwards toward an old Chinese wall policy of isolation."[1]

Wilson failed to win American approval for the League. And the United States was content, during the prosperity of the 1920s and the hard times of the 1930s, to keep the world's quarrels, especially Europe's, at a distance.

That did not mean, however, that the United States had, in fact, moved "backwards toward" a nonexistent past when the nation could seal off the rest of the world. American business, interests, and culture continued to expand overseas after World War I, suggesting that isolationism did not extend to new opportunities to turn a profit. In 1922, the United States joined Britain, France, Italy, and Japan in ratifying an international treaty, negotiated in Washington, to limit the size of naval forces. So if some skeptical American political figures did envision the return of a "Chinese wall policy of isolation," it was a far less daunting obstacle than the original.

As Germany, Italy, and Japan began to make warlike noises in the early and mid-1930s, many Americans had more immediate concerns and, in any case, were not inclined to intervene in the Old World's problems again. The Japanese invasion of Manchuria was followed by Italy's attack against Ethiopia in 1935. Hitler's Germany defied world opinion by rearming in plain violation of limits imposed by the Treaty of Versailles. In March 1936, a revived German army marched into the Rhineland near the French border, a blatant violation of the Treaty's insistence that the region remain demilitarized. Spain erupted that same year.

Speaking in Chautauqua, New York, in the summer of 1936, Roosevelt took note of the new dangers around the globe but made it clear that neither he nor his country were prepared to confront any of the aggressive powers. "I have seen war," he said at Chautauqua. "I have seen war on land and sea. I have seen blood running from the wounded. I have seen men coughing out their gassed lungs. I have seen the dead in the mud. I have seen cities destroyed...I have seen children starving. I have seen the agony of mothers and wives. I hate war."[2]

But there were leaders around the world who had no such qualms. Hitler had seen the same horrors and a good deal more as a corporal on the western front in the German army. The sights, the smells, the agonies of war inspired in him a different sort of hatred, a hatred of those he blamed for his country's defeat, especially Jews, and a burning desire for vengeance. The militarists in Tokyo also had seen, heard, and smelled war, but their memories were of glory and victory when Japan, the rising power of Asia, humiliated Czarist Russia during the Russo-Japanese War in 1904–05. Mussolini bore the scars of war—he was wounded in 1917 when a mortar shell exploded nearby. Dozens of pieces of shrapnel tore through his body. But he did not hate war. He saw it as a means of restoring Italy to greatness.

As the world seemed, incredibly, to be careening towards a new conflagration even while millions still mourned those who perished in the last war, Congress passed legislation designed to ensure American neutrality against the brush fires that erupted around the globe. The neutrality acts barred the United States from selling arms to any nations engaged in combat, even if they were fighting in self-defense. Roosevelt signed the bills without protest. As he often suggested in his speeches about the domestic crisis he inherited, he considered himself at war against poverty, despair, and fear itself at home. He did not need, nor was he willing to consider, a two-front war, one at home, the other overseas.

In July 1937, an ongoing conflict between Japan and China erupted into full-scale war when Japanese forces overran Chinese defenders at the Marco Polo Bridge near Beijing. The invaders quickly seized control of Shanghai and other regions. Hundreds of thousands of troops were rushed into combat, but neither country officially declared war on the other.

The success of the Japanese attack and his sympathies for China prompted FDR to reflect on the nation's insistence on standing aside while the world moved closer to catastrophe. He pointedly declined to bar sales of weapons to either side because, he argued, neither had declared a state of war. The Chinese had the greatest need for weapons, so Roosevelt's refusal to invoke the nation's strict neutrality benefited the victims of Japanese aggression.

Roosevelt's concerns about America's place in a world seemingly intent on going mad led him to schedule a speech in Chicago on October 5, 1937. Chicago was home to one of the nation's leading voices for isolationism, the *Chicago Tribune*, and was a thousand miles removed from the foreign policy establishment of Washington and

New York. It was, then, a good place to see if the nation shared Roosevelt's anxieties.

Known as "The Quarantine Speech," Roosevelt's remarks hinted that the United States could have a role to play in ensuring that war was isolated and stamped out before it could spread. He reminded Americans that innocent civilians and nations were under attack, suggesting that the United States might not be immune from the global disease of war if it were not contained.

The president began by talking about the "prosperous farms, the thriving factories and the busy railroads" he saw on his trip from Washington. From his vantage point, he said, he saw "the happiness and security and peace which covers our wide land."

Those enviable qualities, however, were becoming increasingly scarce in other parts of the world, a situation, he said, which ought to "cause grave concern and anxiety to all the peoples and nations who wish to live in peace and amity with their neighbors."

He acknowledged past hopes that the Great War would be, indeed, a war to end all wars. Following the peace of 1918, nations around the world "solemnly pledged themselves not to resort to arms in furtherance of their national aims and policies." But those hopes, he said, "have of late given way to a haunting fear of calamity."

Without naming names, without citing specific aggressions, Roosevelt reminded his audience that the peaceful scenes of the American heartland were the envy of nations thrust into wars by the aggressive actions of other nations. "Without a declaration of war and without warning or justification of any kind, civilians, including vast numbers of women and children, are being ruthlessly murdered with bombs from the air," he said, an allusion to the war in China. "In times of so-called peace, ships are being attacked and sunk by submarines without cause or notice. Nations are fomenting and taking sides in civil warfare in nations that have never done them any harm. Nations claiming freedom for themselves deny it to others. Innocent peoples, innocent nations, are being cruelly sacrificed to a greed for power and supremacy which is devoid of all sense of justice and humane considerations."

In the modern age, when airplanes made a mockery of conventional defenses, when oceans no longer protected the New World from the feuds and hatreds of the old, the United States could no longer look upon events overseas as beyond its concern, he said. If war continued to break out elsewhere, "let no one imagine that America will escape, that America may expect mercy, that this Western Hemisphere will not be attacked and that it will continue tranquilly and peacefully to carry on the ethics and the arts of civilization."

This, he knew, was not a welcome message. Three thousand miles away, in the House of Commons, a lonely Winston Churchill pleaded with the British government and people to take the threats of Hitler more seriously. But the nation still grieved for its lost generation buried in the fields of France. It would not hear of more war.

The United States was more distant from events in the Old World. Still, Roosevelt said, he and the nation were "compelled, nevertheless, to look ahead. The peace, the freedom and the security of 90 percent of the population of the world is being jeopardized by the remaining 10 percent, who are threatening a breakdown of all international order and law."

How, then, could the peace-loving 90 percent ensure that the warmongering 10 percent did not prevail? Roosevelt deployed the language of disease to describe the ways in which war and violence might be contained. "When an epidemic of physical disease starts to spread," he said, "the community approves and joins in a quarantine of the patients in order to protect the health of the community against the spread of the disease."

Those were dangerous words, for they suggested that Americans ought to join with other nations in order to keep the epidemic of war away from their shores. It suggested the kind of collective security that Woodrow Wilson embraced, and which the U.S. Senate rejected. Roosevelt was quick to note his "determination to pursue a policy of peace," but peace might require something more than a declaration of neutrality.

"War is a contagion, whether it be declared or undeclared," he said. To halt its spread, peace-loving nations must engage in "positive endeavors." They must make their positions clear to other nations "that might be tempted to violate their agreements and the rights of others." They must be persuaded to "desist from such a course."

"America," he said, "hates war. America hopes for peace. Therefore, America actively engages in the search for peace."

But how would that search be conducted? By what means did he propose to quarantine those who carried the virus of war? There were no details in his speech, but even his generalities upset isolationists who saw the rhetoric of Woodrow Wilson in FDR's emphasis on collective security.

The press and political critics attacked the speech while Democrats, still in disarray after the Court debacle, chose to remain silent. Roosevelt told Sam Rosenman, "It's a terrible thing to look over your shoulder when you're trying to lead and to find no one there."[3]

Two months later, the USS *Panay*, a navy gunboat, and three U.S. oil tankers on the Yangtze River in China were attacked and sunk by Japanese warplanes. The Japanese said the attack, which killed three people, was an accident, and they apologized.

Americans wary of the world around them saw the attack not as a blow to their beliefs, but as proof that the United States was better off remaining aloof from the world. The presence of an American gunboat and three oil tankers in China, however, might have suggested that isolation was little more than a pleasant, and dangerous, fantasy.

Labor unions were an important part of the Roosevelt coalition. Here, members of the Congress of Industrial Organizations (CIO) walk a picket line in New York. Worker impatience grew during the "Roosevelt recession" of 1937–38.

CHAPTER 11

A Roosevelt Recession

Fireside Chat

April 14, 1938

TRACK 11

FOR A FEW WEEKS IN THE SPRING OF 1937, AS FRANKLIN ROOSEVELT SOUGHT IN vain to remake the Supreme Court, the nation's economy appeared to be well on its way to a full recovery. Production returned to levels not seen since the stock market crash in 1929. The market itself was moving steadily upward, a sign of increasing investor confidence. The unemployment rate was 12 percent, but that figure may have exaggerated the number of jobless. As several historians have pointed out, the unemployment rate included those without work as well as those working on WPA projects or serving in the Civilian Conservation Corps. Roosevelt biographers Conrad Black and Jean Edward Smith both note that if the unemployment rate took into consideration only those without any kind of work, the figure may have been as low as 4 percent.[1] "The emergency has passed," said South Carolina senator James Byrnes, expressing a widely held sentiment in Washington.[2]

That sense of relief may have reflected not only a desperate desire to cling to better economic figures, but also, according to historians Lawrence W. Levine and Cornelia R. Levine, a collective national belief that the prosperity of the 1920s could never be repeated. Fifty percent of Americans questioned by the American Institution of Public Opinion in July 1937 said that they believed the nation would always have an army of 5 million unemployed. The number of jobless at the time was about 7 million. Harry Hopkins himself wrote that "intelligent people" realized that even when the economy recovered fully, unemployment would remain a persistent problem.[3]

As the sense of emergency eased, workers began to exercise some of the new rights they were given under the Wagner Act. Workers at General Motors went on strike, paralyzing the auto giant. Steelworkers did likewise, leading to deadly confrontations between police and workers and their families. Huge companies like Westinghouse and Ford Motor Company bitterly fought efforts to unionize their work forces despite the protections for unions enshrined in the Wagner Act.

The sense of collective sacrifice and effort that Roosevelt encouraged during his first term appeared to be giving way to dangerous conflict now that the specter of despair and hopelessness was disappearing. Frustrations built up over six or seven years spilled out into the street, pitting law enforcement against workers, capital against labor. The White House kept a lid on tensions through the worst of times. Now, it seemed, those tensions were boiling over.

While labor and capital moved away from cooperation and towards renewed confrontation, Roosevelt sought to look beyond the strikes and sit-ins of 1937. The economy was getting better—the strikes were a function of higher expectations and a reduced sense of emergency—so, he believed, it was time for Washington to roll back some of the emergency measures that were appropriate for more desperate times.

Franklin Roosevelt was never comfortable as a free-spending raider of the federal treasury. While he was not shy about mobilizing the federal government against the economic catastrophe he inherited, he also was wary of the red ink Washington spilled so casually during his watch. Rhetorically anyway, Roosevelt remained committed to the notion of a balanced budget. During his State of the Union speech in 1936, Roosevelt told members of Congress that as a result of New Deal politics, "we approach a balance of the national budget." Months later, he reassured Vice President John Garner, a conservative Texan who was even more wary of government spending, that he meant what he said about stemming Washington's red ink. "I have said fifty times that the budget will be balanced for the fiscal year 1938," he reminded Garner. "If you want me to say it again, I will say it either once or fifty times more."[4] As Alan Brinkley pointed out in his study of the New Deal, *The End of Reform*, Roosevelt appeared to be asserting that a balanced budget would "mark the triumph of the New Deal."[5]

Roosevelt, Brinkley noted, was not the only liberal who was concerned about the federal government's reliance on deficit spending. The editors of the *Nation* magazine, stalwart supporters of Roosevelt, were wary about the combination of increasing inflation—prices rose 7 percent in 1936—and government borrowing. "An unbalanced budget in a period of rapidly rising prices is the surest path to an uncontrolled inflation," the magazine editorialized.[6]

Treasury Secretary Henry Morgenthau could not have agreed more wholeheartedly. Morgenthau was Roosevelt's longtime friend and neighbor whose position in the Cabinet owed more to luck than design. His ambition was to become secretary of agriculture, but Roosevelt passed him over when he assembled his first Cabinet in 1933. But when FDR's first treasury secretary, William Woodin, became ill not long after the administration took office, the president asked his friend Morgenthau to fill in. The job became permanent when Woodin's illness worsened, leading to his death in the spring of 1934.

Morgenthau brought to Washington none of the ideological fervor of some New Dealers. He was loyal to Roosevelt, he knew him longer than most of his other advisors, but he did not go to Washington with any sense that he wished to reorder the relationship between the government and the private sector. He was orthodox in his instincts, and while he accepted the New Deal's desire to stimulate the economy with government spending, he, like Roosevelt himself, never lost his belief in the importance of balanced budgets.

The 1938 federal budget reflected the priorities of the president and treasury secretary as well as the belief that the worst was over. After cutting the deficit from $4.3 billion (about $60 billion today) to $2.7 billion (about $38 billion) in the '37 budget, FDR slashed the gap to just $740 million (about $11 billion today) in his 1938 budget, which would take effect on July 1, 1937. To achieve these reductions,

Washington cut spending drastically. Roosevelt told Congress that Washington ought to be "eliminating or deferring all expenditures not absolutely necessary." His goal, he said, was a balanced budget for fiscal year 1939 (but not FY 1938, as he promised his vice president). Hopkins hacked away at the WPA's budget, Harold Ickes prepared to dismantle the Public Works Administration. Nobody was more pleased than Morgenthau. He said the president had given him "everything" he asked for. The administration, he wrote, could now proceed with further reforms on a "sound financial foundation."[7]

Neither the president not his treasury secretary could have anticipated how quickly that seemingly solid foundation would crumble when another economic storm stuck the nation in October.

The president's new budget priorities quickly proved disastrous. Without the federal government vigorously priming the pump, the nation's recovery began to sputter. Two million people were thrown out of work during the final four months of 1937, and another two million lost their jobs in the first three months of the new year. Steel production collapsed from 80 percent of capacity to 19 percent. The Dow-Jones index fell by 40 percent between August and October. In the midst of these declines, consumers were hit with a $2 billion tax bill (about $30 billion today) to pay for the Social Security program, reducing the amount of money in circulation. All the gains and all the hard work of the previous four years were being wiped out in a recession few in Washington saw coming.

Roosevelt was at a loss as he confronted the prospect of devastating recession. Harold Ickes wrote of his boss, "It is clear that he is greatly disturbed...and doesn't know which way to turn. He is plainly worried."[8]

Roosevelt and his top aides met with business leaders to encourage cooperation rather than confrontation in this new economic crisis. But as the White House desperately sought a way out of the crisis, Roosevelt decided in the spring of 1938 to renew a campaign against monopolistic business practices, hoping that such actions would force businesses to reduce prices in the face of renewed competition.

Through the long, bleak winter of 1938, the press referred to renewed hard times as a "Roosevelt Recession." In late March, the stock market crashed again, sending the Dow-Jones index to 98, from its Depression high of 190 a year earlier. Desperate for a way out, Harry Hopkins visited the president in Warm Springs, Georgia, in early April to make the case for renewed federal spending. Roosevelt, ever the improviser, decided that the anti-monopoly campaign simply wouldn't do. The time had come to dispense with anti-monopoly and balanced budgets. It was time to prime the pump again.

When FDR returned to Washington, he and his aides prepared a new economic stimulus package of $3.4 billion (more than $45 billion today) in emergency spending. Nearly half that sum was designated for Hopkins and the WPA, while the PWA and Ickes received a billion dollars. Roosevelt prepared to forward the proposal to a Congress that was looking ahead to off-year reelection campaigns later in the year. While the legislators figured to be in a cooperative mood, FDR's treasury secretary was not. Morgenthau told the president that he would resign if he sent the spending request to Capitol Hill. He allowed the president, his old friend, to talk him out of quitting.

Roosevelt and his speechwriting team of Harry Hopkins, Thomas Corcoran, and Samuel Rosenman went to work on a message to Congress to accompany the spending plan and on a fireside chat designed to reassure a public that had reason to fear a return to the early 1930s. The group, along with presidential secretary Missy LeHand, worked on the message to Congress on Wednesday night, April 13. They finished the message after midnight, and a satisfied but tired Roosevelt announced that he was ready for sleep. LeHand would have none of it, for the president's work was not finished—at least, not in her view.

"What about the fireside speech, Mr. President," she said in a tone suggesting that Roosevelt was neglecting his duties.

"Oh, I'm tired, let me go to bed," the president replied. He caught the eyes of the other men in the room, looking for support.

"No," LeHand said, "you just have to get something down on paper tonight." He was scheduled to give the speech at ten thirty that evening. [9]

Roosevelt knew he was beaten. He remained seated on a sofa, and after a few quiet minutes, he seemed to doze off. LeHand, Hopkins,

Corcoran, and Rosenman remained quiet until the president opened his eyes and began dictating a draft of his speech. He kept at it until about 2:15 a.m., at which time LeHand allowed the president of the United States to get some sleep. Corcoran and Rosenman, along with secretaries Grace Tully and Dorothy Jones, moved to the Cabinet Room to continue their work. They, too, eventually retired, but were back on the job later in the morning. Finally, at six o'clock, just a few hours before Roosevelt was due to address the nation, Rosenman, Hopkins, and Corcoran finished their draft. "This was the quickest job of speech writing that I had never had anything to do with," Rosenman said.[10]

The final result was a typically folksy, very intimate one-way chat designed to show that the president was aware of the country's anxieties. After his routine of a nap and light dinner in bed, he was wheeled into the broadcast room, where a small group of aides and technicians awaited.

He began by acknowledging that he was speaking during the Christian celebration of Holy Week—the following day was Good Friday. He had hoped to "defer this talk" for a week, but "what I want to say to you, the people of the country, is of such immediate need and relates so closely to the lives of human beings and the prevention of human suffering that I have felt that there should be no delay."

Having established the urgency of his message, there was no point in trying to explain away what he called "a visible setback" to the nation's recovery. He also seemed to concede that his administration had been waiting on events, rather than driving them, during the winter. It had "become apparent," he said, "that government itself can no longer safely fail to take aggressive government steps" to counteract the recession. The first thing he, as president, could do is offer the most basic sort of reassurance. "Your money in the bank is safe," he said, inviting memories of the run on banks that accompanied the panic of the early Depression years. But, he conceded, "I know that many of you have lost your jobs or have seen your friends or members of your families lose their jobs, and I do not propose that the Government shall pretend not to see these things." Roosevelt's use of the first person, the timbre of his voice, the careful crafting of these chats, help create the illusion that he was speaking not to millions, but to individuals gathered in their homes, individuals who wondered if people in power understood their problems.

"I am constantly thinking of all our people—unemployed and employed alike—of their human problems, their human problems of food and clothing and homes and education and health and old age," he said. Inviting his listeners into an imagined conversation, he added: "You and I agree that security is our greatest need—the chance to work, the opportunity of making a reasonable profit in our business—whether it be a very small business or a larger one—the possibility of selling our farm products for enough money for our families to live on decently. I know these are the things that decide the well-being of all our people."

But there was even more at stake than economic well-being. Around the world, totalitarian leaders were taking advantage of hard times to establish dictatorships in former democracies. He cited no specific nations, but his listeners certainly were aware of the rise of Hitler in Germany, Mussolini in Italy, and the militarists in Japan. "Democracy has disappeared in several other great nations—disappeared not because the people of those nations disliked democracy, but because they had grown tired of unemployment and insecurity, of seeing their children hungry while they sat helpless in the face of government confusion, government weakness—weakness through lack of leadership in government," he said. "Finally, in desperation, they chose to sacrifice liberty in the hope of getting something to eat. We in America know that our own democratic institutions can be preserved and made to work. But in order to preserve them we need to act together, to meet the problems of the Nation boldly, and to prove that the practical operation of democratic government is equal to the task of protecting the security of the people."[11]

After explaining his spending plan in detail, and acknowledging that it "is a big program," he once again turned intimate, telling his listeners that he wished "to have a personal word with you."

"I never forget that I live in a house owned by all the American people and that I have been given their trust," he said. "I try always to remember that their deepest problems are human. I constantly talk with those who come to tell me their own points of view—with those who manage the great industries and financial institutions of the country—with those who represent the farmer and the worker—and often, very often with average citizens without high position who come to this house...I can hear your unspoken wonder as to where we are headed in this troubled world. I cannot expect all of the people to understand all of the people's problems; but it is my job to try to understand all of the problems." Turning to the naval imagery he loved, he assured the nation that he planned to continue to "sail ahead."

"For to reach a port, we must sail—sail, not lie at anchor, sail, not drift."

Congress offered little opposition to Roosevelt's new spending. Once the bill was passed, however, the president turned his attention to fellow Democrats he saw as obstacles to further change.

Eleanor Roosevelt often served as her husband's eyes and ears.
Here, she visits a nursery school in the Midwest.
Mrs. Roosevelt was a progressive advocate in her own right and often pushed her husband to the left on domestic issues.

CHAPTER 12

Purging the Democratic Party

Fireside Chat

June 24, 1938

TRACK 12

ALTHOUGH CAPITOL HILL WAS FIRMLY IN THE CONTROL OF FRANKLIN ROOSEVELT'S fellow Democrats, relations between the executive and legislative branches were uneasy at best, tense at worst, in the spring of 1938. Republicans were not the only elected officials emboldened by Roosevelt's failed attempt to pack the Supreme Court. Many Southern Democrats, wary of northern liberals and vigilant in their defense of Jim Crow, were less willing to follow the New Deal line as the off-year elections of 1938 beckoned.

With the nation's economy showing some signs of renewal, FDR set his sights on two major initiatives in early '38. The first was of little interest to most voters—a plan to reorganize and modernize the executive branch. The explosion of new government agencies and programs since 1933 made it necessary, Roosevelt believed, to reconfigure chains of command and to consolidate authority within the executive branch. Many agencies had formed relationships with members of Congress who controlled their purse strings. Representatives and senators had vested interests to protect and patronage to spread, so federal agencies proved useful as employment agencies and as conduits for politically important projects.

Roosevelt and many of his aides saw the relationship between agencies and Capitol Hill as inefficient and, more to the point, as a drain on their own power to articulate and implement federal policy. The idea of a major overhaul of the executive department was not new in 1938—two years earlier, Roosevelt asked a group of experts in public administration to produce a plan to tighten control over the executive department's bureaucracy. The experts recommended a series of technical changes, including the reorganization of dozens of federal bureaus and agencies, the hiring of six administrative assistants in the White House to better supervise the bureaucracy, and the establishment of clear and efficient lines of authority. Roosevelt embraced these recommendations and introduced a reorganization bill to Congress in 1937, but it stalled amid complaints that the president planned to turn over the federal government to "theoretical, intellectual, professorial nincompoops," in the words of one critic, Representative Dewey Short of Missouri.[1] FDR intended to revisit the issue in the new session of Congress in 1938.

His second priority was passage of legislation intended to ban child labor, establish a minimum wage, enshrine the forty-hour workweek, and mandate extra pay for overtime work. The Fair Labor Standards Act, as the bill was called, grew out of Roosevelt's drastic change of course during the recession of 1937. But the legislation grew moldy in the House Rules Committee, opposed by Southern Democrats who worried that measures like the minimum wage could upset the region's racial caste system, giving blacks a claim on equal wages. Also opposed, but for different reasons, was the chairman of the Rules Committee, John J. O'Connor, a Democrat from New York. O'Connor was a thorn in Roosevelt's side, a critic of the New Deal and, given his chairmanship, a formidable obstacle to the president's legislative agenda.

In January 1938, a special Senate election in Alabama produced another ringing endorsement of the New Deal. Lister Hill, a member of the House, defeated a local politician named Tom Heflin to fill a vacancy left when FDR appointed Hugo Black to the Supreme Court. Hill ran as an all-out supporter of Roosevelt, and his victory was interpreted—in the White House especially—as a sign that the public was behind the president even as his critics in Congress seemed louder and bolder than ever. Four months later, in May, another avowed Roosevelt supporter, Claude Pepper, won a Democratic primary race for U.S. senator over a wealthy congressman, J. Mark Wilcox, who made his opposition to the Fair Labor Standards Act a centerpiece of his campaign. Wilcox, the very sort of conservative Southern Democrat who was testing Roosevelt's patience, was the heavy favorite in the race, but the White House intervened by raising money and support for Pepper, helping to turn the race into a referendum on the New Deal.

The Hill and Pepper victories were the 1938 equivalent of Roosevelt's smashing reelection victory in 1936. They convinced the president to lash out against his foes, anticipating that the public would be behind him.

Roosevelt was ready for a confrontation. Weeks before Pepper's victory, the president suffered a major embarrassment on Capitol Hill when his reorganization bill went down to defeat in the House of Representatives after passing the Senate. Public opinion, whipped up by the indefatigable Father Coughlin and other conservatives in the press, forced even a New Deal stalwart like New York senator Robert Wagner to vote against the president. Once again, critics charged that Roosevelt wished to gain dictatorial powers over people's lives, a wild charge that nevertheless carried weight at a time when dictators were on the ascent in Europe and Asia.

Through the spring, the Fair Labor Standards Act remained bottled up in Congressman O'Connor's Rules Committee. Thomas Corcoran, FDR's legislative fixer, was powerless in the face of the determined opposition of O'Connor and the Southern Democrats who opposed the bill.

Claude Pepper's victory, however, caught the attention of Capitol Hill Democrats. The results were barely official when House members began gathering support for a vote to release the Fair Labor Standards Act from O'Connor's committee. The surge of support led to a full floor vote, and it promptly passed the House by a margin of 314 to 97.

Roosevelt turned up the political heat in yet another Democratic primary battle, this one in Iowa, birthplace of presidential advisor Harry

Hopkins. Longtime senator Guy M. Gillette, a conservative Democrat who opposed Roosevelt's effort to pack the Supreme Court, found himself fending off a challenge from U.S. Representative Otha Wearin. Hopkins issued a very public endorsement of Wearin and took an active role in coordinating his campaign, leading to criticism that he manipulated federal WPA spending to aid Wearin's campaign. Gillette won easily despite the administration's overt support for Wearin.

Rather than pause to reflect on Gillette's victory, Roosevelt became even more determined to rid his party of conservative Democrats on Capitol Hill, most of them representing Southern states. The president angered Southerners, who were reliable Democrats, when he described the region's economy as "feudal" and asserted that Southern poverty was the nation's most pressing economic problem. The criticisms stung white Southern leaders who could not help but notice the support the South's blacks gave Roosevelt. A fellow Democrat from Georgia described Roosevelt as "dangerous" because of the support he had "with the lower element," meaning blacks.[2]

As spring turned to summer, Roosevelt decided to put the full weight of his administration behind a purge of Democratic critics in Congress. Egged on by Thomas Corcoran, a superb policymaker but a neophyte in the nuts and bolts of campaign politics, Roosevelt and his top staff made preparations to recruit and support reliable allies to challenge Democratic critics in Congress in a series of primary elections across the country.

Speechwriter Samuel Rosenman recalled years later that the purge was born of the president's "resentment" over the defeat of his reorganization bill and the initial failure of the Fair Labor Standards Act. "There was no doubt of his animosity toward those who were willing to run on a liberal party platform with him and then vote against the very platform pledges on which they had been elected," Rosenman wrote. "I often heard him express himself about such 'shenanigans' in a way that left no doubt about how he felt." Roosevelt, Rosenman wrote, believed that "reactionary Democrats were...blocking the steps that he thought were essential to raise the American standard of living and make the nation strong enough to meet the growing menace from abroad."[3]

Nevertheless, not everyone in the president's inner circle believed in waging war against fellow Democrats. Edward J. Flynn, a longtime Roosevelt confidante and political operative from the Bronx, believed the president was wrong and told him so. Roosevelt was in no mood to hear such advice, not with other advisors, like Corcoran, urging full-scale battle. Roosevelt saw the primary system as a means by which rank-and-file Democrats—the kind of voters who supported Claude Pepper and Lister Hill—took control of the nomination process. In fact, widespread use of primaries, rather than closed conventions, worked to the advantage of candidates with strong campaign organizations. Generally, that meant incumbents.

On June 24, 1938, Roosevelt signed the Fair Labor Standards Act, a measure many historians regard as the last major piece of New Deal legislation. Later that evening, he addressed the nation via radio. It was a hot early summer night, "one of the warmest evenings that I have ever felt in Washington, DC," Roosevelt told his audience, adding, wryly, "and yet this talk tonight will be referred to as a fireside chat."

It was Roosevelt's thirteenth such chat, and he took the occasion to celebrate the passage and signing of the Fair Labor Standards Act. "Except perhaps for the Social Security Act, it is the most far-reaching, the most far-sighted program for the benefit of workers ever adopted here or in any other country," Roosevelt said. "Without question it starts us toward a better standard of living and increases purchasing power to buy the products of farm and factory. Do not let any calamity-howling executive with an income of $1,000.00 a day, who has been turning his employees over to the Government relief rolls in order to preserve his company's undistributed reserves, tell you—using his stockholders' money to pay the postage for his personal opinions—tell you that a wage of $11.00 a week is going to have a disastrous effect on all American industry. Fortunately for business as a whole, and therefore for the nation, that type of executive is a rarity with whom most business executives most heartily disagree."

After that bit of class-warfare rhetoric, Roosevelt moved to the real purpose of this chat—to tell American voters, and his critics, that he intended to move against Democrats who had blocked the

Fair Labor Standards bill for so long, and who could be expected to block future reforms. And, yes, he said, there would be future reforms—even though he was nearly halfway through his second, and presumably his last, term, he had no intention of slowing down and resting on his laurels. "After the election of 1936 I was told, and the Congress was told, by an increasing number of politically—and worldly—wise people that I should coast along, enjoy an easy Presidency for four years, and not take the Democratic platform too seriously," he said. "They told me that people were getting weary of reform through political effort and would no longer oppose that small minority which, in spite of its own disastrous leadership in 1929, is always eager to resume its control over the government of the United States."

That small minority had been particularly active and particularly vocal during the ongoing session of Congress. With a few well-chosen words, Roosevelt made it clear that he had no intention of enjoying an "easy presidency" during what figured to be his last two years in office. He offered his listeners a history lesson, comparing conservative critics to defeatists in Congress during the Civil War. They were known as Copperheads, northern Democrats who sympathized with the plight of the South.

"Never in our lifetime has such a concerted campaign of defeatism been thrown at the heads of the President and the Senators and Congressmen as in the case of this Seventy-Fifth Congress," he said. "Never before have we had so many Copperheads among us—and you will remember that it was the Copperheads who, in the days of the Civil War, the War between the States, tried their best to make President Lincoln and his Congress give up the fight in the middle of the fight, to let the Nation remain split in two and return to peace—yes, peace at any price."

These modern-day Copperheads—the comparison was suggested by Corcoran during a speech-writing session—had been on the wrong side of the debate since 1933, Roosevelt said. After reminding the country once again of how bad things were when he took office—the closed banks, the hunger of the jobless and their families, the desolation in the American heartland—he got to his main point: "I want to say a few words about the coming political primaries...What I am going to say to you tonight does not relate to the primaries of any particular political party, but to matters of principle in all parties—Democratic, Republican, Farmer-Labor, Progressive, Socialist or any other. Let that be clearly understood."

Party labels, then, were not as important as philosophies, which were "generally classified as liberal and conservative." Roosevelt made it clear where he stood: he subscribed to "the liberal school of thought" which "recognizes that the new conditions throughout the world call for new remedies...We believe that we can solve our problems through continuing effort, through democratic processes instead of Fascism or Communism...Be it clearly understood, however, that when I use the word 'liberal,' I mean the believer in progressive principles of democratic, representative government and not the wild man who, in effect, leans in the direction of Communism, for that is just as dangerous to us as Fascism itself."

By focusing on philosophy rather than party labels, Roosevelt challenged listeners to do likewise—a shrewd course of action for a man about to launch an assault on fellow Democrats, without, of course, seeming to do so. As president, it would seem beneath his station to involve himself directly in primary contests designed to allow voters a chance to choose nominees. Roosevelt disingenuously insisted that he had no intention of dirtying his hands with such business, although he said he had "every right" to speak out when his name was being misused—a shot at conservative Democrats who ran as Roosevelt supporters. He was, after all, the "head of the Democratic Party" and was responsible for "carrying out the definitely liberal declaration of principles set forth in the 1936 Democratic platform."

"You and I all know that progress may be blocked by outspoken reactionaries," he said, anticipating that his listeners would glance at each other and nod in agreement. What's more, he said, progress also "can be blocked by those who say 'yes' to a progressive objective, but who always find some reason to oppose any special specific proposal to gain that objective. I call that type of candidate a 'yes, but' fellow."

There was little doubt who the 'yes, but' fellow tended to be: he was a Southern Democrat who was happy to ride Roosevelt's coattails in November, and oppose him when Congress met in January. Political operatives listening to Roosevelt's talk recognized that the president had declared war on conservative Democrats in Congress, and that the formidable resources of the White House would be expended in an all-out purge of the party.

During the weeks that followed, Roosevelt focused his attention on three Southern senators, Millard Tydings of Maryland, Ellison Smith of South Carolina, and Walter George of Georgia, as well as two powerful congressmen, Howard Smith of Virginia and John J. O'Connor of New York. FDR was not reluctant to put his personal prestige behind efforts to unseat these foes of the New Deal—during a ribbon-cutting ceremony in Georgia, Roosevelt publicly endorsed George's opponent, Lawrence Camp, even though George was seated on the same platform.

The primary challenges, coordinated and directed by Corcoran and Hopkins, failed miserably. Ironically, but perhaps not coincidentally, Roosevelt's only success came in New York when Flynn, who opposed the purge, was brought in to manage the campaign against O'Connor, but only after he extracted a promise from Roosevelt that Corcoran would not interfere. Challenger James Fay went on to defeat O'Connor, thus eliminating one of Roosevelt's most powerful Democratic critics.

Elsewhere, however, every other primary challenge failed. In the fall, voters frustrated over the Roosevelt recession made Democrats pay for the return of hard times. Republicans gained eighty seats in the House and eight in the Senate.

While FDR's party still controlled Capitol Hill, the elections of 1938 made Congress a far less friendly place as FDR began the final two years of his second term.

The Nazi campaign against German Jews led Roosevelt to recall his ambassador to Berlin in 1938, a year before Germany invaded Poland to begin World War II.

CHAPTER 13

War

Fireside Chat

September 3, 1939

TRACK 13

Although Franklin Roosevelt's attention was focused on domestic issues, from the court-packing controversy to the stubborn second-term recession to the attempted purge of the Democratic Party, he kept careful tabs on worrisome events overseas. The Japanese were at war with the Chinese, Spain was at war with itself, and Germany and Italy were beating the drums of expansion and conquest.

The president's quarantine speech in the fall of 1937 and the Japanese attack on the gunboat USS *Panay* several weeks later were grave reminders that it would be difficult for the United States to stand aside as the great nations of Europe and Asia moved ever so steadily towards catastrophe. But many Americans saw these conflicts as none of their business and certainly not the concern of their country. Their ancestors had left the Old World in part to escape the unending clash of great powers. The United States, protected by oceans on both flanks, was a safe haven, a refuge from the bloodshed and carnage that was such a constant in the Old World's narrative.

Isolationists in both parties gave voice to the public's determination to avoid a repeat of America's intervention in the Great War. As early as 1935, after the Italian invasion of Ethiopia made it clear that Benito

Mussolini was bent on global conquest, a Democratic congressman from Indiana named Louis Ludlow announced his intention to amend the Constitution to give the voting public, not Congress, the power to declare war. Ludlow's amendment would have required a national referendum on issues of war and peace except when the nation itself came under attack. "You can cast your ballot for a constable, for a dogcatcher, but you have absolutely nothing to say about a declaration of war," Ludlow said.[1]

After Ludlow formally introduced his bill, it was dispatched to the Judiciary Committee, where it was buried. Until, that is, the attack on the *Panay*, when the nation was swept by renewed fear of war. More than two hundred representatives signed a motion to discharge the bill from committee, giving it renewed life and creating an enormous controversy. The bill was brought to the House floor in early 1938. Roosevelt was aghast, he told the House Speaker, William B. Bankhead, that the amendment would "cripple any president in his conduct of our foreign relations, and it would encourage other nations to believe that they could violate American rights with impunity."[2]

Important Republicans, including vanquished presidential candidate Alf Landon, agreed with the president, but some of his reliable allies in the Midwest—the heartland of isolationism—were unmoved. Democrats, Progressives, and other liberals in the region ignored the president's wishes to vote in favor of Ludlow. Ironically, many Southern Democrats voted with the president despite their increasingly vehement opposition to some of FDR's domestic reforms. The Ludlow amendment went down to defeat by a vote of 209–188 in early January, but the fact that the measure saw its way to the House floor and was subject to serious debate was telling. Even with Hitler's Germany rearmed, with Mussolini's legions on the march in Africa, with the Japanese and Chinese engaged in a brutal war, many Americans clung to the belief that oceans still protected them from the contagion of war, that the best way to quarantine the virus was to ignore it.

Weeks later, Hitler's Germany announced its annexation of Austria, a startling development for which the British and the French had no response. The geopolitical map of Central Europe was transformed in an instant. Suddenly Czechoslovakia, a nation created out of the corpse of the Hapsburg Empire after World War I, found itself threatened by the greater Germany that Hitler created when his troops marched into Vienna with the approval of the Austrian people. Czechoslovakia contained 3 million ethnic Germans who lived near the border with Germany and Austria, making it a logical target for Hitler and his goal of an even greater Germany.

As Germany began to issue demands for annexation of a section of Czechoslovakia known as the Sudetenland, home to much of the nation's ethnic German population, Roosevelt once again sought to remind Americans that in a shrinking world, events overseas could no longer be ignored. In August 1938, as war between Germany and an Anglo-French alliance seemed possible, Roosevelt traveled to Canada to deliver a pointed message meant not so much for Canadian consumption as for the ears of his countrymen. "We in the Americas are no longer a far away continent, to which the eddies of controversies beyond the seas could bring no interest or no harm," he said. "The vast amount of our resources, the vigor of our commerce and the strength of our men have made us vital factors in world peace whether we choose it or not."

There was little doubt about where Roosevelt's sympathies lay. He recognized in Hitler a menace quite unlike that of the kaiser a generation earlier. In late August, he put together a secret plan to make it easier for Britain and France to purchase weapons from the United States if the Czech crisis led to war. The plan, however, was aborted when Secretary of State Cordell Hull warned that such a move, combined with public signals of sympathy with France and Britain, would infuriate isolationists who demanded strict neutrality in Europe's affairs.

The plan seemed to be academic in mid-September when the Czechs, under tremendous pressure from the British and French, agreed to turn over the Sudetenland to Germany. But Hitler was not satisfied—he issued further demands about how and when the territory would be turned over to Berlin. War seemed just a moment away. In Washington, far from the great capitals of Europe, Roosevelt engaged in a round of long-distance diplomacy, asking the four nations involved—Britain, France, Germany, and Czechoslovakia—to continue negotiations. He asked Italian dictator Benito Mussolini to take a leading role in bringing the parties together and made a personal appeal to Hitler, suggesting that the talks over Czechoslovakia be broadened to include other powers and other potential areas of conflict. He did not, however, offer his own services as a broker, for such a role would surely have infuriated the nation's vocal, and increasingly wary, isolationists.

The crisis came to an end with the Munich conference at the end of September 1938, when Britain and France essentially abandoned Czechoslovakia to its fate in return for a promise from Hitler that he sought no further territory in Europe. British Prime Minister Neville Chamberlain, who believed Hitler could be appeased and war averted, hailed the Munich accord for bringing "peace for our time." While history has offered a thunderous condemnation of Chamberlain's strategy and judgment, he was not alone in believing that war had been averted. Roosevelt himself thought that the Munich conference might lead to "a new order based on justice and law," a sentiment shared by millions of ordinary Europeans who made Neville Chamberlain a hero in late 1938.

In less than a month, however, Hitler began building up his forces in the west. Roosevelt promptly asked Congress for an additional $300 million in new spending on national defense. That show of determination, however, did little to discourage Hitler's followers. On the night of November 10, 1938, Nazi thugs attacked Jewish homes, businesses, and synagogues on a rampage that became known as Kristallnacht, the night of broken glass. Roosevelt recalled his ambassador to Germany, Hugh Wilson. He never returned to Berlin.

As the fatal year of 1939 began, Roosevelt focused American defense efforts on the production of warplanes for use by the United States and by the British and French. He told his aides that he hoped to sell the two countries as many warplanes as the United States could produce in a hurry. "I hope they will get the best heavy and medium bombers they can buy in this country. And I hope to God they get the planes and get them fast...That is the foreign policy of the United States."[3]

Gone, by necessity he believed, was his intense focus on domestic affairs. As biographer Jean Edward Smith wrote, the "economy was perking along, on five cylinders if not six, and the social revolution had receded in importance."[4] Roosevelt's new priorities led to a shift in his coalition, Smith noted. Southern Democrats who were wary or opposed to New Deal reforms, in large part because they threatened to upset the white supremacy in the region, joined with establishment Republicans in the East in support of Roosevelt's obvious sympathy for Britain and France. But prairie progressives like Robert La Follette Jr. and others found themselves opposing the president's drift away from splendid isolation.

Hampered by neutrality laws and the nation's determination to avoid entanglements that could lead to war, Roosevelt strove mightily to position the United States as a friend of Britain and France as Europe moved ever closer to worldwide conflict. In early June 1939, President Roosevelt and Eleanor Roosevelt played host and hostess to the King George VI of Britain and his queen, Mary. The royal couple flew into Washington and then boarded a train that took them and the Roosevelts to Hyde Park, where they feasted on hot dogs and the president's famous liquor concoctions. After one long session between the two leaders, Roosevelt told the king, "Young man, it's time for you to go to bed."[5] The king later asked: "Why don't my ministers talk to me as the president did tonight? I felt exactly as though a father were giving me his most careful and wise advice."[6]

The royal visit was a sensational and poignant success. On the eve of another conflict in the Old World, Roosevelt had very publicly made it clear where he believed the New World stood. He knew that many of his countrymen, and many on Capitol Hill, adamantly opposed any gesture that seemed to suggest American sympathy for one side or the other. But he was convinced that he was right in publicly embracing the British as they approached the firing line once again.

It was nearly three o'clock in the morning of September 1, 1939, when the telephone rang in the White House. The caller was William Bullitt, the U.S. ambassador to France. He told the president of reports that German troops were pouring into Poland. Later that morning, Roosevelt learned that both France and Britain would no longer stand aside, that they would go to war with Germany. Roosevelt told his Cabinet that "we aren't going into this war."[7] He dismissed a War Department plan to send troops to Europe, saying that such a plan would not be necessary. "We need only think of defending this hemisphere," he said.[8]

After forty-eight hours of uncertainty, the British and French made good on their assurance that they would come to the defense of Poland. They formally declared war on Germany on September 3. That night, Roosevelt addressed the nation about the outbreak of war in Europe, seeking to reassure Americans that he had no intention of becoming involved in the conflict. He told his audience that he had been hoping "that some miracle would prevent a devastating war in Europe and bring to an end the invasion of Poland by Germany." Those hopes, he said, were dashed. Europe was at war again, and there was nothing the United States could do to prevent it. The question was what it would do, what it could do, now that the Old World once again was in flames.

He spoke, as he often did, directly to his audience, conceding that many were skeptical that the nation had any interest in the war. "It is easy for you and for me to shrug our shoulders and to say that conflicts taking place thousands of miles from the continental United States, and, indeed, thousands of miles from the whole American Hemisphere, do not seriously affect the Americas—and that all the United States has to do is to ignore them and go about its own business," he said. "Passionately though we may desire detachment, we are forced to realize that every word that comes through the air, every ship that sails the sea, every battle that is fought does affect the American future."

That said, he immediately made his intentions clear: America would not involve itself in Europe's quarrel. "Let no man or woman thoughtlessly or falsely talk of America sending its armies to European fields," he insisted. The president could not conceive of a scenario when such a measure would be necessary.

While he vowed that America would be "a neutral nation," he acknowledged that the country had an interest in the war's outcome. "I cannot ask that every American remain neutral in thought," he said. Indeed, as the war progressed, he would ask that America choose sides, at least intellectually and even materially. For it was evident that 1939 was not like the Great War of 1914–1918, when Europe's empires slaughtered each other's young in the trenches of France. Through radio and newsreels, Americans were familiar with Hitler's diatribes and his threats against Europe's democracies. Roosevelt hoped Americans would consider which side was right. "Even a neutral has a right to take account of facts," he said. "Even a neutral cannot be asked to close his mind or close his conscience."

But even if America's conscience responded to the plight of Germany's victims, Roosevelt reminded his listeners that the country would remain aloof from the battle. "I have said not once but many times that I have seen war and that I hate war," he said. "I say that again and again."

He ended with a promise he would not be able to keep: "As long as it remains within my power to prevent," he said, "there will be no blackout of peace in the United States."

Long-range bombers turned Europe's cities into battlefields. In this famous photograph, St. Paul's Cathedral is visible amid the smoke and destruction in central London.

CHAPTER 14

A Stab in the Back

Speech in Charlottesville, VA

June 10, 1940

TRACK 14

After the storms of September 1939 brought down Poland's fragile independence, Europe settled into a strange and unexpected tranquility. Great nations were at war, the Czechs, Slovaks, and Poles were under hostile occupation, and the ambitions of dictators were not satisfied. And yet, through the fall and winter of 1939, there was very little fighting between the major powers. Soviet Russia invaded Finland on November 30, earning the Finns great sympathy in America, but Nazi Germany and the Anglo-French alliance did not come to grips with each other's armies on the western front.

In Washington, Roosevelt found himself in a peculiar quandary. The absence of heavy fighting inspired hope that the new conflict would end with a skirmish and not in a catastrophe, even though Germany was massing troops along its border with France and the Low Countries. American political figures like Senator William Borah of Idaho and Senator Robert La Follette Jr. of Wisconsin continued to preach from the gospel of isolation, while others hoped against hope that the storm had passed. Roosevelt, however, understood that the war had only just begun, that Nazi aggression remained a deadly menace to France and Great Britain, and that America's fate was inextricably linked to the fortunes of those democracies aligned against Adolf Hitler.

Conveying those apprehensions, however, was no small task as weeks went by without major engagements, without appalling casualties, without a sense of urgency. Even Europeans—save for the Poles and Finns, who suffered enormous casualties in a doomed defense of their country—wondered if the storm had passed. The conflict became known as the "phony war."

Roosevelt believed it was anything but phony, and that the United States had to shore up its armed forces and take other defensive measures to ensure its security while, at the same time, preserving its neutrality. The delicacy of Roosevelt's task was brought home after the Soviet invasion of Finland, when isolationists in Congress rewrote a bill that would have allowed the Finns to borrow $60 million to purchase weapons and other military hardware to help resist the invaders. After the bill's revisions, Finland was granted $20 million in credit to buy non-military goods, even as the Finns gallant resistance was beginning to falter. Congress and a good portion of the American people may have sympathized with the Finns, but sympathy did not extend to active intervention on their behalf.

Roosevelt was well aware of the nation's temper, and yet he also believed the status quo was unacceptable and unrealistic. The issue, he told famed newspaper editor William Allen White, was convincing Americans that they needed to build up their defenses while, at the same time, reassuring them that the nation would remain neutral. "I am almost literally walking on eggs," he said.[1]

Small steps, then, were the order of the day. Roosevelt asked Congress to repeal an arms embargo that prohibited the United States from selling weapons to combatants. Critics saw repeal as a move towards war, but in early November, Congress overwhelmingly approved the measure. The new Neutrality Act of 1939 allowed the United States to sell weapons to France and Great Britain, but the belligerent nations had to pay up front in cash and were required to transport the materiel in their own ships, with their own crews.

In the meantime, Roosevelt continued to do battle with those who viewed such measures as a presidential trick designed to get the United

States into the war on the side of the Allies. One of the isolationist movement's chief spokesmen was aviator Charles Lindbergh, an authentic American hero based on his historic solo flight across the Atlantic Ocean in 1927. Lindbergh portrayed himself as an expert in air power and production, the newest and most important means of projecting military power over vast distances. Roosevelt, sensing Lindbergh's popularity and credibility, sent private signals suggesting that he might ask the aviator to help supervise the nation's air defense buildup. Lindbergh rejected the overture, speaking out publicly and with great passion against any American involvement in what he saw as just another conflict between competing European powers and not as a struggle over ideology and freedom.

Lindbergh declared, "This is simply one of those age-old struggles within our own family of nations—a quarrel arising from the errors of the last war, from the failure of the victors to follow a consistent policy either of fairness or force."[2] A furious Roosevelt privately accused Lindbergh of Nazi sympathies. (Lindbergh visited Berlin in 1936 and accepted an award from the head of the German Luftwaffe, Hermann Goering, on behalf of Hitler.)[3] But as the German army overran Poland with astonishing speed and lethal results, Roosevelt won the support of critics like Alfred E. Smith and U.S. Senator Millard Tydings of Maryland—one of the senators Roosevelt sought to purge from the Democratic Party in 1938.

As the year turned and winter neared an end, the arguments over America's role, or lack thereof, in the conflict took on the quality of an academic exercise, for there was no war to speak of in Europe. British Prime Minister Neville Chamberlain asserted that "Hitler missed the bus." Historian William E. Leuchtenburg noted that the sense of crisis and impending doom in Europe seemed to fade even in nations technically at war.[4] Civilians went to work, as they did before September 1939. Children played in schoolyards. Strollers soaked in the springtime sun of Paris and London. "The character of the European war," Leuchtenburg wrote, "served to reinforce the illusion of [American] isolation."

Talk of war gave way to chatter about Franklin Roosevelt's future. Would he break precedent and tradition by running for a third term? He refused to rule out the possibility, but privately, he seemed eager to return home to Hyde Park. "I am tired," he said. "I have to have a rest."[5] But he also added a caveat: if the situation in Europe got worse, he said, he could change his mind.

On April 9, 1940, the phony war came to a shocking end. With lightning speed, Germany marched through undefended Denmark and attacked Norway by land, sea, and air. Britain and France were unprepared for the German thrust. They could only look on with horror as Germany completed its conquest in two weeks. On May 10, the German war machine brought its might and precision to bear on Belgium, the Netherlands, and France as the German army and air force crashed through its western frontier. The very existence of France and Great Britain was in peril.

Almost overnight, America's mood changed from complacency to panic. The speed and ruthlessness of the German offensive led to frenzied concerns about a possible cross-Atlantic invasion by paratroopers and amphibious forces. In a speech on May 16, as German troops were moving towards Paris, Roosevelt spoke of the possibility of long-range bombers crossing the Atlantic and hitting targets in the American Midwest.

The president seized the opportunity to push through billions of dollars in additional defense spending for thousands of new warplanes, tanks, and ships. As the advancing Germans cut to pieces the French army and the British Expeditionary Force, America organized civil defense groups to prepare for a possible German invasion by sea or air. The British, outmanned and outgeneraled, evacuated France in late May from the port of Dunkirk. Some 350,000 British soldiers escaped the German onslaught, but they left behind their tanks, their artillery, their ammunition, and their weapons. Without debate and without delay, Washington arranged to sell the British an enormous cache of weapons and munitions to replace what was lost in northern France.

Days after the Dunkirk evacuation, with France's defeat inevitable and a German attack on Great Britain surely to follow, the new British Prime Minister Winston Churchill addressed the House of Commons to speak about the horrors that lay ahead. "Even though large tracts of Europe and many old and famous States have fallen or may fall into the grip of the Gestapo and all the odious apparatus of Nazi rule, we shall not flag or fail," he said. "We shall go on to the end, we shall fight in France, we shall fight on the seas and oceans, we shall fight with growing confidence and growing strength in the air, we shall defend our Island, whatever the cost may be, we shall fight on the beaches, we shall fight on the landing grounds, we shall fight in the fields and in the streets, we shall fight in the hills; we shall never surrender…" But if the worst happened, if Britain were to fall, Germany still would know no rest. The British Empire, "armed and guarded by the British Fleet, would carry on the struggle, until, in God's good time, the New World, with all its power and might, steps forth to the rescue and the liberation of the old."[6]

The message to Americans, listening to the speech via radio, was clear.

With disaster unfolding in France and Germany seemingly unstoppable, Roosevelt sought to keep Hitler's ally, Italian dictator Benito Mussolini, out of the war. As the Battle of France drew to a close, Roosevelt dispatched a message to Rome, offering to serve as a mediator between Italy and the Allied powers. The offer was coldly ignored.

On June 10, 1940, Roosevelt traveled by train to deliver a commencement address at the University of Virginia's law school in Charlottesville. His son, Franklin D. Roosevelt Jr., was among the graduates. The president carried with him a speech written not by his usual speechwriters, but by State Department personnel. The speech was designed to firmly align the United States with embattled Britain and suffering France, still fighting but only days away from capitulation. As Roosevelt left Washington, he learned that Mussolini, ravenous for the crumbs of Hitler's impending victory, had declared war on France. More than thirty Italian divisions were on the march.

Bitter and angry over Mussolini's duplicity and opportunism, Roosevelt went through the text of his prepared remarks and inserted a sentence in his own handwriting. "On this tenth day of June, 1940," he wrote near the speech's conclusion, "the hand that held the dagger has struck it into the back of its neighbor." Delivered in a sarcastic, contemptuous tone, the phrase gave the speech its name: the stab-in-the-back speech.

While the reference was memorable, the speech in its entirety was important not because it allowed Roosevelt to display his temper, but because, in the words of historian, Jean Edward Smith, it "marked the decisive turning point in American policy."[7] Roosevelt made it clear that American neutrality would not and could not be simple evenhandedness. American interests and American freedom were at stake in the fight against Hitler.

He began with references to the American Revolution and to what he called "the seemingly endless years of the War Between the States." During both of those conflicts, America's young men and women concerned themselves not with their careers and personal lives, but with the life and survival of their county. "There is such a time again today," he said. The United States was not at war, as it was in 1861 and 1776. But Roosevelt sought to persuade his listeners that the moment was just as perilous, the stakes just as enormous. The conflict in Europe was not about what kind of new order would emerge after the war. It was about the future of the United States as well, because forces from afar were capable of bringing conflict to America as never before.

"We see today in stark reality some of the consequences of what we call the machine age," he said. Machines, capable of mass destruction, were "in the control of infinitely small groups of individuals who rule without a single one of the democratic sanctions that we have known. The machine in hands of irresponsible conquerors becomes the master; mankind is not only the servant; it is the victim, too. Such mastery abandons with deliberate contempt all the moral values to which even this young country for more than three hundred years has been accustomed and dedicated."

While the success and brutality of the Nazi war machine had changed the nation's "perception of danger," Roosevelt acknowledged that some Americans continued to hold onto the "delusion that we of the United States can safely permit the United States to become a lone island, a lone island in a world dominated by the philosophy of force. Such an island may be the dream of those who still talk and vote as isolationists." But, he said, such an island "represents to me and to the overwhelming majority of Americans today a helpless nightmare of a people without freedom—the nightmare of a people lodged in prison, handcuffed, hungry, and fed through the bars from day to day by the contemptuous, unpitying masters of other continents." Isolationism, then, offered not escape, but imprisonment. Americans had to ask "how now we can prevent the building of that prison and the placing of ourselves in the midst of it."

Preventing the nation's imprisonment required a public acknowledgment of "certain truths." The sympathies of the United States, he said, were with "those nations that are giving their life blood in combat" against "the gods of force and hate." On this day in June, with Mussolini's legions marching on France, Roosevelt placed Italy among the "gods of force and hate."

"The people and the Government of the United States have seen with the utmost regret and with grave disquiet the decision of the Italian Government to engage in the hostilities now raging in Europe," he noted, adding that he and Mussolini had exchanged messages in an apparent effort to restore peace to Europe. "I proposed that if Italy would refrain from entering the war I would be willing to ask assurances from the other powers concerned that they would faithfully execute any agreement so reached and that Italy's voice in any future peace conference would have the same authority as if Italy had actually taken part in the war, as a belligerent."

Instead, Italy had entered the war, had launched an attack on a neighbor on the verge of collapse. His voice rising with anger, Roosevelt uttered the phrase he wrote into the text: "On this tenth day of June, 1940, the hand that held the dagger has struck it into the back of its neighbor."

There was no longer any question about America's sympathies, or its view of those who had brought war and carnage to Europe for the second time in a quarter century. The enemies of Germany and Italy were engaged in a "battle for freedom," and that battle was America's as well.

"In our American unity," he said, "we will pursue two obvious and simultaneous courses; we will extend to the opponents of force the material resources of this nation; and, at the same time, we will harness and speed up the use of those resources in order that we ourselves in the Americas may have equipment and training equal to the task of any emergency and every defense."

Everything short of a declaration of war would be marshaled on behalf of "the opponents of force." American neutrality would not be the neutrality of the disinterested.

The question was whether American actions would be too little, too late, for Great Britain.

News photographers refrained from photographing Roosevelt in a wheelchair. However, several such images exist. Here, Roosevelt enjoys a moment at Hyde Park with the child of a family friend.

CHAPTER 15

Breaking with Tradition

Speech at the Democratic National Convention

July 19, 1940

TRACK 15

There was no constitutional limit on a president's tenure in 1940, so only tradition stood in the way of Franklin Roosevelt seeking a third term. But that two-terms-and-out tradition was strong and revered. Every two-term president in the nation's history followed in the footsteps of George Washington, who retired from office in 1797 after serving two terms.

Under ordinary circumstances, then, Franklin Roosevelt should have been considered a lame duck as the election year of 1940 got underway. Certainly many of his fellow Democrats considered him to be exactly that, and were making plans, with various degrees of discretion, to become his successor. Among them was FDR's own vice president, John Garner of Texas, who openly declared his candidacy in December 1939. Roosevelt was bemused, noting during a Cabinet meeting that the hard-drinking Garner had "thrown his bottle—I mean his hat—into the ring."[1] Others who saw themselves as presidential timber were James Farley, chairman of the Democratic National Committee and a longtime Roosevelt aide, Secretary of State Cordell Hull, Attorney General Robert Jackson, and Agriculture Secretary Henry Wallace.

At the age of fifty-eight, Roosevelt was hardly ready for retirement. But there were days when he longed to return to the Hudson Valley, or so he told friends. In a move that must have heartened his would-be successors, the president signed a contract with *Collier's* magazine, a mass-circulation periodical covering news and politics, for $75,000 a year (more than a million dollars in today's money) as a contract writer and editor beginning in 1941, when he presumably would leave office. *Collier's* actually offered a higher salary in exchange for Roosevelt's services, but the president insisted on accepting a salary no higher than what he was making as the nation's chief executive.

But if politicians and voters expected a definitive word from the president, they ought to have known better. Coy as ever, Roosevelt sent out mixed signals about his future. He told Cordell Hull's wife that her husband had better get used to giving political speeches—a sign that he not only was preparing to retire, but considered Hull a possible heir. He told allies that he wanted nothing more than rest and a chance to write. But there were no public announcements, no formal statements about his intentions.

Months passed without any word from the White House about a third term. This was long before presidential campaigns began two years, or more, before the end of a term, long before the explosion of primary contests and party caucuses. Candidates were actually chosen at a party's national convention. The Democratic convention was scheduled for July, so there was no need to rush into a decision during eventful winter and spring of 1940.

Political advisor Edward J. Flynn, an old friend from the president's days as governor of New York, believed that Roosevelt ought to retire. "It was obvious to me even then that the President's health was beginning to suffer," he wrote, adding that Roosevelt "lacked some of the early resilience and power of quick reaction he once had."[2] Flynn believed that he and the president's wife, Eleanor, were among the very few people close to Roosevelt who didn't advise him to run for a third term.

Larger events, of course, were unfolding in Europe while the nation waited on Roosevelt's decision. Speechwriter Samuel Rosenman become convinced that Roosevelt would run for a third term, in part because of the dangers lurking abroad, and in part because Roosevelt was not satisfied with any of the Democrats who might succeed him. Farley was not considered an enthusiastic New Dealer, at least in Rosenman's eyes, and his Catholicism was seen as a major drawback just twelve years after Al Smith's defeat at the hands of Herbert Hoover. Hull, too, was not liberal enough on domestic issues, and Garner was downright hostile to many New Deal reforms. Roosevelt, according to Rosenman, was convinced that the Republican old guard or conservative Democrats would try to roll back the New Deal, touching off social strife and dividing the country at a dangerous, unstable time.

In mid-June, days before the Republican National Convention was to begin, Roosevelt pulled off an election-year masterstroke. Convinced that the crisis in Europe would require drastic action and unity of purpose in the United States, Roosevelt announced a Cabinet-level shakeup. Two prominent Republicans, Frank Knox and Henry Stimson, were brought into the president's inner circle, Knox as secretary of the navy and Stimson as secretary of war, a position he filled during the administration of William Howard Taft three decades earlier.

Republicans were stunned, but Roosevelt's choices made sense. Unlike many rank-and-file Republicans, both Knox and Stimson were in general agreement with Roosevelt's policy towards the embattled Allies. Indeed, only a month after the war's outbreak, Stimson delivered a speech in which he stated bluntly that if Britain and France were defeated, the United States would have to take up the fight against Germany. Knox spoke publicly about the need for a draft, a massive military buildup, and full support for the British in their fight against Hitler.

At their convention in Philadelphia, Republicans—angry over the loss of two of their most prominent spokesmen on foreign policy—nominated a political unknown named Wendell Willkie, a lawyer who presided over a utility company named Commonwealth and Southern. Willkie actually was a Democrat who quickly reregistered as a Republican. He had few profound disagreements with the New Deal, although he was not particularly fond of Franklin Roosevelt, in part because of the president's strong condemnations of businessmen in the early and mid-1930s. Like Knox and Stimson, Willkie was no isolationist; his nomination meant that if Roosevelt did indeed run for a third term, his opponent would not make an issue of aid to Britain.

After the Republicans dispersed from Philadelphia and all political eyes began to turn to Chicago, site of the Democratic convention, Rosenman was summoned to the White House just before he was scheduled to take a vacation in Montana with his family. He arrived in sweltering, humid Washington on July 10, five days before the convention started, while his family headed west without him.

Roosevelt still had made no statement about his intentions, for he wanted the delegates to rise as one to draft him as their nominee without any prompting from the White House. He didn't wish to be seen actively campaigning for the nomination. Rather, if the third-term taboo were to be broken, it would be at the insistence of the party. Roosevelt "wanted it made clear that he was not actively seeking a third term," Rosenman wrote.[3]

But there was no question that he wanted the nomination. Conversation in the White House among Roosevelt, Rosenman, Harry Hopkins, and secretaries Grace Tully and Missy LeHand focused on the vice presidency. Three candidates emerged—Wallace, Hull, and Senator James Byrnes of South Carolina. Wallace's enthusiastic support for the New Deal made him a favorite, but many rank-and-file Democrats were suspicious of him. He had been a Republican until 1933, and he had a reputation as an impractical idealist, not the sort of man who could relate to urban Democratic bosses.

On the eve of the convention, with Hopkins on his way to Chicago to monitor events, Roosevelt took some of his aides for a cruise along the Potomac in the presidential yacht that bore the river's name. Rosenman went along to begin writing the president's acceptance speech, even as FDR insisted on sending a personal message to the convention, releasing delegates to vote for whomever they wished. He wanted his nomination to seem freely given, not orchestrated. That message was delivered to the Democrats gathered in Chicago Stadium on July 16, the second night of the convention. The delegates, stunned at first, broke into spontaneous chants in support of Roosevelt. That was precisely what the president desired. Roosevelt was renominated the following day.

Still, the proceedings in Chicago did not go smoothly. Flynn, the Bronx political boss and confidante of FDR, found the convention joyless. Farley, the party chairman, was sulking, his ambitions thwarted by Roosevelt's covert campaign for a third term. Many of Flynn's colleagues were dubious about breaking the two-term tradition. Others resented the presence of Hopkins as Roosevelt's stand-in, for he was considered a policymaker, not a political professional.

The mood grew worse when Wallace emerged as Roosevelt's choice for the vice presidency. Flynn's colleagues barely knew the man, and those who did know him considered him unreliable. But Roosevelt saw him as a loyal New Dealer who had worked long and hard for him as secretary of agriculture, and he was determined to get his way despite the developing opposition. The president's allies worked the convention floor as a full-fledged battle broke out over the vice-presidency. On the final night of the convention, Roosevelt sat by a radio in the White House—he did not go to Chicago, but he did send Eleanor to deliver a speech—and played cards while he monitored the roll-call vote. The room was unbearably warm because Roosevelt refused to use air-conditioning. It bothered his sinuses, he said.

The mood in the Oval Office was as tense as the room was hot, for Wallace faced a serious challenge from House Speaker William Bankhead of Alabama. As the voting dragged on, Roosevelt handed Rosenman a short statement, telling him to "smooth it out and get it ready for delivery," he said. The statement asserted that the party was "divided" and seemed unwilling to take a "stand in favor of liberalism." He charged that "certain influences of conservatism and reaction have been busily engaged in the promotion of discord" since the convention started. The party would have to decide which road it would travel.

"Therefore," the statement concluded, "I give the Democratic Party the opportunity to make that historic decision by declining the honor of the nomination for the presidency."[4]

Roosevelt continued to play solitaire while Rosenman drafted a longer version of the speech. The president looked it over and indicated his approval. He was prepared to stand down if the convention rejected Wallace. Chief of Staff Edwin "Pa" Watson was nearly in tears as the president kept a tally of the vote on a scrap of paper.

After enormous arm-twisting and deal-cutting, Wallace prevailed over Bankhead, winning the votes of 627 of the convention's 1,100 delegates. Back in the Oval Office, the president's relieved aides gathered up copies of the speech FDR would not have to deliver. The president, his shirt soaked in sweat, retired to his bedroom for a quick change while his aides called Chicago to let the delegates know that the president would address the convention, and the nation, by radio at ten o'clock Washington time.

The speech was a collective effort by Rosenman, Thomas Corcoran, and Ben Cohen, with some input by Supreme Court Justice Felix Frankfurter and speechwriter Archibald MacLeish. Roosevelt delivered it from the White House broadcast room, where, as usual, several aides gathered to watch and listen.

It was a speech no president had ever given, a third-term acceptance speech. Roosevelt dealt with the defiance of tradition immediately, telling delegates of his "mixed feelings." He longed for retirement, he said, but he also heard the call of "that quiet, invisible thing called 'conscience.'" In 1936, when he was reelected to a second term, he had intended to retire after the 1940 elections. "Eight years in the Presidency, following a period of bleak depression, and covering one world crisis after another, would normally entitle any man to the relaxation that comes from honorable retirement."

Even when war broke out in Europe in September 1939, Roosevelt said, "it was still my intention to announce clearly and simply, at an early date, that under no conditions would I accept reelection. This fact was well known to my friends, and I think was understood by many citizens." Such a statement, he insisted, would have hampered his ability to respond to momentous events abroad, so he chose to wait until the beginning of the convention to announce that he did not wish a third term.

Roosevelt wanted to be seen as a reluctant warrior summoned to service by party and country at a time of national peril. He reminded his listeners that "we in the United States have been taking steps to implement the total defense of America," including the establishment of a peacetime draft beginning in September that required the services of "many men and women" who would be taken away "from important private affairs...from their homes and their businesses."

"Lying awake, as I have, on many nights, I have asked myself whether I have the right, as Commander-in-Chief of the Army and

Navy, to call on men and women to serve their country or to train themselves to serve and, at the same time, decline to serve my country in my own personal capacity, if I am called upon to do so by the people of my country."

Minutes earlier, he had been prepared to issue a statement rejecting the chance to continue his service. But his listeners, of course, knew nothing of that. "Like most men of my age," he said, "I had made plans for myself, plans for a private life of my own choice and for my own satisfaction, a life of that kind to begin in January 1941.

"These plans, like so many other plans, had been made in a world which now seems as distant as another planet. Today all private plans, all private lives, have been in a sense repealed by an overriding public danger. In the face of that public danger all those who can be of service to the Republic have no choice but to offer themselves for service in those capacities for which they may be fitted.

"Those, my friends, are the reasons why I have had to admit to myself, and now to state to you, that my conscience will not let me turn my back upon a call to service."

Roosevelt wanted to emphasize service over ambition, so he emphasized the burdens that would be his even as his opponents carried out their campaigns in the fall. He, however, would have no time to campaign. "I shall not have the time or the inclination to engage in purely political debate," he said. Such a promise was doomed from the start, as Rosenman recognized. So Roosevelt added a line, saying that he would "never be loath to call the attention of the nation to deliberate or unwitting falsifications of fact, which are sometimes made by political candidates." That allowed him wiggle room when he did, in fact, campaign as the election neared.

After justifying his decision to do what no president had done before, he turned his attention more closely to the war that so many Americans sought so desperately to avoid. With Willkie at the top of the Republican ticket, Roosevelt knew that his pro-British neutrality was not likely to become a campaign issue. That knowledge offered him the luxury of defending his policy in a straightforward, unapologetic manner, and in a way that put Americans on notice again that Britain's struggle was America's struggle, and the struggle of all free people.

"I do not recant the sentiments of sympathy with all free peoples resisting...aggression, or begrudge the material aid that we have given to them. I do not regret my consistent endeavor to awaken this country to the menace for us and for all we hold dear." In surprisingly bitter tones, he condemned those who "charged me with hysteria and war-mongering" as "appeaser fifth columnists." If that characterization seemed harsh, that was because of the stakes involved. Like the more eloquent Churchill, Roosevelt saw the struggle in Europe not as a conflict between empires, but as a clash of civilizations.

The United States, he said, had to make a choice, not about who would be its president, but where it would stand in the conflict overseas.

"We face one of the great choices of history," he said. "It is the continuance of civilization as we know it versus the ultimate destruction of all that we have held dear—religion against godlessness; the ideal of justice against the practice of force; moral decency versus the firing squad; courage to speak out, and to act, versus the false lullaby of appeasement."

The American people would have to decide accordingly, he said, but they ought to know that he had made his own choice.

President Roosevelt envisioned America as the arsenal of democracy. The Ford Motor Company's famous Willow Run plant in Michigan churned out thousands of B-24E bombers, better known as "Liberators."

CHAPTER 16

The Arsenal of Democracy

Fireside Chat

December 29, 1940

TRACK 16

As the Roosevelt Administration prepared for the uncharted territory of a third term, the situation in Europe grew even more dire. Northern France was in the hands of German armed forces while British cities were under assault from the air as the Luftwaffe crossed the English Channel and bombed civilian targets in an effort to break Britain's will to fight. Hitler had postponed his plans to invade Britain in September, after the heroic pilots of the Royal Air Force fought a desperate and successful battle to control the air above Britain. But the change in plans brought an ominous shift in tactics: rather than focus the German aerial assault on military targets, Hitler directed that his air force take its campaign to Britain's cities, especially London.

For the next fifty-seven consecutive nights, Britons scurried to air-raid shelters as German bombers unleashed fire and death from above. In the weeks just after Roosevelt's reelection, German air raids over Coventry and Birmingham killed nearly two thousand people and caused enormous damage to property.

The German threat was not confined to the air. On the high seas, German submarines sunk British merchant vessels with near impunity. The toll was appalling: more than 2 million tons of supplies were sent to the bottom of the Atlantic Ocean at a time when Britain desperately needed the goods and was struggling to find the cash for such shipments.

In early December, British Prime Minister Winston Churchill dispatched a four-thousand-word letter to FDR, the first communication between the two men since the president's reelection victory in November. Churchill later recalled that the letter to Roosevelt was among the most important he ever wrote. In it, he offered the president an assessment of Britain's prospects in 1941, confident, he declared, that "the vast majority of American citizens have recorded their conviction that the safety of the United States, as well as the future of our two Democracies and the kind of civilization for which they stand, is bound up with the survival and independence of the British Commonwealth of Nations."[1] Roosevelt's reelection, which followed his assertions that America's fate was inseparable from Britain's, provided Churchill with the evidence of American support for Britain's struggle.

The Prime Minister then went on to detail the strategic burdens his nation would bear in 1941 as it continued to face the might of Nazi Germany alone. The key to Britain's survival, he wrote, was shipping. "The decision for 1941 lies upon the seas," he wrote. "Unless we can establish our ability to feed this island, to import...munitions of all kinds...we may fall by the way, and the time needed by the United States to complete her defensive preparations may not be forthcoming."[2]

With that invocation of American self-interest, Churchill laid out a series of requests by which the United States could help itself by assisting Britain in its hour of peril. The Prime Minister asked the president to invoke the notion of freedom of the seas to carry out lawful trade with any nation. In conjunction with that request, he suggested that American warships, not Royal Navy vessels, be used to protect trade between Britain and the United States. If those measures were not possible, Churchill wrote, perhaps the president would consider the "gift, loan, or supply of a large number of American vessels of war" so that the overstretched Royal Navy could protect Britain's Atlantic lifeline.[3]

Gifts and loans were the operative words in that request, because Britain was running out of the hard cash required to pay for war materiel made in the United States. He warned the president that the "moment approaches when we shall no longer be able to pay cash for shipping and other supplies...While we will do our utmost," he wrote, "and shrink from no proper sacrifice to make payments across the exchange, I believe you will agree that it would be wrong in principle and mutually disadvantageous in effect if at the height of this struggle Great Britain were to be divested of saleable assets, so that after the victory was won with our blood, civilization saved, and the time gained for the United States to be fully armed for all eventualities, we should stand stripped to the bone."[4]

In Washington, Roosevelt's aides were well aware of Britain's financial predicament. During a meeting on December 3 in the office of the Department of the Treasury, Cabinet officials reckoned that Britain would run out of cash by year's end. By the first week in January 1941, the Americans figured, Britain would have no more money to pay for any further shipments of desperately needed materiel.

Treasury Secretary Henry Morgenthau, a fiscal conservative who saw himself as a prudent steward of the nation's finances, was aghast. "What are we going to do," he asked. "Are we going to let them place more orders?"[5]

Frank Knox, the new secretary of the navy, quickly replied. Washington had no choice, he said. It could not halt sales to Britain even if the British were flat broke.

Roosevelt embarked on an early December cruise to the Caribbean with the issue of British payments, and Britain's future, undecided. He indulged his love of fishing and poker in the company of a few selected aides, including Harry Hopkins, who noted that the president seemed oddly disconnected from the great struggle underway across the Atlantic. On December 9, a navy seaplane delivered Churchill's long letter to Roosevelt. Hopkins noted that FDR read it several times while seated in his deck chair. He became quiet, no longer interested in fishing. The following day, Roosevelt received word from Washington that the British had less than $2 billion in gold and currency on hand, but they were liable for $5 billion in orders for materiel and supplies.

Roosevelt kept his own counsel. Finally, though, he revealed his thoughts to Hopkins as they continued their cruise. Without consulting staff or precedent, Roosevelt came up with a way to keep Britain supplied without draining its treasury. What if Washington loaned Britain the supplies it needed in return for leases of British-controlled territory? "He didn't seem to have any clear idea how it could be done legally," Hopkins wrote. "But there wasn't a doubt in his mind that he'd find a way to do it."[6]

When he returned to Washington, Roosevelt shared his idea with his Cabinet and then, on December 17, with the national press corps. During a regularly scheduled session with reporters, Roosevelt said he had little news to report. But the reporters didn't believe him, according to historian James McGregor Burns. They "could tell from his airs—the uptilted cigarette holder, rolled eyes, puffing cheeks, bantering tone—that something was up."[7]

In these informal sessions between the president and the press, there were few formalities as there are today, with questions and answers delivered in a set-piece ritual. Reporters and Roosevelt enjoyed each other's company, relishing the give-and-take that didn't always make its way into the following day's newspaper.

Roosevelt got things going with a few seemingly innocuous remarks about finances, and the lack thereof. He wanted to get past traditional ideas about the exchange of money for goods or services. "Now what I am trying to do is eliminate the dollar sign," he said. "That is something brand new in the thoughts of practically everybody in this room, I think—get rid of the silly, foolish old dollar sign."[8]

He then launched into one of his most famous metaphors. "Well, let me give you an illustration," he told the reporters. "Suppose my neighbor's home catches on fire, and I have a length of garden hose four or five hundred feet away. If he can take my garden hose and connect it up with his hydrant, I may help him to put out his fire. Now, what do I do? I don't say to him before that operation, 'Neighbor, my garden hose cost me fifteen dollars; you have to pay me fifteen dollars for it'...I don't want fifteen dollars—I want my garden hose back after the fire is over...If it goes through the fire all right, intact, without much damage to it, he gives it back to me and thanks me very much for the use of it."

He said he was outlining a "gentleman's obligation" in an effort to provide Britain with whatever it needed—ships, ammunition, the materiel of war—regardless of its current ability to pay. The materiel would be "loaned" to Britain, rather than purchased, with Britain agreeing to lease military bases to the United States throughout its flagging empire. Although an obvious response to Churchill's long letter, Roosevelt did not inform the Prime Minister of his plans, which were still being formalized. Churchill learned of the president's interest second hand. He was taken by surprise, and, not surprisingly, he was delighted.

The American public's reaction, however, was less predictable. Inside the White House, some aides fretted that the president was moving the country too close to war, and too fast. The president's proposal to aid Britain was not one of a dispassionate neutral, but one of an ally in a war the United States still sought to avoid—officially, in any case.

Roosevelt decided to make his case to the nation with a fireside chat. Sam Rosenman, Harry Hopkins, and Robert Sherwood were summoned to the White House on December 26 to begin work on the speech. The three aides had unusual access to the president, in part because of the gravity of the subject, in part because so many other aides were on vacation over the Christmas holidays. Roosevelt told his writers that he wished to make his case for arming the nation's democratic allies as simply and plainly as possible.

The White House announced that Roosevelt would deliver a talk on national security on Sunday night, December 29, at nine o'clock Washington time. Anticipation of the president's address was so high that people left movie theaters and restaurants early in order to get home in time for the speech. The usual small crowd of aides filled the White House broadcast room as airtime approached, although two new faces—two very well-known faces—were on hand for the occasion. Actor Clark Gable and his wife, actress Carole Lombard, joined the intimate gathering.

The speech is remembered today for its description of America's role as "the arsenal of democracy." The phrase was not original—French diplomat Jean Monnet used it during a conversation with Supreme Court Justice Felix Frankfurter earlier in the year. Roosevelt spotted the phrase in a speech drafted by the War Department. He brought it to the attention of his speechwriters, saying, "I love it."[9]

FDR's speechwriters went through six drafts before it was sent to the State Department for vetting purposes. The diplomats made several changes and suggestions that the president adopted, but one annoyed him. Roosevelt and his writers wished to point fingers at isolationists who were, in effect, aiding the Nazi war effort. Roosevelt wanted to say that there were "American citizens, many of them in high places," who were "aiding and abetting" the Nazis. The State Department struck out the phrase "many of them in high places." Roosevelt "snorted" when he read the proposed deletion, Rosenman wrote. "Leave it in," he told his writers. "In fact, I'm very much tempted to say 'many of them in high places—including the State Department.'"[10] He managed to resist that temptation.

The final version of the speech left no doubt about Roosevelt's sympathies. It firmly established the United States as an ally of Britain and of any nation resisting Nazi tyranny.

He opened on a conservative note, insisting that he wished to talk not about war, but about "national security," because "the whole purpose of your President is to keep you now, and your children later, and your grandchildren much later, out of a last-ditch war for the preservation of American independence and all of the things that American independence means to you and to me and to ours." The sentiments were a variation of his own themes, and of Churchill's: America's freedom was inextricably connected to the struggle in Europe.

He brought his listeners back to another perilous time, when the nation's banks were on the verge of collapse and FDR stepped in to declare a bank holiday. When he spoke to the nation about that crisis in 1933, he said, he sought to "convey to the great mass of American people what the banking crisis meant to them in their daily lives.

"Tonight, I want to do the same thing, with the same people, in this new crisis which faces America." Not since Jamestown and Plymouth Rock, he said, "has our American civilization been in such danger as now." He was setting the stage to argue that aid to Britain was not just a magnanimous gesture to a friend, but an essential part of America's national defense.

"The Nazi masters of Germany have made it clear that they intend not only to dominate all life and thought in their own country, but also to enslave the whole of Europe, and then to use the resources of Europe to dominate the rest of the world," he said. The "rest of the world," of course, included the United States; the Nazis, then, were enemies of the United States.

"If Great Britain goes down, the Axis powers will control the continents of Europe, Asia, Africa, Australia, and the high seas—and they will be in a position to bring enormous military and naval resources against this hemisphere," he added. "It is no exaggeration to say that all of us, in all the Americas, would be living at the point of a gun—a gun loaded with explosive bullets, economic as well as military." The two oceans that had served America so well in the past were no longer enough. They provided defense "in the days of the clipper ships," but not in the more frightening era of the long-range bomber.

After making the case against Nazi Germany with more urgency and greater strength than ever before, and aligning himself with Britain even more definitively than in the past, Roosevelt faced the question begging to be asked: what could, what should, America do to resist the Nazis and aid the British?

"Thinking in terms of today and tomorrow," he said, "I make the direct statement to the American people that there is far less chance of the United States getting into war if we do all we can now to support the nations defending themselves against attack by the Axis than if we acquiesce in their defeat, submit tamely to an Axis victory, and wait our turn to be the object of attack in another war later on."

The embattled peoples of Europe were not asking Americans to send armies across the Atlantic. Rather, they sought "the implements of war...which will enable them to fight for their liberty and our security." It was a well-chosen formulation: their liberty; our security. It was imperative that Americans "get these weapons to them...so that we and our children will be saved the agony and suffering of war which others have had to endure." Producing those weapons, he warned, would require "great effort," which in turn would demand "great sacrifice." Here, Roosevelt issued a pointed message to American industry—labor and management alike. Defense industries, he said, should not be hampered by strikes or lockouts. Owners and workers should be expected to settle their differences peacefully and without an interruption in production. America's rearmament and its commitment to the defense of Great Britain required nothing less than full commitment to the cause of freedom.

Then came the memorable phrase. "We must be the great arsenal of democracy," he said. "For us this is an emergency as serious as war itself. We must apply ourselves to our task with the same resolution, the same sense of urgency, the same spirit of patriotism and sacrifice as we would show were we at war.

"We have furnished the British great material support and we will furnish far more in the future. There will be no 'bottlenecks' in our determination to aid Great Britain. No dictator, no combination of dictators, will weaken that determination by threats of how they will construe that determination."

Safely reelected, Roosevelt saw no need to hide his sympathies or his policy. With this speech, he made it clear that American neutrality meant only that it would not send troops into combat alongside the British. Anything else, however, was fair game if it meant assisting the British and defeating the Axis powers.

Days later, a new Gallup Poll reported that 68 percent of Americans favored Roosevelt's Lend-Lease proposal to aid Great Britain. Roosevelt's words, delivered through the intimate medium of radio and heard in living rooms throughout the nation, moved the nation away from isolation and toward confrontation with the forces of darkness in Europe.

PART THREE:
Freedom's Champion, 1941–1945

Introduction

As Franklin Roosevelt began his third term, wars in Europe and Asia continued to rage and America continued to stand aside. The president's sympathies were clear: he was intent to help Britain in its lonely battle against Nazi Germany. But he was not prepared to commit his country to war.

Instead of troops, Roosevelt sent Britain ships and weapons under a creative program called Lend-Lease. The cash-strapped British agreed to lease military bases to the United States in exchange for a "loan" of vital military equipment. Although no troops were involved, the nation was another step closer to war.

The worldwide conflict became unavoidable when Japan attacked the U.S. Pacific Fleet in Pearl Harbor, Hawaii, on December 7, 1941. In a dramatic speech the following day, Roosevelt asked Congress for a declaration of war against Japan. Approval was swift and nearly unanimous.

The war years saw an end to the stubborn economic maladies of the 1930s. But during his third term, Roosevelt sought, at least at times, to balance the nation's war needs with his determination to continue economic and social reforms. Roosevelt famously described the nation as under the care of Dr. New Deal and Dr. Win-the-War. To the chagrin of some New Dealers, he suggested Dr. Win-the-War had priority, at least for the time being. Nevertheless, Roosevelt used his third term to introduce one of the greatest pieces of domestic legislation in the twentieth century, the Serviceman's Readjustment Act, better known as the G.I. Bill.

The nation and its military recovered quickly after Pearl Harbor, and by 1944, Roosevelt and his wartime allies, Winston Churchill and the Soviet Union's Joseph Stalin, were preparing for the new world order that would follow the war. Roosevelt hoped to build a lasting peace through a new international organization that would emphasize collective security—the United Nations. Determined to play a role in building that new order, Roosevelt ran for a fourth term in 1944.

He was a sick man by the time voters returned him to the White House. Years of effort took a visible toll on his once ebullient smile. Political operatives, fearing the worst, took it upon themselves to make Harry Truman the new vice president, pushing aside Henry Wallace, a man they regarded as unreliable.

The end came on April 12, 1945, with victory in Europe only weeks away.

A jubilant Adolf Hitler celebrated the Nazi conquest of France in 1940. In Washington, Franklin Roosevelt struggled to win the public's approval for aid to embattled Great Britain, Hitler's next target.

CHAPTER 17

The Four Freedoms

State of the Union Address

January 6, 1941

TRACK 17

As the fateful year of 1941 began, prominent voices continued to challenge Franklin Roosevelt's assertion that the United States had a stake in Britain's battle with Nazi Germany. While Republican presidential candidate Wendell Willkie did not make an issue of Roosevelt's pro-British tilt—many Eastern Establishment Republicans agreed with FDR's policy—isolationists in both parties remained skeptical at best, hostile at worst, as Washington moved ahead with plans to aid London.

The America First Committee, created as Britain fought for its life in the skies above London and other cities, recruited nearly a million members in more than four hundred chapters across the country. As historians Lawrence and Cornelia Levine pointed out in their study of the Roosevelt presidency, the America First Committee included not only Charles Lindbergh, its most famous recruit, but dozens of other well-known Americans, including Alice Roosevelt Longworth (Theodore Roosevelt's daughter), film actress Lillian Gish, businessman Robert Wood, and World War I flying ace Eddie Rickenbacker.[1]

The America First group was just one of several organized to oppose anything except strict, dispassionate neutrality. Historian James McGregor Burns identified several categories of isolationists, including

Americans of German and Italian descent who objected to popular bias against their ancestral homelands, and Irish Americans who found it difficult to see Britain as a paragon of freedom and liberty. Other isolationists, Burns argued, opposed intervention on ideological grounds—some liberals saw the war as an Old World struggle between imperial oppressors, and some conservatives feared that war would further increase the power of the federal government, particularly the president's office.[2]

In an effort to counter the organized isolationists, pro-Administration voices created groups of their own. The largest and best known was the Committee to Defend America by Aiding the Allies. William Allen White of Kansas, one of the nation's most famous newspaper editors and a Republican, served as the committee's chairman, but his cautious approach to intervention—similar to Roosevelt's during the 1940 campaign—led to splits in the committee between those who believed American involvement should stop with arms shipments and those who advocated for armed intervention on the side of the Allies. Allen resigned from the committee in early 1941.

The public responded favorably to Roosevelt's vision of the United States as an arsenal of democracy, but it was clear, as the president neared the beginning of his third term, that significant opposition remained. What's more, even those who supported his views were divided over just how far the United States ought to go to ensure the survival of Great Britain.

Roosevelt planned to use his annual State of the Union message to formally present his Lend-Lease plan to Congress and to make the case yet again for all aid short of outright war to help the British. With that in mind, staff at the State Department prepared a draft of the annual message that continued the administration's intense focus on America's interest in Britain's survival. Roosevelt and his speechwriters—Ben Cohen, Samuel Rosenman, and Robert Sherwood—spent the first week of 1941 on several drafts of the message and its renewed clarion call for an Anglo-American partnership in the face of Axis aggression. But the speech was more than an argument about Lend-Lease. Roosevelt and his writers asserted that the battle for democracy required not only a strong defense against dictators, but social justice, too. Roosevelt wished to make the point, Rosenman wrote, that "what we were fighting for was economic as well as political democracy."[3]

Several months earlier, during the height of the German blitz on Britain, Roosevelt received a memo from Interior Secretary Harold Ickes summarizing a debate in the British press about the need for an "economic bill of rights to defeat Hitlerism in the world forever."[4] Several commentators argued that just as Britain and other democracies advocated free speech and freedom of religion, they ought to establish minimal standards for housing, education, and access to medical care. A more equitable economic system, the British commentators argued, would create a stronger society, one better equipped to resist the appeals of dictators. Roosevelt forwarded the Ickes memo to his assistant, Grace Tully, telling her to include it in a file she was building for the State of the Union message.

As Roosevelt and his speechwriters worked on a fourth draft of the speech, the president with an original copy and his aides working off carbon copies, he announced that he had an idea for a grand statement near the speech's conclusion. Rosenman, Sherwood, Hopkins, and Cohen watched as Roosevelt looked up at the White House ceiling for a long time—so long, in fact, that Rosenman began to feel uncomfortable as he awaited the president's words. At last, Roosevelt returned his gaze to his aides and asked one of his secretaries to take notes as he spoke. Usually, at this stage of one of FDR's speeches, the hard work was over and all that remained was a few additions made in pencil to the typewritten script. Rosenman and the other writers were taken by surprise as Roosevelt dictated a long passage—the words by which the speech would become famous.

"We must look forward to a world based on four essential freedoms," he began, creating a construction—the four freedoms—that would serve as a moral framework for the war and the peace that would follow.[5]

The four freedoms, as Roosevelt enunciated them, were freedom of speech, freedom of religion, freedom from want, and freedom from fear. The words, Rosenman wrote, "seemed now to roll of his tongue as though he had rehearsed them many times to himself." The words Roosevelt dictated to Brady were almost exactly the words he would deliver to Congress. "Nobody ghost-wrote those words," said Sherwood, one of FDR's speechwriters.[6]

Rosenman copied down Roosevelt's words on a legal pad. When the president was finished, he asked his aides for their opinions. Hopkins expressed some concerns about a phrase Roosevelt used twice in describing the first two freedoms. Freedom of speech and freedom of religion, Roosevelt had said, should be allowed "everywhere in the world."[7]

"That covers an awful lot of territory, Mr. President," Hopkins said. "I don't know how interested Americans are going to be in the people of Java."

"I'm afraid they'll have to be some day, Harry," the president replied, according to Rosenman's account. "The world is getting so small that even the people in Java are getting to be our neighbors now."

The phrase made its way into the finished copy of the speech.

On January 9, 1941, Franklin Roosevelt went to Capitol Hill to deliver the speech, the final major address of his second term. The atmosphere was sober, and Roosevelt's message was suitably grave. The nation, he said, faced an "unprecedented" crisis, for "at no previous time has American security been as seriously threatened from without as it is today." He offered members of Congress a brief history lesson of the crises faced by Americans in the past. The new crisis differed from those of the past, he said, because "the future and the safety of our country and of our democracy are overwhelmingly involved in events far beyond our borders." Democracies were under siege; dictators were on the march. If democracy failed abroad, American democracy would come under direct attack. "In times like these it is immature—and incidentally, untrue—for anybody to brag that an unprepared America, single-handed, and with one hand tied behind its back, can hold off the whole world," he said. "No realistic American can expect from a dictator's peace international generosity, or return of true independence, or world disarmament, or freedom of expression, or freedom of religion, or even good business."

The United States, then, had no choice but to prepare to defend itself. It must be wary not only of appeasers—a familiar enough warning by now—but also "that small group of selfish men who would clip the wings of the American eagle in order to feather their own nests." Roosevelt and his aides expected a strong reaction to his characterization of rich and influential isolationists, who, Roosevelt implied, were willing to sacrifice America's defense so they could grow rich doing business with Hitler and his ilk. "The President and all of us thought [the phrase] was fine, and it was beautifully delivered," Rosenman wrote. "But no one ever noticed the sentence, and, to our keen disappointment, it made no impression at all."

No doubt it was lost in the dark scenario Roosevelt offered Congress as he described what might follow a British defeat. With the Royal Navy gone from the Atlantic, he said, it was not impossible to rule out a full-scale invasion of the United States or the Western Hemisphere. "The first phase of the invasion of this Hemisphere would not be the landing of regular troops," he said. "The necessary strategic points would be occupied by secret agents and their dupes—and great numbers of them are already here, and in Latin America. As long as the aggressor nations maintain the offensive, they—not we—will choose the time and the place and the method of their attack.

"That is why the future of all the American Republics is today in serious danger. That is why this Annual Message to the Congress is unique in our history."

America's first line of defense, then, was not the East Coast, not even the Atlantic Ocean, but the embattled island nation of Great Britain. Roosevelt formally asked Congress "for authority and for funds sufficient to manufacture additional munitions and war supplies of many kinds, to be turned over to those nations which are now in actual war with aggressor nations. Our most useful and immediate role is to act as an arsenal for them as well as for ourselves. They do not need manpower, but they do need billions of dollars worth of the weapons of defense." He acknowledged that they would not be able to pay for the weapons in cash. Instead, he said, "we shall be repaid within a reasonable time following the close of hostilities, in similar materials, or, at our option, in other goods of many kinds, which they can produce and which we need."

In a direct challenge to Hitler, Roosevelt asserted that such assistance "is not an act of war, even if a dictator should unilaterally proclaim it to be so." Roosevelt's proposal was hardly the action of a neutral. But in the president's view, that argument was over. The United States was not, in fact, neutral. It had firmly cast its lot, its future, with democracies under siege.

Still, at such a dire moment in the nation's history, it was appropriate, he said, to think about the "social and economic problems which are the root cause of the social revolution which is today a supreme factor in the world." If democracies were to prevail in the face of that revolution, they had to ensure that their citizens enjoyed equality of opportunity, employment, security, the "ending of special privilege for the few," civil liberties, and a "constantly rising standard of living." This was a New Deal formulation writ large, a restatement of a social contract that enshrined economic rights as well as political rights. And it applied not only to other nations, but to the United States as well. Roosevelt used this virtual wartime speech to advocate for an increase in "old-age pensions and unemployment insurance," greater opportunities for "adequate medical care," and a "better system" of providing employment. The war, then, was part of a larger struggle for basic freedoms and rights throughout the world.

It was in this context that Roosevelt enunciated his Four Freedoms, the blueprint for a postwar world in which, he hoped, the guarantee of justice would provide no recruits for future would-be dictators, in which peace would flower from the seeds of genuine equality.

"In the future days," he said, "which we seek to make secure, we look forward to a world founded upon four essential human freedoms.

"The first is freedom of speech and expression—everywhere in the world.

"The second is freedom of every person to worship God in his own way—everywhere in the world.

"The third is freedom from want—which, translated into world terms, means economic understandings which will secure to every nation a healthy peacetime life for its inhabitants—everywhere in the world.

"The fourth is freedom from fear—which, translated into world terms, means a world-wide reduction of armaments to such a point and in such a thorough fashion that no nation will be in a position to commit an act of physical aggression against any neighbor—anywhere in the world."

The Four Freedoms became, almost instantly, an iconic statement of a new and better world order. The artist Norman Rockwell rendered a series of four portraits for the *Saturday Evening Post*, illustrating each of the freedoms Roosevelt enunciated. But those freedoms were contested not only on the battlefield, but at home as well. African Americans in the South and elsewhere were systematically denied the freedoms of which the president spoke. They attended segregated schools, risked violent assault if they attempted to vote, and were barred from lunch counters, hotels, swimming pools, and other public accommodations. As commander in chief, Franklin Roosevelt presided over a segregated military, a practice he did not challenge during his long tenure. He was slow to support anti-lynching legislation, fearful that he would alienate Southern Democrats whose support he needed during the glory days of the New Deal. Roosevelt finally supported an anti-lynching bill in 1938, but Southern senators launched a filibuster, leading Roosevelt to surrender. Anti-lynching legislation never made it to Roosevelt's desk.

But African Americans in the North were an important part of the Roosevelt coalition, and the president knew it. He encouraged his wife to speak out forcefully on civil rights issues, and she did. Southern politicians feared that Roosevelt's liberal agenda would lead him to attack segregation and white supremacy. Ironically enough, African Americans seemed to agree with the white South's conclusions, for Roosevelt was enormously popular with African Americans in both the North and South. The New Deal was not color-blind, but for many African Americans, it offered an opportunity to advance, to take a step towards Franklin Roosevelt's four freedoms.

Roosevelt's Lend-Lease program allowed the United States to re-arm the British despite their low cash reserves. These bombers are being loaded onto a ship bound for Britain.

CHAPTER 18

Lend-Lease

Speech to the White House Correspondents Association

March 15, 1941

TRACK 18

ON A SUNNY, COLD MONDAY MORNING IN WASHINGTON, DC, FRANKLIN Roosevelt took the oath of office for the third time, officially shattering the two-term tradition that governed presidential ambitions for a century and a half. His inaugural address was unlike his first two, both of which focused relentlessly on the nation's domestic problems. With the world at war and Britain fighting for its life, with the United States aggressively committed to Britain's defense, Roosevelt used the first speech of his third term to reemphasize the country's stake in the war in Europe, and to warn against those who insisted that America could remain safely on the sidelines.

"There are men who believe that democracy, as a form of government and a frame of life, is limited or measured by a kind of mystical and artificial fate, that for some unexplained reason, tyranny and slavery have become the surging wave of the future—and that freedom is an ebbing tide," he said.[1] Anne Murrow Lindbergh, the journalist wife of the hero aviator and isolationist Charles Lindbergh, was among those who believed democracy was flagging. Her book, *The Wave of the Future*, took a pessimistic view of the struggle between authoritarianism and democracy, making the case that democracies were too inefficient, too cumbersome, in an age that demanded strong leadership.

Roosevelt offered a more sanguine picture, based, he said, on America's recent struggle against the forces of fear and economic oppression at home. "Eight years ago, when the life of this Republic seemed frozen by a fatalistic terror, we proved that this is not true," he told the thousands gathered outside the East Portico of the Capitol. "We were in the midst of shock—but we acted. We acted quickly, boldly, decisively."

A few days earlier, while he worked on his inaugural address, FDR met privately with his vanquished opponent, Willkie. The president respected Willkie and appreciated the Republican's refusal to pander to his party's isolationist wing during the campaign. When a British diplomat suggested that the president send his onetime foe to Britain on a goodwill mission—and as a sign of bipartisan support for the president's foreign policy—Roosevelt seized the opportunity.

The two men spent about an hour together, discussing the upcoming mission to Britain and, not surprisingly, talking politics. The conversation must have become friendlier and more intimate than either man expected, leading Willkie to ask the president why he relied so much on Harry Hopkins, who was not the most popular member of FDR's inner circle. The impolitic question did not ruffle the president. Rather, he replied to Willkie as a colleague and peer, not a beaten foe. "Someday," he told Willkie, "you may well be sitting here where I am now. And when you are, you'll realize what a lonely job it is." That sense of loneliness—that vulnerability—led presidents to embrace an aide like Hopkins, who, Roosevelt said, "asks for nothing except to serve you."[2]

Roosevelt handwrote a letter of introduction for Willkie to present to Prime Minister Churchill. He then attached a verse from a poem by the American writer Henry Wadsworth Longfellow that summed up the president's view of the struggle in Europe. Roosevelt had memorized the poem, entitled "Building of the Ship," when he was a schoolboy. He chose the poem's most poignant lines, which, he wrote, "applies to your people as it does to us."[3]

Sail on, O Ship of State!
Sail on, O Union, strong and great!
Humanity with all its fears,
With all the hope of future years
Is hanging breathless on thy fate.

After receiving Roosevelt's letter from Willkie's hand, Churchill spoke to the House of Commons and British people about the war situation in North Africa, where troops from around the Empire were routing a large Italian army in Libya. The success of British arms against one of Hitler's partners offered Churchill an opportunity to revel in success rather than dwell on defiance, but he warned his listeners that Hitler still posed a grave threat. Germany, he said, "may be forced, by the strategic, economic and political stresses in Europe, to try to invade these islands in the near future...In order to win the war Hitler must destroy Great Britain."[4]

With that sobering message, Churchill took note of the letter he received from Roosevelt, and read aloud, in his marvelous growl, Longfellow's words. What answer should he give, what reply might he make, Churchill asked.

"Here is the answer which I will give to President Roosevelt: Put your confidence in us. Give us your faith and your blessing, and, under Providence, all will be well." He continued, and then closed with a plea, delivered with an actor's sense of drama and timing: "Give us the tools, and we will finish the job."

Even as Churchill spoke, Congress was debating whether the British would receive those tools. Majority Leader John McCormick of Massachusetts introduced the Lend-Lease bill in the House of Representatives in mid-January. His prominent role was not an accident; the Roosevelt Administration believed that McCormick's Irish ancestry would help persuade Irish-Americans to back aid to their homeland's ancient foe. The bill's urgency only increased during each week of debate as Britain's lifeline became more and more tenuous. During the first three months of the new year, German submarines sent 142 British vessels, carrying 800,000 tons of supplies, to the bottom of the ocean.

The House responded to the crisis with surprising speed, approving the bill by a 260–165 margin on February 8, the day before Churchill's "give us the tools" speech in London. But the measure faced a sterner test in the Senate.

Wendell Willkie was among those asked to testify about Lend-Lease during hearings in the Senate Foreign Relations Committee. He was just back from his mission to London and was more than agreeable to amending some of his campaign rhetoric, when he charged that Roosevelt was intent on dragging the United States into the world war. A Senator asked if Willkie still believed what he said months earlier. "It was a bit of campaign oratory," he said, to the amusement of a crowd gathered in the hearing room's gallery. "I'm very glad you read my speeches because the president said he did not."[5] Willkie's steadfast support for Lend-Lease took some of the partisan edge off the debate, for it made it harder for Republicans to block the bill when their own party's candidate for president in 1940, Willkie, endorsed it. Nevertheless, the bill prompted several jagged exchanges, such as when Republican Senator Burton Wheeler of Montana, a staunch isolationist, charged that Lend-Lease was to foreign policy what the Agricultural Adjustment Administration was to the New Deal. "It will plow under every fourth American boy."[6] Roosevelt called Wheeler's remark "the rottenest thing that has been said in public life in my generation."

Public opinion was with Roosevelt. A Gallup Poll showed that 59 percent of respondents supported Lend-Lease, and that support was ratified on Capitol Hill. Lend-Lease won the Senate's approval on March 8 by a vote of 60–31, and the House approved the Senate's version of the bill by a 317–71 vote on March 11. Roosevelt signed the bill thirty minutes after receiving it. Seven billion dollars worth of war materiel was soon on its way to Britain. "There are not many dates in the history of the world as important as that one," speechwriter Sam Rosenman wrote of March 11, 1941.[7] Lend-Lease became a reality despite "the great split" in America over how far the United States ought to go in assisting Hitler's enemies.

On March 15, as ships laden with supplies for Britain were crossing the ocean, President Roosevelt attended the annual dinner sponsored by the White House Correspondents Association. The affair was, and remains, lighthearted, with an emphasis on wit and gossip rather than public policy and political debates. In past appearances at the event, Roosevelt joined in the laughter and festivities but refrained from speaking. On this occasion, however, he chose to deliver a speech about Lend-Lease.

It was a comfortable setting for the president, because he seemed to enjoy the company of many of the dozens of journalists who covered him—even if his relations with publishers tended to be somewhat tenser. He met with reporters in the Oval Office twice a week in a scene right out of a 1940s newspaper movie: Roosevelt, seated behind his desk, calling on or nodding to his inquisitors, the reporters, in white shirts and narrow ties, gathered almost literally at the president's feet, notebooks in hand. Inevitably, the room became shrouded in cigarette smoke, some of it spiraling from the tip of the president's elegant cigarette holder. Roosevelt delighted in political gossip, and it was freely exchanged during these informal sessions. He also was a master of the off-the-record quote, to the delight and occasional frustration of those who chronicled his administration.

The annual correspondents' dinner was a more formal, ritualized affair than the average Oval Office press conference. Roosevelt spoke from a podium, to an audience gathered in evening clothes. He acknowledged the difference right away, noting that the occasion was "unique" because it "differs from the press conferences that you and I hold twice a week, for you cannot ask me any questions tonight; and everything that I have to say is word for word 'on the record.'" His audience, all of them insiders in their own way, chuckled at the reference to his predilection for off-the-record comments.

There were not many laughs during the remainder of Roosevelt's speech, for he chose this occasion and this audience to remind the American people that with the passage of Lend-Lease, they had crossed an important threshold. They were not formally at war, but they certainly were not at peace.

Playing to his audience's language and sensibilities, he said, "The big news story of this week is this: The world has been told that we, as a united nation, realize the danger that confronts us—and that to meet that danger our democracy has gone into action." Britain would become the beneficiary not only of American words and American thoughts, but of American materiel as well. He used the occasion to unleash pointed references to the Nazis and to Hitler, references that were absent during his gentle-persuasion speeches of 1940. "Nazi forces are not seeking mere modifications in colonial maps or in minor European boundaries," he said, drawing an implicit distinction between the European wars of the past and the Nazi conquest of 1939–41. "They openly seek the destruction of all elective systems of government on every continent—including our own; they seek to establish systems of government based on the regimentation of all human beings by a handful of individual rulers who have seized power by force."

Because they had only contempt for democracy and personal liberty, they believed the democratic nations would be unable to resist their "new world order."

"They believed that democracy, because of its profound respect for the rights of man, would never arm itself to fight," he said. "They believed that democracy, because of its will to live at peace with its neighbors, could not mobilize its energies even in its own defense."

The now-concluded debate over what he called the "aid to democracies bill" had taken place "in every newspaper, on every wave length, over every cracker barrel in all the land; and it was finally settled and decided by the American people themselves," he said. The world no longer had reason to doubt where America's sympathies lay.

But sympathies were no longer enough. More tangible assistance was on its way, with much more to come. "Here in Washington, we are thinking in terms of speed, and speed now," he said. "And I hope that that watchword—'Speed, and speed now'—will find its way into every home in the Nation."

One of Roosevelt's greatest strengths as a speaker was the way in which he seemed to talk directly to his listeners, even when he was speaking to tens of millions. In this room of Washington journalists, while millions listened on the radio, he described the ways in which the lives of Americans would change as a result of America's new commitment to the defense of democracy. He did so by speaking to each one of his listeners, in simple phrases and homey touches that conveyed the urgency of his message.

"I must tell you tonight in plain language what this undertaking means to you—to you in your daily life," he said. "Whether you are in the armed services; whether you are a steel worker or a stevedore; a machinist or a housewife; a farmer or a banker; a storekeeper or a manufacturer—to all of you it will mean sacrifice in behalf of your country and your liberties. Yes, you will feel the impact of this gigantic effort in your daily lives. You will feel it in a way that will cause, to you, many inconveniences."

Businessmen, he said, would have to be happy with lower profits because taxes will be higher. Workers will have to put in longer hours, whether they worked at a machine, a bench, a desk, or behind a plow. They would have to work harder and longer, for fewer material rewards, and they would have to do so without complaint. "A halfhearted effort on our part will lead to failure," he said. "This is no part-time job. The concepts of 'business as usual,' of 'normalcy,' must be forgotten until the task is finished. Yes, it's an all-out effort—and nothing short of an all-out effort will win."

At stake, he said, was the "light of democracy" which could be kept burning only through the collective effort of the entire nation. "And there are many more millions in Britain and elsewhere bravely shielding the great flame of democracy from the blackout of barbarism," he said. "It is not enough for us merely to trim the wick, or polish the glass. The time has come when we must provide the fuel in ever-increasing amounts to keep that flame alight."

And nowhere was that flame more threatened than in Britain, where "plain people—civilians as well as soldiers and sailors and airmen, women and girls as well as men and boys" were preparing "for invasion whenever such attempt may come."

The British and their allies needed ships, he said. "From America, they will get ships." He promised, too, that they would get planes, food, tanks, guns, and ammunition.

The words were stirring, but they avoided the next difficult issue: getting those ships, planes, food, tanks, guns, and ammunition safely across the Atlantic.

Winston Churchill, shown here with his wife, Winnie, and military aides, formed an historic partnership with Franklin Roosevelt during their conference off Newfoundland in 1941.

CHAPTER 19

Closer to the Edge

Fireside Chat

September 11, 1941

TRACK 19

THROUGH THE SPRING AND SUMMER OF 1941, FRANKLIN ROOSEVELT WAVERED over a critical question arising from his Lend-Lease plan. If America was determined to provide the British with the arms, food, ships, tanks, and ammunition they needed, was it equally determined to provide protection for those shipments? German submarines already had turned the North Atlantic into a killing zone. The Battle of Britain gave way to the Battle of the Atlantic as the British fought desperately to avoid starvation and deprivation.

The Royal Air Force's gallant defense of Britain's skies has gone down in history as a symbol of the island nation's defiance of Hitler and Nazism. But the conflict in the North Atlantic in 1941 posed an equally dire threat to Britain's existence, for the British were dependent on shipping to feed soldiers and civilians alike and to obtain the war materiel they needed to defend their homeland against invasion. British convoys sailing from North America were subjected to relentless assault from groups of submarines patrolling together, looking for easy targets. A convoy of twenty-two ships was reduced to just a dozen during an attack in early April. Such losses, continued over time, would mean that "our days would be numbered," Winston Churchill wrote.[1]

In mid-April 1941, United States armed forces took possession of Greenland, the massive island in the far north Atlantic and a particularly strategic site for naval bases. The government of Denmark administered Greenland, but the Danish leadership fled Copenhagen in the spring of 1940 when the Nazis overran the country during the larger campaign against Norway. The Danish government in exile approved the bold American move and thus the United States established a military presence in an increasingly important combat zone.

Roosevelt followed up the occupation of Greenland with a declaration that the U.S. Navy patrols of the Atlantic would push farther east and would inform the British of all vessels it spotted in a self-declared security zone. While this measure added a greater American presence in the Atlantic, Roosevelt refused to allow navy vessels to escort convoys crossing the Atlantic with supplies for Britain. Protecting the merchant vessels remained "solely a British responsibility," Churchill wrote. Americans favored Lend-Lease, but as Roosevelt knew, they were not prepared to put American lives on the line for Britain. Polls showed about half of respondents opposed the use of U.S. Navy vessels on convoy duty, and more than three-quarters were opposed to American entry into the war.

Treasury Secretary Henry Morgenthau, Interior Secretary Harold Ickes, Navy Secretary Frank Knox, and War Secretary Henry Stimson were disappointed in Roosevelt's apparent failure of nerve. "The president is loath to get us into this war," Morgenthau wrote. "He would rather follow public opinion than lead it."[2] Morgenthau, a staunch supporter of Britain's fight, could not see, or simply would not see, just how much Roosevelt had done to change public opinion. His speeches, especially since winning reelection, helped move the country in favor of Lend-Lease and thus of Britain's cause. Isolationists were not silent, but they did not command the following they once had. Events had helped turn public opinion, but so had Roosevelt's actions, and his words. Still, he was not ready to act on Churchill's plea, written in early May, that the United States formally declare war on Germany.

The president would not necessarily have disagreed with Morgenthau's dour assessment. He was loath indeed to enter the war. He told his aides that he was unwilling to fire the first shot—but he also conceded that a shot might well be fired. "I am waiting to be pushed into this situation," he told Morgenthau in mid-May.[3]

Less than two weeks later, on May 27, the president delivered his first fireside chat of his third term. Anticipation was high, a reflection of his long absence from the nation's living rooms and of increased anxiety about the war and its consequences for the United States. About 85 million people tuned into the broadcast. Historians Lawrence and Cornelia Levine noted that the country seemed to come to a standstill as the president began speaking from the White House. "There was scant traffic in Times Square; crowds gathered around taxicabs and storefronts to hear the address...jukeboxes in bars and restaurants fell silent..."[4] A baseball game in New York's Polo Grounds between the New York Giants and the Boston Braves was halted after the seventh inning so the crowd and the players could listen to the president.

The fireside chat did not contain a request for a declaration of war, which Churchill sought, or an announcement that U.S. Navy vessels would perform convoy duty across the Atlantic, as many of his advisors wished. But the address was dramatic and sober all the same, the moral equivalent of a wartime speech. The president revisited his arguments in favor of aid to Britain, turned up the rhetorical heat on Hitler and the Nazis, and once again linked America's fate to Britain's. It sounded very much like a variation on a theme, until he announced that he had declared an "unlimited national emergency" requiring the further buildup of the nation's armed forces.

The declaration sounded urgent, as it was meant to be, but its practical effect was uncertain. The navy was assigned no new responsibilities in the Atlantic. Roosevelt did not ask for a repeal of the Neutrality Act, which, in any case, had not prevented him from moving the country so clearly to Britain's side. But the very phrase "unlimited national emergency" did signal the president's increased anxiety about the war. His words may have broken little ground, but they reasserted his advocacy for Britain at a time when American public opinion overwhelmingly opposed entrance into the war. Churchill later contended that FDR's speech "greatly disturbed" German military leaders, particularly Admirals Raeder and Doenitz, who asked Hitler to approve more aggressive U-boat patrols near the U.S. coast. Hitler, however, refused permission, fearing a widening of the war.[5]

American pubic opinion began to follow the president, not, as some of his Cabinet suggested, the other way around. In polls taken after his fireside chat of May 27, a majority of respondents said they would support American naval protection for convoys in the Atlantic. All the while, the Battle of the Atlantic raged to Britain's disadvantage. The Germans sunk 136,000 tons of shipping in the Atlantic in May, leading to further pleas from London for more aggressive American help in protecting the convoys. Washington prepared top-secret plans to dispatch several thousand troops to Iceland to replace British troops who were guarding the strategic island. But before the deployment could take place, the contours of the war changed dramatically.

Hitler launched a massive invasion of the Soviet Union on June 22, catching the Red Army by complete surprise. Suddenly, communist-ruled Russia, led by a brutal dictator, Joseph Stalin, joined the roster of nations violated by Hitler. Churchill immediately announced his support for the Soviets; Roosevelt followed on June 24 with a pledge to assist the Soviets just as America was assisting Britain. But first Roosevelt had to navigate the anticipated opposition of Americans who saw Soviet communism as an evil no less threatening than fascism. A diplomatic outreach to Pope Pius XII helped lead to a Vatican statement that cautiously approved assistance to the Russian people, as opposed to Soviet communists. The papal statement was designed to tamp down American Catholic opposition to Roosevelt's plan to extend Lend-Lease to Moscow.

With the war widened and with Britain still in mortal peril, Franklin Roosevelt and Winston Churchill agreed to meet formally in early August off the coast of Newfoundland. The conference was kept so secret that even Eleanor Roosevelt and the Cabinet assumed, as the rest of the country did, that the president was enjoying a fishing vacation on the waters off Cape Cod. The presidential yacht was conspicuous by its presence, but the president himself was sailing north on a warship, bound for Placentia Bay in Newfoundland.

Churchill's journey was kept just as secret, and it was a good deal more hazardous, for he and his party, which included Britain's top political and military leaders, had to make the same dangerous crossing that produced so many casualties. During two stormy days, the battleship carrying Churchill and other leaders steamed ahead of its escorts, as alone and vulnerable as the island nation itself was.

The first summit meeting between the two leaders began aboard the USS *Augusta*, a heavy cruiser, on August 9. Roosevelt stood in his heavy braces, leaning on the arm of his son, Elliott, as the British leader climbed aboard. The following day, Roosevelt returned the favor, visiting Churchill aboard the HMS *Prince of Wales*, a battleship whose captain and crew were sunk four months later. Roosevelt and Churchill sat side by side on the ship's deck for a Sunday prayer service, Roosevelt in a dark suit and white shirt, Churchill in a naval uniform, the bill of his officer's cap mischievously off center. The two men joined their aides and hundreds of sailors standing on the massive ship's wooden deck in singing hymns Churchill chose for the occasion—"For Those in Peril on the Sea," "Onward Christian Soldiers," and "O God, Our Help in Ages Past." Although neither man was particularly observant, both were moved by the ceremony and the power of the moment. "If nothing else had happened while we were here," Roosevelt said of the service, "that would have cemented us."[6]

The conference produced a joint statement of purpose that became known as the Atlantic Charter. In it, Roosevelt and Churchill announced that they sought no new territories, sought no territorial changes without "the freely expressed wishes of the peoples concerned," would respect the right of all peoples to choose their own government, would strive for access to goods and trade for all nations, and asserted their belief that, once the war ended in Nazi Germany's defeat, all nations should abandon "the use of force."[7] The Atlantic Charter sought to provide a moral framework for the war and the peace that would follow. More practically, however, it further bound the United States and Great Britain to a common cause. Churchill wrote, "The fact alone of the United States, still technically neutral, joining with a belligerent power in making such a declaration was astonishing."[8]

The question was: just how long would the United States remain technically neutral? An incident in early September put that question to the test.

On September 4, 1941, the USS *Greer*, a destroyer carrying supplies to American troops recently deployed to Iceland, cooperated with British aircraft in tracking down a German submarine in the North Atlantic. The submarine fired torpedoes at the *Greer* after it was attacked by British warplanes. The *Greer* fired back with depth charges. None hit the mark.

Although the *Greer* incident produced no casualties, President Roosevelt seized the opportunity to take yet another step towards the war he and most Americans still hoped they could avoid. He asked Sam Rosenman to prepare a fireside chat explaining why the Atlantic convoys required U.S. Navy protection—the very move he had been resisting all summer. Rosenman and other aides prepared a speech for delivery on September 8, but Roosevelt's beloved mother, Sara, died on September 7 with her distraught son at her side. The speech was postponed while the grieving president buried his mother next to his father in Hyde Park.

Rosenman and Harry Hopkins produced a strong document justifying the use of armed American warships to protect the convoys. The State Department churned out four drafts of its own, and the president wrote a draft while riding the train that took him from Hyde Park back to Washington. White House staff worked long into the night of September 10, rewriting the speech and making copies for the president to read the following morning. Roosevelt read the working draft to congressional leaders at ten o'clock that morning—the moment was grave, and the step momentous. Roosevelt rejected the State Department's request to tone down passages that seemed too militant, according to Rosenman.

That evening, the president told the nation of his decision. He opened with a recapitulation of the *Greer* incident. "She was flying the American flag. Her identity as an American ship was unmistakable," he said. "She was then and there attacked by a submarine. Germany admits that it was a German submarine...I tell you the blunt fact that the German submarine fired first upon this American destroyer without warning, and with deliberate design to sink her."

Absent from this version was the *Greer*'s role in tracking the submarine, and the British warplane's assault on the vessel, which prompted the sub to fire at the *Greer*. Roosevelt's version of the story, told in sober, firm tones, was yet another indication of the people's anxiety about the nation's direction. In order to justify a more aggressive U.S. presence in the Atlantic, Roosevelt felt obliged to tell a version of the *Greer* incident designed to provoke maximum outrage, to dispel lingering doubts. "Our destroyer, at the time, was in waters which the Government of the United States had declared to be waters of self-defense—surrounding outposts of American protection in the Atlantic," he said. The attack, he said, was either "deliberate" or it was carried out with disregard for the ship's identity, which, he said, would be "even more outrageous." It was, he added, "piracy—piracy legally and morally," and it was only the latest in a series of similar attacks in the Atlantic.

He asserted that the United States was "not becoming hysterical or losing our sense of proportion" in light of the incident and others like it. And it would be, he said, "unworthy of a great nation to exaggerate an isolated incident." But he used the *Greer* episode to once again make the argument that the war in Europe was unlike the last war, and, indeed, the kinds of wars that the ancestors of so many Americans sought to escape when they fled the Old World for the New.

"The Nazi danger to our Western world has long ceased to be a mere possibility," he said. "The danger is here now—not only from a military enemy but from an enemy of all law, all liberty, all morality, all religion." Roosevelt was well aware of Hitler's barbaric war within the war—the Nazi campaign to exterminate Europe's Jews. The final solution, that is, Hitler's decision to round up Jews and send them to concentration camps, had not yet been implemented, but the Nazis' murderous intentions were clear enough. Roosevelt vigorously condemned Nazi outrages against German Jews, particularly the 1938 rampage known as Kristallnacht, when mobs destroyed Jewish-owned businesses in Berlin and elsewhere.

Some modern scholars have suggested that Roosevelt and other western leaders were far too slow—perhaps even unwilling—to confront Hitler's war against the Jews. One example of apparent Western callousness was the famous voyage of the SS *St. Louis*, a passenger ship that brought more than nine hundred German Jews from Germany to

Cuba in 1939. The Cuban government refused to allow most of the passengers to land, forcing the ship to search for another safe harbor. Roosevelt, hampered by strict immigration law, refused to allow the ship to dock in an American port. Canada also refused entry, forcing it to return to Europe. Hundreds of passengers were resettled in Britain, France, Belgium, and the Netherlands, but about half perished during German occupation in the 1940s.

While Roosevelt's actions before and during the Holocaust remain contested, his condemnations of Nazi ideology were unambiguous.

"There has now come a time," he told his audience, "when you and I must see the cold inexorable necessity of saying to these inhuman, unrestrained seekers of world conquest and permanent world domination by the sword: 'You seek to throw our children and our children's children into your form of terrorism and slavery. You have now attacked our own safety. You shall go no further.'"

The time for the niceties of diplomacy, of exchanges of notes, had long since passed, he said. Entire nations lay under the jackboot of Nazism because they had relied on notes rather than force, diplomacy rather than confrontation. The United States, he said, "will not make that fatal mistake."

He then read a passage that the State Department sought to edit hours earlier, but which he insisted on keeping in the text. "We have sought no shooting war with Hitler. We do not seek it now. But neither do we want peace so much, that we are willing to pay for it by permitting him to attack our naval and merchant ships while they are on legitimate business." Secretary of State Cordell Hull and his colleagues thought the passage was too militant, that the reference to "shooting war" ought to be struck. It was not. And there was more to come. Roosevelt turned once again to a simple and effective word picture to get his point across. Summoning up an image from the American West, he noted that nobody waits for a rattlesnake to strike. "These Nazi submarines and raiders are the rattlesnakes of the Atlantic. They are a menace to the free pathways of the high seas. They are a challenge to our own sovereignty. They hammer at our most precious rights when they attack ships of the American flag—symbols of our independence, our freedom, our very life."

Striking the rattlesnake, then, was an act of self-defense. Likewise, the time had come for what he called "active defense." American vessels could no longer simply wait to be attacked. "That means, very simply, and very clearly, that our patrolling vessels and planes will protect all merchant ships—not only American ships but ships of any flag—engaged in commerce in our defensive waters. They will protect them from submarines; they will protect them from surface raiders."

Offering such protection was not an act of war, he argued, but a legitimate defensive action. But it would be an active defense, a defense that would not wait for a potential enemy to fire the proverbial first shot. He issued a warning: if German or Italian vessels entered waters that the United States claimed as part of its defensive security zone, "they do so at their peril."

He conceded the "gravity of this step," but he insisted that he had no choice. The German threat in the Atlantic was real, he said, as the *Greer* incident proved.

But there were other threats he did not mention, threats half a world away that were becoming more serious by the day.

The USS *Arizona* took a direct hit during the Japanese attack on Pearl Harbor on Dec. 7, 1941. Nearly 3,000 Americans died, leading Roosevelt to ask for a declaration of war against Japan.

CHAPTER 20

Day of Infamy

Speech to Congress

December 8, 1941

TRACK 20

THE WAR THAT THE UNITED STATES HOPED TO AVOID ARRIVED ON DECEMBER 7, 1941, in a place few Americans recognized. Pearl Harbor, a deep-water naval base on the Hawaiian island of Oahu, was the new home of the U.S. Navy's Pacific Fleet. The fleet's headquarters had been in San Diego for years, but in 1940, the War Department transferred the massive fleet three thousand miles to the west as a buffer against Japanese expansion in the Pacific.

Relations between Japan and the United States had been deteriorating for some time, but few Americans were paying attention. The stunning triumphs of Nazi Germany, the gallant defiance of Great Britain and, beginning in June, the titanic clash between Germany and the Soviet Union monopolized the nation's conversation about the war and America's interests. The president's public statements, speeches, and fireside chats warned of the threat from Hitler and the Nazis. He said little about potential threats to the west, from an island nation seeking to replace European colonial powers as masters of the Pacific.

Behind the scenes, however, the president and his advisors had been tracking Japan's aggression with increasing alarm. Japan lacked a conspicuous personification of its ambitions and its ideology—Hideki Tojo, the Japanese Prime Minister since September 1940 and a career army officer, was unknown in the United States. Roosevelt's bellicose rhetoric after his reelection in 1940 excoriated Hitler by name, helping the public to see the Führer as a personal threat to their liberty. There was no Japanese equivalent of Hitler or, perhaps more to the point, Roosevelt had not tried to create one.

Nevertheless, Roosevelt, his advisors, and America's military strategists were well aware that Japan was every bit as intent on conquest as Germany was. They knew, too, that American sea power in the Pacific posed a formidable obstacle to Japan's territorial ambitions. As the island nation turned its attention to the resources of Indochina, ruled by the French, the East Indies, controlled by the Dutch, and Malaya, governed by the British, the presence of a powerful American Pacific fleet became increasingly intolerable to Japanese expansionists.

Although the Japanese invasion of China preceded the outbreak of war in Europe by two years, most Westerners saw the conflict as a regional dispute, unlike, say, Hitler's territorial demands in Europe before 1939, which were perceived to be a threat to world peace and stability. Roosevelt biographer Frank Freidel noted that FDR "was nervous but not frightened about Japan."[1] As assistant secretary of the navy for seven years, he was well aware that naval officers viewed Japan as a possible source of conflict as long ago as World War I. But like so many Westerners, he underestimated Japan's ambitions and abilities, even after the Japanese so thoroughly drubbed the Russians in the Russo-Japanese war of 1904–05.

The conflict in Asia became more ominous in 1940. With the conquest of China far from complete, American military planners expanded their maps, and their thinking. Finishing off China meant choking off supplies and isolating the resistance. That would involve closing down supply lines leading from Indochina, still controlled by the Vichy French government.

In late September, Japanese forces invaded northern French Indochina and quickly assumed control of the strategic port city of Haiphong in today's Vietnam, a major source of Chinese supplies. Within days, Tokyo signed a formal agreement with Hitler's Germany and Mussolini's Italy, each promising to consider an attack on one to be an attack on all. The war in Asia was no longer a regional conflict, if it indeed ever was.

Preoccupied with his reelection and with moving public opinion to Britain's side, FDR took no drastic actions and issued no stern warnings in the face of new Japanese aggression. He cut off supplies of scrap metal to Japan, but resisted playing his most provocative card, a cutoff of U.S. oil. Such a move, many Americans believed, would only lead Japan to invade the oil-rich Dutch West Indies.

The president chose diplomacy over confrontation, meeting personally with Japan's new ambassador to the United States, Admiral Kichisaburo Nomura, in February. Roosevelt told the admiral that there was "plenty of room in the Pacific area for everybody."[2] Neither country would gain anything from a war, Roosevelt said. Nomura did not dispute the president's assertion. Privately, he, too, was worried about the possibility of war.

Roosevelt held an advantage over Nomura, who continued to hold regular conversations with Secretary of State Cordell Hull. American intelligence cracked the Japanese diplomatic code, allowing Roosevelt to read intercepted cable messages from Tokyo to its diplomats around the world. After Germany invaded the Soviet Union, Tokyo was divided over how it ought to react: some believed Japan ought to strike Siberia, while others believed the widened war offered Japan a chance to move south to further seal off the Chinese and gain vital resources in Europe's colonial possessions in Asia and the Pacific. Roosevelt followed the deliberations by reading intercepts. "The Japs are having a real drag-down and knock-out fight trying to decide which way to jump," he told aide Harold Ickes in early July.[3] Regardless of what Tokyo decided, Roosevelt added, the United States had to do what it could to prevent a clash between Japan and Washington. "I simply do not have enough navy to go around," he said.

In Japan, a plan to further reduce America's naval power was under discussion. Admiral Isoroku Yamamoto, who opposed Japan's pact with Nazi Germany and Italy and who was dubious about an armed confrontation with Washington, put aside his misgivings to devise a plan to attack and wipe out the American Pacific Fleet in

Hawaii with one daring assault. The plan was at odds with Japanese naval orthodoxy, which called for a series of encounters that would draw the American fleet into a climactic battle against a superior force. Yamamoto, who studied at Harvard University from 1919 to 1921, had greater appreciation for America's industrial capacity. He insisted that the climactic battle had to be the first battle, with an equally devastating follow-up action. Otherwise, he feared, America's vast resources eventually would overwhelm Japan.

As this plan was formulated, Japan raised the stakes in Asia. Late July 1941 saw Japanese troops march into southern Indochina after Japan signed a treaty with Vichy France granting it use of airfields and navy bases in today's southern Vietnam. Almost overnight, Japan was poised to threaten the rest of Southeast Asia and the resources—especially oil and rubber—of the Dutch East Indies. Roosevelt knew about the Japanese move into southern Indochina in advance thanks to the intercepts, but he did nothing to stop them, fearing that further provocation would lead to a shooting war between the United States and Japan. With the United States fully engaged in helping Britain survive the Battle of the Atlantic, Roosevelt believed America had little choice but to avoid a confrontation in the Pacific. Harold Ickes wrote that the president "was still unwilling to draw the noose tight."[4]

The trigger for war would be oil. An American embargo, Roosevelt said repeatedly, would only inflame a dangerous situation, and so he was opposed to it. Before leaving for his meeting with Winston Churchill off Newfoundland, however, Roosevelt ordered that Japanese assets in the United States should be frozen; that is, Japan would be denied access to their cash and assets in America. In addition, he said, there would be no increase in oil exports.

While the president was away from Washington, his edict was interpreted so broadly that Japan could not get access to cash and assets to pay for oil shipments. An oil embargo, unauthorized by direct presidential action, took effect in Roosevelt's absence. Upon his return, he chose not to reverse the policy, in part because he feared Tokyo would interpret a reversal as weakness or indecision.

In Tokyo, a divided government sent conciliatory messages to Washington through the U.S. ambassador to Japan, Joseph Grew.

But Roosevelt's government was divided, too, with confrontationists like Knox and Stimson on the ascent. They and others helped scuttle a proposal for Roosevelt to meet with the Japanese Prime Minister, Fumimaro Konoye, fearing that the president might concede too much during such an intimate setting.

Konoye resigned in mid-October. His replacement was General Tojo. Roosevelt's top military advisors said they anticipated no radical changes in Japan's policy. But in early November, the Japanese cabinet prepared for war with the United States.

Diplomatic negotiations between the State Department and the Japanese embassy in Washington continued through November. Roosevelt and Congress fought a bitter and, for Roosevelt, a successful battle to repeal the nation's Neutrality Act, which the president saw as a bar to sending all aid short of armed force to those who fought Hitler's aggression. Congress repealed the act, at last, on November 4.

Three weeks later, Japanese forces were steaming toward the Philippine Islands, Guam, Malaya, and Pearl Harbor.

The attack on the American fleet began at about eight o'clock on Sunday morning, December 7. By the time it was over, two hours later, eight U.S. battleships and ten other vessels were destroyed or damaged. Hundreds of planes were attacked on the ground. More than two thousand people were dead.

Roosevelt learned of the attack while he was eating lunch with Harry Hopkins in a White House study. Stunned by the magnitude of U.S. losses, furious that the fleet had been such an easy target, he called his top civilian and military advisors into a meeting at three o'clock. An overseas call came in; it was Winston Churchill, asking if what he heard about the attack was true. Roosevelt confirmed the news. "We are all in the same boat now," he told the Prime Minister.

When the meeting broke up, Roosevelt asked to see his secretary, Grace Tully. He wanted her to take dictation of a message he would deliver to Congress the following day. Drawing on a freshly lighted cigarette, he began dictating not only the words he wished to say, but the way he wished them to be punctuated. No speechwriters were present; none would be consulted. The message he delivered the following day essentially was the message he dictated to Tully on the afternoon of December 7, including the speech's most famous phrase, describing December 7, 1941, as "a date which will live in infamy."

Roosevelt met with Congressional leaders that night to brief them on the terrible details. For a man who was proud of the U.S. Navy and his personal connection to the service as an assistant secretary, the details were almost too much to bear. "Find out, for God's sake, why the ships were tied up in rows," he told Secretary of Navy Knox.[5]

The following day, he and Eleanor drove from the White House to Capitol Hill at noon. At 12:30 p.m., with the House chamber packed with members of Congress and other government officials sitting in a semicircle in front of him, Roosevelt began his speech. He spoke deliberately, with the force of righteous indignation. "Yesterday, December 7, 1941—a date which will live in infamy—the United States of America was suddenly and deliberately attacked by naval and air forces of the Empire of Japan." He emphasized the words suddenly and deliberately, making clear that the attack was a surprise and that it had been no accident.

Speechwriters Samuel Rosenman and Robert Sherwood were among those listening intently to the president's words. Neither had been consulted about the speech. The words were Roosevelt's. They offered few memorable phrases aside from the first line. They drew no inspiring word pictures. There was little of Churchill in this speech. It was presented to the court of world opinion, a brief on behalf of a wounded nation. "It will be recorded that the distance of Hawaii from Japan makes it obvious that the attack was deliberately planned many days or even weeks ago," he said. "During the intervening time the Japanese Government has deliberately sought to deceive the United States by false statements and expressions of hope for continued peace."

Roosevelt sought to catalog not only the attack on Pearl, but the simultaneous Japanese assaults on the Philippine Islands, on Guam. The conflict, then, was not simply between the United States and Japan. Like that in Europe, it was between democracies and militarists intent on aggression and conquest.

"Yesterday the Japanese Government also launched an attack against Malaya.

"Last night Japanese forces attacked Hong Kong.

"Last night Japanese forces attacked Guam.

"Last night Japanese forces attacked the Philippine Islands.

"Last night the Japanese attacked Wake Island. And this morning the Japanese attacked Midway Island."

The Japanese threat was real, and it was aimed at all those who stood in their way. Americans gathered around their radios to hear the president were told that he had "directed that all measures be taken for our defense." He urged them to "remember the character of the onslaught against us."

Then, in the six-minute speech's most ringing phrases, he promised that "no matter how long it may take us to overcome this premeditated invasion, the American people in their righteous might will win through to absolute victory." The House burst into sustained applause.

Finally, the words he wished he would not have to say, words that now seemed merely pro forma. Lowering his voice, he told Congress and the nation what would come next: "I ask that the Congress declare that since the unprovoked and dastardly attack by Japan on Sunday, December 7, 1941, a state of war has existed between the United States and the Japanese Empire."

The motion passed with only one vote of dissent. The United States was at war.

American industry quickly converted to a wartime footing. Here, a finished B-17 warplane receives a final inspection.

CHAPTER 21

Fear, Again

Fireside Chat

February 23, 1942

TRACK 21

THE WINTER OF 1941–42 WAS DREARY, ANXIOUS, AND DEPRESSING FOR AN American public still dealing with the shock of Pearl Harbor and reality of war. Roosevelt himself, ever the optimist in public, later confessed that he was often depressed during the war's early months. Little good news flowed into the White House. But there was no shortage of bad news. The Axis powers were extending their conquests from the Pacific Ocean to the Russian front, and there was little, it seemed, that the United States, Britain, and the Soviet Union could do about it.

Pearl Harbor was, of course, a strike by only one member of the Axis alliance, Japan. Roosevelt pointedly did not say a word about Japan's partners when he asked for a declaration of war against the Japanese empire. Left unstated in FDR's address to Congress on December 8, 1941, was America's position in the European war. Was it now a full belligerent against Germany and Italy, or would Washington turn all of its might against Japan only?

The question became moot on December 11 when first Nazi Germany and then Italy declared war on the United States. Both nations believed that Japan's attack on the U.S. Pacific Fleet marked a new phase of the war, one that would lead to inevitable victory. "Now it is impossible to lose the war," Hitler said after Pearl Harbor.[1] "We have an ally who has never been vanquished in three thousand years." Roosevelt's request that Congress declare war against Germany and Italy was made matter-of-factly, not with a formal speech but with a note delivered to Capitol Hill hours after the Axis acted. Congress approved the declaration with no opposition. And with that action, the United States was plunged into a two-front, two-ocean war, a formidable task for any nation but one especially daunting for a country as unprepared for global war as the United States was in the winter of 1941.

Winston Churchill, now Roosevelt's formal wartime partner, fretted that the United States might turn the bulk of its attention to Japan as it sought to avenge the dead of Pearl Harbor. He was relieved, however, to learn that Roosevelt believed that Germany, not Japan, posed the greater threat. America would pursue a Germany-first strategy, but one that would not preclude advances when possible against Japanese ambitions in the Pacific and in Asia.

Regardless of which front came first, the news was bad from all fronts. Just days after the Pearl Harbor attack, Japanese warplanes attacked and sank two British battleships, the HMS *Prince of Wales*—which had transported Churchill from Britain to Newfoundland the previous summer—and the HMS *Repulse*. The loss of two capital ships in a single attack demonstrated the vulnerability of surface vessels, however well armed, to aircraft armed with torpedoes. Air power now trumped Britain's greatest military asset, sea power.

With the U.S. Pacific Fleet out of commission, the Japanese offensive in the Pacific moved forward with all the speed and success of Germany's blitzkrieg attacks in Europe in 1939 and 1940. Within a matter of weeks, Japan wrapped up its conquests of Guam, Wake Island, and Hong Kong. Japanese landings in the Philippines overwhelmed local and American opposition, forcing the United States and its Filipino allies to retreat to Bataan and Corregidor, a fortified island in Manila Bay. The embattled U.S. garrison there received extensive attention in the U.S. media thanks to radio broadcasts directly from the island outpost, so Americans eagerly followed the efforts by General Douglas MacArthur to hold off the Japanese invaders.

Winston Churchill sailed across the dangerous Atlantic Ocean yet again in mid-December to have another face-to-face meeting with Roosevelt. He planned to stay a week; he stayed in America for nearly a month, seizing the opportunity to cement his relationship with Roosevelt and to influence American public opinion. He spoke to a joint session of Congress the day after Christmas, reminding his live audience and those listening on radio that he understood their anxiety, and their determination. "The greatest military power in Europe, the greatest military power in Asia...have all declared, and are making, war upon you...But here in Washington, in these memorable days, I had found an Olympian fortitude which, far from being based upon complacency, is only the mask of an inflexible purpose and the proof of a sure and well-grounded confidence in the final outcome." Britain, he reminded Americans, "had the same feeling in our darkest days," a phrase which notably suggested that the island nation's darkest days were in the past.[2]

Churchill lived in the White House during most of his time in America, tearing apart the rhythm and rhyme of the Roosevelt order with the blank verse of spontaneous performance and chaotic hours. He slept late and was at his post well past midnight. He drank with enthusiasm, to the astonishment of a president who generally confined himself to one or two cocktails at six o'clock in the evening. Roosevelt took delight in Churchill's assault on the White House routine, although he half-jokingly said he was looking forward to getting some sleep after Churchill finally departed. Nevertheless, he ignored his wife's concerns that the naughty visitor might have a bad influence on her disciplined husband.

Amid the highballs and unifying public appearances, however, serious work took place as the Atlantic Alliance moved to its next stage, preparing for joint operations in Europe and Asia. Roosevelt and Churchill and their military advisors agreed on a plan to launch an Anglo-American invasion of Axis-occupied North Africa in late 1942. A two-nation command structure called the Combined Chiefs of Staff would work together on preparations and strategy. And documents from the meetings coined the phrase "United Nations" to describe all those countries engaged together in the fight against the Axis.

In the midst of Churchill's visit, Roosevelt went to Capitol Hill on January 6 to deliver his annual State of the Union message. Continued disaster had followed his last trip to the Hill, on December 8, but Roosevelt delivered a defiant speech using the simple, spare language of his fireside chats. "We have not been stunned," he said, a counterintuitive reading of the country's mood since Pearl Harbor. "We have not been terrified or confused." The mere fact that Congress was in session, was gathered before him for the occasion, was proof that the nation's quiet resolve "bodes ill for those who conspired and collaborated to murder world peace."

Those conspirators roused an industrial giant bent on liberating the world of conquest, and Roosevelt laid out a spectacular plan of production to arm the forces of righteous indignation. Over the next year, he said, the United States would aim to produce 60,000 planes; the following year, 125,000. In 1942, the United States would build 45,000 tanks; in 1943, that number would increase to 75,000. Production of merchant ships would increase from about a million tons in 1941 to 6 million tons in 1942 and to 10 million tons in 1943. "These figures and similar figures...will give the Japanese and the Nazis a little idea of just what they accomplished in the attack on Pearl Harbor," he said, brimming with confidence.

Those figures, however, made guesswork look scientific. Roosevelt extrapolated from figures given him by Britain's Lord Beaverbrook, who came up with the estimates based on comparing Canadian and American production capacity and resources. Roosevelt told Harry Hopkins, "Oh, the production people can do it if they really try."[3]

Despite the defiance and optimism of FDR's annual message, the nation's mood was not nearly as resolute and determined as both the president and Prime Minister asserted it was. Sam Rosenman recalled that many Americans were afraid that "our own cities [would] be attacked," and so preferred that the United States withdraw into a defensive shell rather than carry the war to its enemies. The weeks following FDR's speech on January 6 brought fresh rounds of bad news. German submarines continued to assail Allied shipping in the Atlantic with devastating results. Americans and Filipinos were fighting a losing battle in the Philippines. Roosevelt chose this time of fear and anxiety to carry out the most shameful act of his presidency—on February 19, 1942, he ordered the internment of Japanese immigrants and their U.S.-born children, about 120,000 men, women, and children in total. They were evacuated from their homes on the West Coast, a likely target of Japanese invaders, and dispatched to camps far from their homes. With little time to prepare for their forced removal, the detainees sold their property for prices far below fair market value.

It was a move driven by panic and fear, difficult to justify even at the time. J. Edgar Hoover, the director of the Federal Bureau of Investigation and no civil libertarian, opposed the president's actions.

There was no denying, however, that fear had returned to American living rooms. It had been there before, as recently as 1933, when Franklin Roosevelt argued against the power of fear itself. "The president was beginning to feel concerned lest a spirit of defeatism settle over the American people," Rosenman wrote. "Americans had become accustomed to thinking that they could lick any nation with one hand tied behind their back. Now...we were being thoroughly smeared by the Japanese, about whose power and fighting ability a great many Americans had for years felt contemptuous."[4]

Roosevelt decided to address the nation's fears directly in a fireside chat on Monday night, February 23, the day the nation celebrated Washington's birthday. Roosevelt and his aides believed the speech would be just as important as the president's very first fireside chat in March 1933, in the depths of the Depression. Circumstances surely were different, but the need for reassurance was the same. Although "the outlook seemed hopelessly dismal," Rosenman wrote, Roosevelt was determined to persuade Americans that "liberation and victory were bound to come."[5]

FDR told his aides he wanted his listeners to have maps in front of them as they listened to his speech in their living rooms and kitchens. "I'm going to speak about strange places that many of them never heard of—places that are now the battleground for civilization," he told Rosenman. "I'm going to ask the newspapers to print maps of the whole world. I want to explain to the people something about geography—what our problem is and what the overall strategy of this war has to be...I want to explain this war in laymen's language. If they understand the problem and what we are driving at, I am sure that they can take any kind of bad news right on the chin."[6]

Harry Hopkins, Robert Sherwood, and Rosenman spent hours in the White House Cabinet Room working through seven drafts of the speech. Other White House aides were in contact with newspaper editors around the country, asking them to print maps of the world so the American people could follow the president as he took them on a virtual tour of the war's battlegrounds. Most editors obliged.

The speechwriters labored through the night of February 21, a Saturday. Sheets of paper—copies of discarded drafts—covered a large table in the center of the Cabinet Room. Roosevelt joined them for a while, but Sherwood, Hopkins, and Rosenman remained at their post after the president went to bed. They fortified themselves with coffee, sandwiches, and soft drinks, although Sherwood and Hopkins helped themselves to something stronger—bourbon—as midnight approached. At one point, Rosenman let his thoughts drift from the task at hand. "What's the war news like," he asked Hopkins.

"It's all terrible," Hopkins replied. "We're getting one hell of a licking all over the Pacific."

"If the American people ever needed a shot in the arm, this is the time," Sherwood said. "I hope this speech can do it."[7]

They worked until three o'clock in the morning, leaving a draft for the president to read with his breakfast. The final draft did not include a long passage Roosevelt wrote himself, telling his writers to "stick it in somewhere, boys." It was a long, defensive explanation about an incident in which three German warships managed to elude the Royal Navy in the English Channel—the latest humiliation for America's ally. The speechwriters thought FDR's passage was overly defensive and apologetic, and they persuaded him to discard it.

Finally, as the nation celebrated the anniversary of Washington's birth (which actually fell on Sunday and so was commemorated on Monday, the 23rd), Roosevelt delivered one of the most critical fireside chats of his tenure. Listeners by the tens of millions held maps in their hands in preparation for the president's promised world tour of places and nations that were unfamiliar to them, but which loomed large in the fight against the Axis enemy.

As if to underscore the urgency of the moment, Roosevelt began the speech with a reference to the bleak prospects that confronted Washington and his soldiers during another crisis, the American Revolution. "For eight years," he reminded listeners, "General Washington and his Continental Army were faced continually with formidable odds and recurring defeats. Supplies and equipment were lacking...Washington's conduct in those hard times has provided the model for all Americans ever since—a model of moral stamina. He held to his course, as it had been charted in the Declaration of Independence. He and the brave men who served with him knew that no man's life or fortune was secure without freedom and free institutions." The parallels between the 1770s and the 1940s were, in Roosevelt's telling, clear.

But there were differences as well. Warfare itself was far more deadly, far more dangerous, than it was in the eighteenth century. "This war is a new kind of war," he said. "It is different from all other wars of the past, not only in its methods and weapons but also in its geography. It is warfare in terms of every continent, every island, every sea, every air-lane in the world." It was for that reason, he explained, that he asked his listeners to "take out and spread before you a map of the whole earth." This was Roosevelt at his most intimate, talking to one person at a time, holding a conversation, albeit one-sided, with millions of Americans gathered collectively in front of their radios. His informal delivery, warm baritone, and use of the second person—"you"—invited listeners to be participants in this chat, not merely spectators.

Before embarking on his tour of the world's battlefields and trouble spots, he addressed himself to the geographic feature that protected America from the Old World's conflict so effectively for so long. But no longer. "The broad oceans which have been heralded in the past as our protection from attack," he said, "have become endless battlefields on which we are constantly being challenged by our enemies. We must all understand and face the hard fact that our job now is to fight at distances which extend all the way around the globe." World war meant that the United States had to protect supply lines, shipping lanes, and airspace that spanned the globe itself. The nation could no longer hunker down behind an imagined Fortress America.

"Look at your map," he said. "Look at the vast area of China, with its millions of fighting men. Look at the vast area of Russia, with its powerful armies and proven military might. Look at the islands of Britain, Australia, New Zealand, the Dutch Indies, India, the Near East and the Continent of Africa, with...their resources of raw materials, and of peoples determined to resist Axis domination. Look too at North America, Central America and South America."

As the American people directed their gaze from their radios to their maps, Roosevelt explained that if any of these nations and regions were "cut off from each other," disaster would follow. If the United States could no longer aid China, the war against Japan would become immensely more difficult. If the Japanese isolated Australia, they could move east towards the American West Coast. If British and Russian forces in the Mediterranean were cut off from American aid, the Nazis would move into West Africa, "putting Germany within easy striking distance of South America—fifteen hundred miles away." Americans followed the president from region to region, seeing the ways in which the world had shrunk, comprehending why failure in one country, one region, could bring a shooting war closer to America's vulnerable shores.

He offered one last argument against the logic of isolationists. "Those Americans who believed that we could live under the illusion of isolationism wanted the American eagle to imitate the tactics of the ostrich," he said. "Now, many of those same people, afraid that we may be sticking our necks out, want our national bird to be turned into a turtle. But we prefer to retain the eagle as it is—flying high and striking hard.

"I know [that] I speak for the mass of the American people when I say that we reject the turtle policy and will continue increasingly the policy of carrying the war to the enemy in distant lands and distant waters—as far away as possible from our own home grounds."

He continued to prompt his audience to consult their maps as he described the Japanese assault on the Philippine Islands, where, he said, American and Filipino forces were "making Japan pay an increasingly terrible price for her ambitions..." He revisited the attack on Pearl Harbor, insisting that the "consequences of the attack...have been wildly exaggerated" and that "these exaggerations come originally from Axis propagandists; but they have been repeated, I regret to say, by Americans in and out of public life." Those Americans who chose to believe Axis exaggerations deserved only "contempt."

It would have been foolhardy to insist that all was well, that the nation's plight in the winter of 1942 was not as grim as it appeared to be. Roosevelt acknowledged that his listeners knew that the war news was grave indeed, but he characteristically insisted that he had confidence in "your ability to hear the worst, without flinching or losing heart." The nation had been forced to "yield ground" in the Pacific, but, he insisted, "we will regain it." That task would be made easier if Americans put individual gain aside for the collective good—they should never cease production even for a day in a labor dispute; they should not demand "special privileges" for any group or occupation, and they should "give up conveniences" if "our country asks us to."

The nation's enemies, he said, believed Americans were incapable of adhering to these selfless goals. Berlin, Rome, and Tokyo described America as "soft and decadent...a nation of weaklings—'playboys'—who would hire British soldiers, or Russian soldiers, or Chinese soldiers to do our fighting for us." His conversational tone shifted, his voice rose, as he voiced the nation's defiance:

"Let them repeat that now!

"Let them tell that to General MacArthur and his men...

"Let them tell that to the Marines!"

He concluded by recalling the words of Thomas Paine, who, during the Continental Army's long, cold retreat through New Jersey in 1776, wrote that "these are the times that try men's souls."

Men's souls were being tried again, but, as Paine wrote, "the harder the sacrifice, the more glorious the triumph."

But more sacrifice would be required before Americans could imagine triumph. On March 12, Roosevelt ordered General Douglas MacArthur to leave the Philippines as the Japanese pressed their attack on the Bataan peninsula and on Corregidor. Trapped U.S. forces surrendered on May 6. The bad news of winter did not break with the coming of spring, but Roosevelt's candid words on February 23 helped prepare the nation for the worst even as they dared to imagine renewal and final victory.

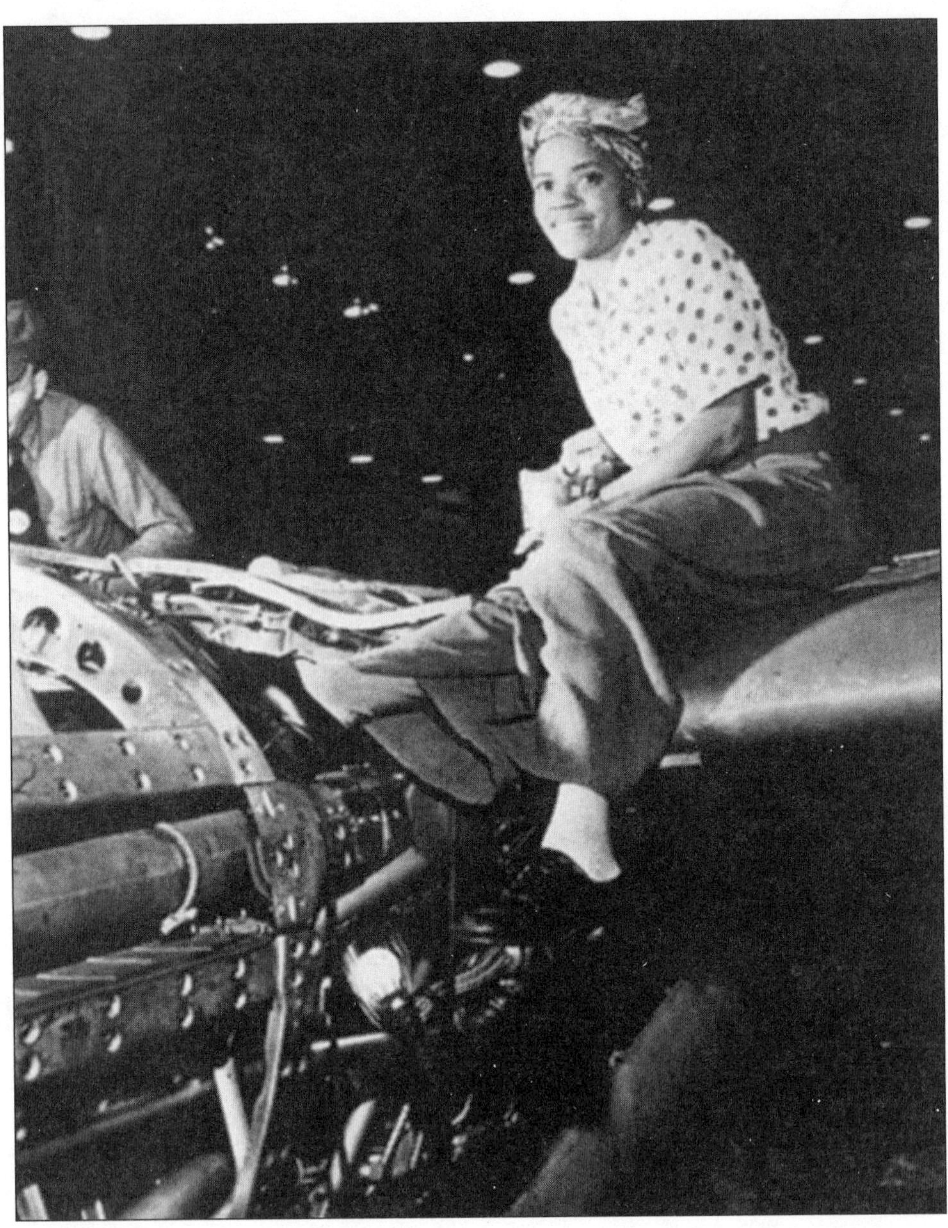

With millions of American men in uniform (along with thousands of women), industry turned to women to provide much-needed labor. While many women returned to more traditional roles after the war, the experience helped change America's work culture and set the stage for new career opportunities for women.

CHAPTER 22

The Folks Back Home

Fireside Chat

September 7, 1942

TRACK 22

Filled with confidence after finishing their conquest of the Philippine Islands, the Japanese ventured farther into the Pacific in the spring of 1942, preparing for a decisive victory over the U.S. fleet. Amid the defeats and setbacks, President Roosevelt sought desperately for some victory, however small, to rally American public opinion. He found it in a risky mission that figured to deliver little in the way of military success, but much in the form of higher spirits at home.

Towards the end of the long winter of 1941–42, Roosevelt asked his commanders about the possibility of attacking Tokyo from the air. It was an audacious suggestion at a time when Japan was advancing on all fronts and the U.S. Pacific Fleet was so gravely reduced. But no aircraft carriers were at Pearl Harbor on December 7. They were capable of delivering U.S. air power far into the Pacific.

But how far? Roosevelt wished to project a small show of force across the vast ocean and into the enemy's home territory. Despite initial skepticism from top military brass, the plan took shape during the late winter, and in mid-April, Lieutenant Colonel James Doolittle led a force of sixteen B-25 bombers from the deck of the carrier USS *Hornet* on an eight-hundred-mile mission to Tokyo. The planes dropped their bombs and then, with little fuel left, they parachuted out of their planes over Chinese air space. Nine crew members were killed or captured, but seventy-one survived. The success of the Doolittle mission picked up the country's spirits and infuriated the Japanese.

The Doolittle raid, inspired by Roosevelt's wish for a display of American defiance, added urgency to Admiral Yamamoto's renewed offensive. He sought a final, decisive destruction of U.S. forces before they could recover from the blows of December 7. Yamamoto focused his attention on the American base on Midway Island, while another Japanese force moved south to threaten Australia.

Yamamoto hoped to achieve complete surprise yet again, as he did at Pearl. But U.S. intelligence broke the Japanese code, and the American high command followed every move the Japanese made. A two-carrier force under Admiral Chester Nimitz sailed towards New Guinea to intercept a would-be Japanese invasion force. During the ensuing battle in the Coral Sea in early May, surface ships never fired a shot at each other. Instead, the three-day battle was fought by carrier-based aircraft defending or attacking other carriers or warships.

One of the U.S. pilots involved in the battle was Lieutenant John James Powers, who flew a dive bomber with extraordinary skill and success during the engagement's first two days. His attacks destroyed one Japanese vessel and severely damaged several others. During the battle's final day, after Powers was briefed on his latest target, a Japanese aircraft carrier, he told his fellow pilots, "Remember, the folks back home are counting on us. I am going to get a hit if I have to lay it down on their flight deck."

He did just that, careening towards his target in spite of a barrage of antiaircraft fire. He was last seen trying to pull out of his dive, but the bomb scored a direct hit, destroying the carrier. Powers was never seen again. But the Japanese invasion force turned away, and a month later, on June 4, the U.S. Navy devastated Yamamoto's fleet at the Battle of Midway, sinking three carriers and damaging another beyond repair.

Roosevelt read about Powers's heroics in a letter from Navy Secretary Knox, who recommended that Powers received the Medal of

Honor. The pilot's final words about the folks back home resonated with the president. During the summer of 1942, the folks at home were very much in his thoughts, even as the United States began to strike back in the Pacific and prepared to go on the offensive in North Africa.

Mobilization in the age of global conflict involved more than simply marshaling men and materiel for combat. It meant conscripting large sectors of the economy into the war effort. It meant extraordinary government intervention into the marketplace. It meant sacrifice in even the humblest home, and a sense that all citizens were called to do their duty. The folks at home were not necessarily in uniform, but they were very much a part of a collective effort like no other in the nation's history.

Just a few months after Pearl Harbor, Roosevelt began his offensive on the home front when he asked for the public's help in reducing the nation's use of rubber. The Japanese onslaught in the Pacific reduced rubber imports by 90 percent, leading FDR to plead with citizens to bring their spare tires, garden hoses, and boots to collection points so they could be converted into war materiel. Actor/crooner Bing Crosby donated a box of golf balls to the cause. Speed limits were reduced to 35 miles per hour to conserve on tire use, and tires themselves were extremely hard to find.

But that was only the beginning of the sacrifices and changes Washington would ask of civilians. The government began rationing sugar and coffee in mid-1942, and soon would extend rationing to meat and dairy products. A new federal agency, the Office of Price Administration, froze the prices of some goods to avoid inflation. The OPA and another new agency, the War Production Board, supervised the rationing system.

Well aware that Americans did not like limits—the rationing of gasoline was particularly unpopular—the Roosevelt administration set out on a propaganda campaign to inculcate a spirit of shared sacrifice. A poster showing a stricken tanker sinking into the sea asked if brave men should die "so you can drive." Another showed a picture of a healthy G.I. eating a battlefield meal, with the words, "Do with less—so they'll have enough."

War on the home front meant other kinds of sacrifices as well. Roosevelt established the National War Labor Board to mediate labor disputes and thus avoid strikes that might affect the production of war materiel—and in 1942, nearly all production had some kind of military usage.

Roosevelt understood that Americans would have a hard time getting used to sacrifice, coming hard on the heels of the calamitous 1930s. But in a two-ocean war certain to strain the resources even of a continental nation like the United States, Americans would have little choice but to give up luxuries and even necessities in order to defeat their enemies. And, in a break with the American tradition of limited government and rugged individualism, Washington would enforce those sacrifices through an unprecedented intervention into the marketplace. For example, the War Production Board policed men's and women's fashions in an effort to save wool for military use. Men's clothing stores were barred from including an extra pair of pants with suits. The length of women's skirts was regulated not by taste or preference, but by government regulators. It was an astonishing and rapid assertion of federal power into every facet of American economic life.

In a fireside chat on April 28, Roosevelt put the struggle in dramatic, almost Churchillian, terms. "The price for civilization must be paid in hard work and sorrow and blood," he said. "The price is not too high. If you doubt it, ask those millions who live today under the tyranny of Hitlerism...Ask the women and children whom Hitler is starving whether the rationing of tires and gasoline and sugar is too great a 'sacrifice.'"

Roosevelt sought to lead by example. When coffee was placed on the government's ration list, the president publicized his own formula for reusing old coffee grounds. A character on humorist Fred Allen's popular radio program said that the president's coffee tasted "like low tide at Coney Island."[1]

Through the summer of 1942, the president remained concerned about inflation. Government measures were not working to his satisfaction, and Congress, its eyes focused on reelection campaigns in the fall, debated in leisurely fashion his request for a tax increase of nearly $9 billion to help prevent excess civilian purchasing power from driving up prices, which were continuing to increase despite his administration's efforts to keep the cost of living under control. Congress was particularly skeptical of giving the administration power to put a ceiling on agricultural prices. In fact, Congress passed a law designed to keep farm prices no lower than 110 percent of what was called "parity" value. Parity was a national standard for farm prices, so the congressional action allowed farmers to increase prices above what the White House considered a decent standard of living. Those price increases were driving inflation despite the president's best efforts. Treasury Secretary Morgenthau told Roosevelt that he had better act quickly, "because this thing is getting away from you."[2]

Roosevelt wanted congressional approval for his bid to put a lid on price increases, but some of his aides, including Sam Rosenman, now a legal aide as well as a speechwriter, insisted that the president ought to do so unilaterally if Congress would not act. The president's war powers, Rosenman and others argued, gave him the authority to impose controls on prices. But Roosevelt was reluctant to act without Congress.

As summer drew to a close—as the fall elections neared, and as the United States moved closer to a planned invasion of North Africa codenamed Operation Torch—Roosevelt decided to take the battle against inflation directly to Congress and the people. He and his top advisors, including Rosenman, spent long hours in three locations—Washington, Hyde Park, and the presidential retreat in the Maryland mountains that FDR called Shangri-La (Dwight Eisenhower would rename the getaway "Camp David")—working on a message to Congress and a fireside chat. Both would focus on the dangers of inflation, and would present the case for price controls on agricultural goods. He would tell Congress that if it refused to act by October 1, he would do so on his own, using his war powers. In his long message to Congress, delivered in writing, he vowed that when "farm prices are stabilized, wages can and will be stabilized."[3] The message also focused on the unpopular issue of taxes—everyone, he said, save for the very poor, should have to pay more to the government. The president's proposal was radical; he asserted that nobody in America should make more than $25,000 after taxes in a single year.

The president opened his chat with the story of Lieutenant John James Powers, one of the heroes of the Battle of the Coral Sea, where the seemingly inevitable Japanese advance towards Australia and the western United States came to an abrupt halt. Roosevelt told listeners of Powers's courage under fire, his determination to sink a Japanese carrier even if it cost him his life, and his reminder to his fellow pilots that "the folks back home are counting on us."

"You and I are 'the folks back home' for whose protection Lieutenant Powers fought and repeatedly risked his life," Roosevelt said. "He said that we counted on him and his men. We did not count in vain."

But if heroes like Lieutenant Powers were sacrificing for the "folks back home," what were those folks doing to deserve such dedication? "How are we playing our part back home in winning this war?" the president asked. "The answer is that we are not doing enough." Listeners who grumbled about government rationing and government regulation of goods, who resented the inconveniences of war, might have recognized themselves in the president's speech. That was precisely his intent.

Roosevelt made his point clear: controlling the cost of living was critical to the war effort, but it could be achieved only through collective action and a spirit of self-sacrifice. He took dead aim at the farm lobby's insistence that prices should be no lower than 110 percent of parity value. "This act of favoritism for one particular group in the community increased the cost of food to everybody—not only to the workers in the city or in the munitions plans, and their families, but also to the families of the farmers themselves." Such special treatment, he said, had to come to an end, for if farmers continued to raise the price of food, "the wage earner, particularly in the lower brackets, will have a right to an increase in his wages." Roosevelt conceded that the wage earner's demand would be "essential justice and a practical necessity."

Such demands, however, could prove ruinous in an economy devoted to winning a world war. "If the vicious spiral of inflation ever gets under way, the whole economic system will stagger...The cost of the war, paid by taxpayers, will jump beyond all present calculations."

The cost of nearly everything would increase, perhaps as much as 20 percent. "I need not tell you that this would have a demoralizing effect on our people, soldiers and civilians alike," he said.

He told listeners of the message he sent to Congress hours earlier, demanding that members take further steps to control the cost of living, including the imposition of a ceiling on farm prices. If farm prices were stabilized, he said, "I will stabilize wages. That is plain justice—and plain common sense." If common sense did not prevail on Capitol Hill by October 1, he said, he would impose it himself.

After softening his rhetoric to pay tribute to the patriotism of the nation's farmers, he then moved to the more radical part of his address: his proposal to raise taxes and limit the net income of the nation's highest earners to $25,000 per year, or about $375,000 in today's money. "The nation must have more money to run the war," he said. "People must stop spending for luxuries. Our country needs a far greater share of our incomes."

With the nation finally wriggling free of deprivation and sacrifice, this was a harsh message, indeed. But Roosevelt believed that it was necessary.

The sacrifice of Lt. John James Powers, the deaths of thousands of Americans in combat, cried out for greater American appreciation of the threat it faced from abroad.

"All of us here at home are being tested—for our fortitude, for our selfless devotion to our country and to our cause," he said.

Roosevelt's listeners were chastened. Once again, his words, delivered into millions of living rooms, changed the political dynamics. Congress quickly passed an anti-inflation package that did not go as far as the president wished—net annual incomes were not limited to $25,000 a year after all—but which nevertheless granted the White House extraordinary power to intervene in the marketplace. On October 3, 1942, Roosevelt established the Office of Economic Stabilization to oversee the regulation of prices and wages.

American troops storm the beaches of North Africa
as Operation Torch gets underway in 1942.

CHAPTER 23

The Sands of North Africa

State of the Union Address

January 7, 1943

TRACK 23

FRANKLIN ROOSEVELT COULD NOT HIDE HIS ANXIETY. HE WAS AT SHANGRI-LA, THE presidential retreat in the Maryland mountains, for a much-needed postelection weekend away from the White House. The Democrats had taken a beating in the off-year contests earlier in the week, losing fifty seats in the House and eight Senate seats. But Roosevelt's concerns on Saturday night, November 7, had little to do with election results. A joint Anglo-American armada was heading towards North Africa with thousands of American citizen-soldiers who were about to undergo their baptism of fire.

Roosevelt was awaiting a telephone call with news of the invasion. When it finally came that night, Roosevelt's hands shook as he picked up the phone. Aides and friends heard only his end of the conversation, but what they heard sounded encouraging. "Thank God," he said. "Thank God. That sounds grand." He put down the phone and turned to his guests. "We have landed in North Africa," he said. "Casualties are below expectations. We are striking back."[1]

American and British armed forces were storming beaches in Morocco and Algeria with great success. Opposing them were French forces loyal to the collaborationist government based in Vichy. They did not put up much of a fight and stopped firing completely when the United States worked out a deal with the French commander, Admiral Jean Darlan, an Anglophobe whose previous service included a stint as the head of the Vichy government. The agreement allowed Darlan, whom the French resistance regarded as a traitor, to assume political control over French North Africa. In exchange, Darlan persuaded other Vichy French generals to accept a cease-fire. The deal led to bitter criticism of Roosevelt, who was perceived to be cooperating with Nazi sympathizers. Churchill told Roosevelt, "We must not overlook the serious political injury which may be done to our cause, not only in France but throughout Europe, by the feeling that we are ready to make terms with local Quislings," a reference to the notorious Norwegian collaborator.[2]

The president, however, believed he had no choice. The deal with Darlan saved American lives, Roosevelt said. He explained to skeptics that the arrangement meant that the Anglo-American conquest of North Africa would last only "a couple of weeks with very few lives lost."[3] According to historian Robert Dallek, Roosevelt saw the alliance with Darlan as a temporary arrangement, one that could be dissolved when the Allies had military and civil control over the region. He told Eisenhower, who planned the invasion, that "we do not trust Darlan."[4]

Roosevelt's critics, however, did not accept his pragmatic justification of the Darlan deal. Walter Lippman and other influential journalists continued to hammer away at what they perceived to be a betrayal of the war's moral purpose, a turning away from the president's idealistic Four Freedoms speech. The bitterness extended to Roosevelt's cabinet and inner circle—the president's seemingly cavalier association with an unapologetic Nazi collaborator horrified Treasury Secretary Morgenthau and Supreme Court Justice Felix Frankfurter.

According to speechwriter Sam Rosenman, FDR bitterly resented the criticism. "He showed more resentment and more impatience with his critics throughout this period than at any other time I know about," Rosenman said. That is a startling claim, given the ferocity of criticism leveled at FDR during the 1930s over the New Deal and in 1939–1940, when isolationists opposed Roosevelt's efforts to aid Great

Britain. Rosenman said FDR sometimes "bitterly read aloud what some columnist had written" about the Darlan deal, and he "expressed his resentment."[5]

Darlan had more dangerous enemies than American journalists, and they had resentments of their own to express. On December 24, 1942, an assassin shot and killed Darlan in Algiers, removing him as a political lightning rod as the Allies moved to strengthen their position in North Africa.

The North African campaign was the result of extensive planning, which, in turn, followed weeks of wrangling between American and British military and political leaders. Top American generals, including Dwight Eisenhower, believed the Anglo-Americans should take the war to Germany in the most immediate way possible—by crossing the English Channel and opening a second front in France. Churchill and the British, mindful of the generation they lost in the abattoir of World War I, refused to go along with what was, in retrospect, a foolhardy American rush to throw unprepared troops at the best-equipped army in the world.

The British persuaded Roosevelt that the best way to strike the Axis was on the periphery, in what Churchill called the "underbelly" of the Nazi empire. The British Eighth Army already had German forces under the command of the brilliant German commander Erwin Rommel on the defensive after a stunning victory at El Alamein in Egypt in October. The Britons' arguments against a cross-Channel operation carried extra weight because the United States simply did not have the manpower and materiel yet to mount a major offensive in France. If the Allies were to invade France, the British would have to take the lead. And the British believed such an invasion would end in disaster.

In pressing their argument, the British had to tread carefully, making sure that they did not offend Roosevelt or his chief military advisor, George C. Marshall, both of whom were sympathetic, at least conceptually, to a cross-Channel operation in 1942. There was always the danger, at least in British eyes, that the United States might throw the bulk of its resources against the power that had attacked them, Japan, if they lost confidence in British resolve. So Churchill parried, rather than explicitly ruled out, American ideas for a frontal assault on France, constantly turning the conversation to the opportunities awaiting the Allies in North Africa. Churchill and the British knew that Roosevelt desired action; he wanted Americans to see that the country was on the offensive, striking back at the enemy, when they went to the polls in November's off-year congressional elections. An invasion of North Africa, then, seemed to satisfy the concerns of both parties. The Americans would get a chance to go on the offensive against Hitler and his allies; the British could avoid what they saw as a foolhardy invasion of France.

After the war, General Marshall conceded that the North Africa campaign was planned with an eye on domestic political concerns. "The people demand action," Marshall recalled. "We couldn't wait to be completely ready."[6]

If the Americans weren't completely ready, as Marshall admitted, it surely would have been foolish, if not criminal, to hurl unprepared forces across the English Channel in 1942. North Africa, however, presented a much softer target. The success of the initial assault in early November and the rapid capitulation of Vichy forces gave the Anglo-Americans a quick victory, something they could not possibly have won in northern France. Within a week of the invasion, the Allies were firmly in charge of Morocco and Algeria, preparing to move against German forces in Tunisia. Hitler quickly dispatched additional warplanes, tanks, and troops to support Rommel at a time when a titanic struggle with Soviet forces was unfolding near Stalingrad. The Soviets had pressed Roosevelt and Churchill for a broad second front in France to help relieve pressure on the Red Army. While North Africa was not what Stalin had in mind, Anglo-American successes in the Mediterranean forced Hitler to spread his defenses at a critical moment in the war.

Although there still was hard fighting to be done in North Africa, and victory over a canny foe like Rommel was hardly assured, Roosevelt seemed confident and relaxed as 1942 drew to a close. Historian James MacGregor Burns, in his study of Roosevelt's war leadership, noted that Roosevelt believed a turning point in the war was at hand. The successful landings in North Africa followed the sensational victory over Japan near Midway Island, while on another front Hitler was bogged down outside of Stalingrad on the eve of a Russian winter. A year after Pearl Harbor, the United States and the Allies were indeed striking back.

As he prepared to face a joint session of Congress for his annual State of the Union message, Roosevelt believed the time was right to begin a conversation about the sort of world that would follow an Allied victory.

The senators and representatives who gathered in the House chamber on January 7, 1943, to hear FDR's message was by far the most hostile congressional audience he had faced since his election. Republicans enjoyed historic gains in the fall elections, slicing into the Democrats' majorities in both houses and persuading some conservative Democrats that the New Deal had gone far enough. Roosevelt was well aware that many of the smiling faces in the crowd were anything but friendly. The smiles were part of political protocol; they indicated neither approval nor support.

Roosevelt began by according them a place in history. They had assembled, he said, during "one of the great moments in the history of the nation." Decisions they made would have historical importance because 1943 figured to be a year of hard-earned victories, opening a path that would lead to final victory. "The Axis powers knew that they must win the war in 1942—or eventually lose everything," he said, reminding them that "our enemies did not win the war in 1942." The war of "defensive attrition" in the Pacific was "drawing to a close," while Russian victories and the Allied invasion of North Africa turned momentum in the Allies' favor. Roosevelt made it clear that the new year would bring renewed defeat for the Axis, a judgment he could make, he said, thanks to the bravery of Allied soldiers and the astonishing productivity of American civilian workers.

He told listeners that the Allies would soon take the battle to the Axis powers in Europe. "I cannot tell you whether we are going to hit them in Norway, or through the Low Countries, or in France, or through Sardinia or Sicily, or through the Balkans, or through Poland, or at several points simultaneously. But I can tell you that no matter where and when we strike by land, we and the British and the Russians will hit them from the air heavily and relentlessly. Day in and day out we shall heap tons upon tons of high explosives on their war factories and utilities and seaports."

Like Churchill, Roosevelt could barely disguise his contempt for the nation's enemies and the causes they represented. He focused specifically on the ways in which the air war had changed. Germany could no longer bomb civilian targets without expecting treatment in kind. "Hitler and Mussolini will understand now the enormity of their miscalculations—that the Nazis would always have the advantage of superior air power as they did when they bombed Warsaw, and Rotterdam, and London and Coventry," he said. "That superiority has gone forever. Yes, the Nazis and the Fascists have asked for it—and they are going to get it."

With the fortunes of war favoring the Allies, then, Roosevelt insisted that it was important for Americans to remember "the things we are fighting for." Yes, American troops were fighting for a permanent peace, but they also wanted "permanent employment for themselves, their families, and their neighbors...

"They do not want a postwar America which suffers from undernourishment or slums, or the dole. They want no get-rich-quick era of bogus 'prosperity' which will end for them in selling apples on a street corner, as happened after the bursting of the boom in 1929."

It was a pointed message, delivered to a Congress that included nearly sixty new Republicans. If the new Congress was spoiling for a fight, Roosevelt made it clear he was willing to play the Depression/Hoover card. The question was whether this was an appropriate time to "speak of a better America after the war. I am told it is a grave error on my part. I dissent."

He also believed it was time to speak of a better world, a world in which Americans would play a leading role in the world affairs, side by side with other peace-loving nations. "Today the United Nations are the mightiest military coalition in all history," he said. "They represent an overwhelming majority of the population of the world. Bound together in solemn agreement that they themselves will not commit acts of aggression or conquest against any of their neighbors, the United Nations can and must remain united for the maintenance of peace by preventing any attempt to rearm in Germany, in Japan, in Italy, or in any other Nation which seeks to violate the Tenth Commandment—'Thou shalt not covet.'" He conceded that some "cynics" and "skeptics" would argue that "it cannot be done." But "all the freedom-loving peoples of this earth are now demanding that it must be done. And the will of these people shall prevail."

After delivering his broad vision of the postwar world, Roosevelt met with Churchill in Casablanca. There, Roosevelt announced that the Allies would accept nothing less than unconditional surrender from the Axis. A seemingly spontaneous remark, it reflected precisely what he told Congress on January 7. There would be no quarter given to the enemies of mankind.

Their visions of the world were incompatible with his, and with those of "all freedom-living peoples."

Although President Roosevelt framed World War II as a struggle for freedom, injustice continued to oppress African Americans at home. Segregation was a way of life, as this sign indicates.

CHAPTER 24

The G.I. Bill

Fireside Chat

July 28, 1943

TRACK 24

As commander in chief of a great global military enterprise upon which nothing less than the world's future depended, Franklin Roosevelt was, of course, immersed in the political, strategic, diplomatic, and logistical details of the sprawling Allied effort against Germany, Italy, and Japan. But his role as a wartime leader was not confined to strategy and tactics, enunciating great principles, and consulting with generals and heads of governments. The war surely changed the priorities of his administration, but Franklin Roosevelt still was the author and administrator of some of the greatest domestic reforms in American history.

The president demonstrated in his annual message to Congress in January 1943, that he had not entirely forgotten about the ways in which his administration transformed relations between labor and capital, between disparate groups of Americans, during his first years in office. After watching big business leaders—the targets of some of Roosevelt's most stinging rhetoric—come to Washington to take over wartime production boards, after observing the apparent decline in the influence of New Dealers like Interior Secretary Harold Ickes and Vice President Henry Wallace, some New Dealers had concluded that the age of reform was over. David Lilienthal, head of the Tennessee

Valley Authority, was among them. In his view, domestic reformers felt defeated and marginalized at the end of 1942. Perhaps sensing Lilienthal's low spirits, Roosevelt took him aside and assured him that he had not forgotten the issues that animated his first two terms. He would fight opposition in Congress, he promised, and would see to it that the nation's fighting men would not "come back to fear about jobs, to worry about the things a man can't prevent, like accident [and] sickness..."[1]

Roosevelt's State of the Union message offered a hint of the president's plans for a postwar America, but as 1943 proceeded, bringing little but good news from the world's battlefields, Roosevelt began to flesh out his vision for a renewed burst of reform at home.

Some of the president's attention to domestic affairs in mid-1943 was forced on him. Racial violence broke out in Detroit and Los Angeles, directed at African Americans and Mexicans. Twenty-five blacks and nine whites died in the Detroit riots. An official with the National Association for the Advancement of Colored People warned that without aggressive presidential action, more violence was sure to follow.

Meanwhile, on the labor front, one of Roosevelt's most accomplished antagonists, John L. Lewis, head of the United Mine Workers, threatened to disrupt the nation's supply of coal. With his bushy eyebrows and confrontational manner, Lewis was among the best-known—and most vilified—labor leaders of the war years.

In early 1943, some fifteen thousand mine workers went on strike in an unauthorized job action that soon led to disruptions in other industries. Although the nation's unions signed a no-strike pledge for the duration of the war, labor stoppages did not disappear as workers demanded higher wages, sometimes in response to price increases granted to industry by Roosevelt's regulators.

Most strikes were short and quickly resolved. But the spring of 1943 promised a more ominous development. A two-year contract with the United Mine Workers, some six hundred thousand strong working in the nation's vital coal mines, was due to expire. Lewis made it clear that he was ready for a confrontation. He wanted a two-dollar-a-day wage increase for his members, arguing that the cost of living had gone up despite government controls and that mine owners had been granted price increases for the coal his men extracted from the bowels of the earth. It was hard and dangerous work.

As Lewis ramped up the rhetoric of confrontation with Roosevelt, whom he despised, miners began walking off the job in late April. The president pleaded with them "not as president, not as commander in chief, but as the friend of the men who worked in the coal mines."[2] Roosevelt's description of himself was not without merit. In 1940, the mine workers overwhelmingly supported FDR despite Lewis's hostility.

This time, however, friendship took a backseat to the miners' insistence on a wage increase. Faced with a shutdown of one of the nation's most important industries, Roosevelt ordered his government to seize the nation's coal mines on May 6. He devoted a fireside chat the following day to the crisis in the coal mines. He stressed that the nation's war effort was achieving a miracle of production, and the beneficiaries of that effort were America's fighting men and women. But if the coal mines were shut down, American production might grind to a halt, risking the lives of troops around the world. Every striking miner, he said, was "obstructing our war effort."

That was a harsh charge, and Roosevelt intended it to be. Lewis, already one of the nation's favorite villains, was subjected to further public scorn, although in the end, after months of back-and-forth negotiations, he did win a wage increase for his union.

Through this crisis and other wartime labor disputes, Roosevelt reminded the public of his affinity for the nation's working people and the support he received from unions in his three election campaigns. But the necessities of war precluded, at least in Roosevelt's view, the generosity and advocacy he offered the union movement in the past.

Once the war was over, however, there was going to be a place for Dr. New Deal again.

During the eventful summer of 1943, as American armed forces continued to push back the Germans in the Mediterranean and the Japanese in the Pacific, Roosevelt received a report detailing plans to extend educational benefits to veterans upon their return home. The report contained the broad outlines of a domestic reform that would profoundly affect the lives of millions of Americans—the G.I. Bill of Rights.

Known formally as the Servicemen's Readjustment Act, the G.I. Bill offered veterans a chance to attend college, purchase homes, and otherwise improve their lives with the help and support of their government. The program was as transformative as Social Security and other pieces of the social welfare system that are more closely connected to the New Deal.

The report that Roosevelt received in 1943 was not nearly as ambitious as the G.I. Bill. It recommended federal funding for a year of college, not four, as the bill eventually included. It said nothing about making federal funds available for home purchases—that, too, was added during the legislative process leading to passage of the bill in 1944. But the report set in motion one of the most famous pieces of domestic legislation in the twentieth century, a bill that would allow nearly 8 million veterans to attend college and 4 million to buy homes with federal loans. The chance for a college degree would no longer be confined to the privileged; home ownership became a rite of passage for a generation of urban dwellers that exchanged a rental apartment for a patch of grass in the suburbs.

On July 28, the president spoke to the nation about the plan that would become the G.I. Bill. He began by celebrating a milestone in the war against the Axis—the collapse of Benito Mussolini's Fascist government and the dictator's arrest, ordered by Italy's head of state, King Victor Emmanuel III. With Allied bombers bringing the war to Rome and an invasion imminent after successful Anglo-American operations in Sicily, public opinion turned on Mussolini, a turn of events Roosevelt was delighted to revel in as he began his fireside chat.

"The criminal, corrupt Fascist regime in Italy is going to pieces," he said, and Mussolini knew that "the jig was up," adding that Il Duce and his allies would be "punished for their crimes against humanity."

"No criminal," he pointedly warned, "will be allowed to escape by the expedient of 'resignation.'" For officials in Berlin and Tokyo, Roosevelt's words were sobering indeed. This war would not end with an armistice or even surrender. It would not end until the political leaders who started the war were called to account, regardless of whether they still were in power. Roosevelt's strong and purposeful delivery indicated that this was no mere posture on his part. He meant what he said. "We will have no truck with Fascism in any way, in any shape or manner. We will permit no vestige of Fascism to remain."

Before moving to the heart of his speech—his plan for veterans' benefits—FDR showed that he had been thinking about how the world, not just the United States, would change after the war. The Four Freedoms, he said, applied as much to the victims of fascism as they did to his fellow Americans. "It is our determination to restore these conquered peoples to the dignity of human beings, masters of their own fate, entitled to freedom of speech, freedom of religion, freedom from want, and freedom from fear."

That determination would mean that unlike the last world war, the United States would not turn inward once the instruments of surrender were signed. Ensuring a global program of Four Freedoms would mean active American engagement with the rest of the globe. And nobody knew better than Roosevelt that some Americans resisted the idea of exporting democracy abroad. "I am sorry if I step on the toes of those Americans who, playing party politics at home, call that kind of foreign policy 'crazy altruism' and 'starry-eyed dreaming,'" he said in a voice that suggested he was not sorry at all.

After reviewing the success of Allied arms in North Africa and Sicily, praising the nation's "almost unbelievable" war production, and singling out the "devotion, determination and self-sacrifice...displayed by the Russian people and their armies," Roosevelt moved seamlessly to his vision of a postwar America, after the demobilization of some 14 million men and women.

"They must not be demobilized into an environment of inflation and unemployment, to a place on a bread line, or on a corner selling apples," he said, conjuring memories, all too recent, of the America he inherited when he became president in 1933. "I have assured our men in the armed forces that the American people would not let them down when the war is won."

But his assurance was not enough, and he knew it. Any new program that involved the expenditure of vast resources would require the approval of Congress, and Congress, in mid-1943, had turned more conservative, more hostile to a revival of New Deal-type reforms. But FDR knew that even such a Congress would be reluctant to deny benefits for returning veterans.

He then sketched out what he had in mind: mustering-out pay for every soldier honorably discharged; unemployment insurance for all veterans; "an opportunity for members of the armed services to get further education or trade training at the cost of the government"; greater access to medical care; and pensions for wounded veterans.

With those words, Roosevelt set in motion a legislative package that would transform the nation within a decade of his death. He was correct in believing that Congress would not resist a massive social-spending program if it were targeted at veterans. Indeed, Congress eventually passed an even more ambitious program, one that was shaped in part by the nation's most powerful veterans organization, the American Legion. Generally conservative and suspicious of New Deal-type spending programs, the Legion was made up of World War I veterans who were deprived of such benefits when they returned home. They were determined to make sure that veterans would never again have to march on Washington in futile pursuit of government assistance.

The Servicemen's Readjustment Act went from talking points in a fireside chat to legislation to law in less than a year. America was never the same.

Roosevelt joined Winston Churchill and Chinese leader Chiang Kai-Shek to discuss the war in Asia. FDR considered the war in Europe his first priority, but America had the power to roll back Japanese gains in the Pacific even as it took the offensive in Africa and Europe.

CHAPTER 25

Managing the Alliance

Fireside Chat

December 24, 1943

TRACK 25

WELL AFTER SUNDOWN ON NOVEMBER 11—THE ANNIVERSARY OF THE END OF World War I—Franklin Roosevelt, Harry Hopkins, and other aides left the White House for a drive to Quantico Marine base in Virginia. There, they boarded the presidential yacht, the *Potomac*, for what appeared to be just another one of the president's many working vacations at sea. There were fish to be caught, no doubt, and cocktails to be made.

In fact, the yacht was destined not for some fishing location, but for the USS *Iowa*, a huge new battleship that was waiting for the president and his party in deeper waters. The *Iowa* and an escort of destroyers would take the president across the dangerous Atlantic Ocean to North Africa, for a series of meetings with Winston Churchill, Joseph Stalin, and the head of the Chinese nationalist movement, Chiang Kai-shek.

The presidential journey went beyond top secret. Intense discussions took place as key White House advisors sought to ensure that there were no leaks, however unintended, to the press while the president was in transit. Sam Rosenman, the president's counsel and speechwriter, was given the task of figuring out what to do if Congress approved legislation and sent it on to the president for his signature during his absence. According to the Constitution, the president has ten days (excluding Sundays) to sign a bill. If he or she does not act in that time frame, the bill automatically becomes law as long as Congress remains in session.

Roosevelt was scheduled to be overseas for several weeks, but his whereabouts were supposed to be secret. What to do, then, with legislation that might find its way to the White House in his absence? In those days before jet travel, ships would have had a hard time making a round-trip journey from Washington to North Africa in ten days. There were, of course, no fax machines in 1943, never mind electronic correspondence. The president decided that the ten-day clock should start when he physically received the bill, not when the bill was delivered to the White House. That formula still did not explain why Roosevelt might not see a piece of legislation within the ten-day time frame. Rosenman met with top congressional leaders to explain why Roosevelt might be unable to act within ten days. They discreetly agreed to the new arrangement.

As Roosevelt sailed the Atlantic on his way to the port of Oran in Algeria, the Anglo-American offensive in the Mediterranean was beginning to take a backseat to the massive buildup in Great Britain as the Allies prepared for Operation Overlord, the invasion of northern France. In the English countryside, in the moors of Scotland, along the coast of Wales, American, British, and Canadian troops prepared for the greatest amphibious assault in human history. Paratroopers practiced for their perilous jumps behind the Nazi front line. Front-line troops studied the terrain of northern France, from the cliffs along the beaches to the hedgerows that awaited them in the Norman countryside. Landing craft disgorged troops in mock exercises along the English coastline.

But even as these preparations took on added urgency, hard fighting was underway in Italy. The Mediterranean campaign reached its logical and bloody climax in September with an Anglo-American invasion of Italy. Although Mussolini had been thrown out of power, he remained influential in the area, supported by tens of thousands of German troops that used the peninsula's mountains as a strategic ally in the effort to stall the Allies' momentum.

Hard fighting would continue in Italy. And there promised to be even more ferocious fighting in France once the invasion got underway—that is, if it succeeded. More battles loomed on the eastern front even after the Germans suffered a catastrophic loss in Stalingrad in early 1943. In the Pacific, American, British, and Dutch troops continued to push back the Japanese, while the Chinese, under the command of Chiang Kai-shek, sought a place for themselves in the grand Allied strategy.

To resolve some of the diplomatic tensions among the Allies and to begin more intense planning for the war's end, Roosevelt chose to cross the Atlantic to meet with Chiang and Churchill in Cairo, Egypt, and then, momentously, with Churchill and Joseph Stalin in Tehran, Iran, in what would be the first face-to-face meeting of the three main Allied heads of government.

The president and his party were at sea no more than two days when a torpedo was fired mistakenly from one of the *Iowa*'s escorts. It just missed the huge battleship. Roosevelt, who witnessed the near-catastrophe, did not betray any misgivings in a letter to his wife. In fact, he reported with characteristic joviality that it was "a relief to have no newspapers" during the sea journey.[1] Rather than newspapers, Roosevelt focused on his vision of a postwar Germany. During the transatlantic crossing, FDR told aides, including General George Marshall, that Germany ought to be divided into zones after the war, with U.S. armed forces in charge of occupying a huge swath of the country, including its capital, Berlin. "There is going to be a race for Berlin, and the United States should have Berlin," he said.[2]

Roosevelt landed in Oran, where the greeting party included his sons, Elliot, who was in the Army Air Corps, and Franklin Jr., an officer in the navy. He then flew to Cairo to meet with Chiang and Churchill, an arrangement that displeased the Prime Minister. He wished a solo audience with the president so that they could better prepare for their forthcoming meeting with Stalin in Iran, but that was precisely what Roosevelt wished to avoid. He didn't want Stalin thinking that he and Churchill were meeting separately, perhaps to adopt a common line on discussions with an ally. Chiang's presence offered Roosevelt cover against an outbreak of Stalinesque paranoia.

Roosevelt and Chiang met several times over the course of four days in the Egyptian capital. The president told him that China would take its place among the four conquering powers—along with the United States, Britain, and the Soviet Union—after the war, meaning that it would have a full voice in the postwar settlement. It was the war's end, not so much the battles still to be fought, which weighed on the president's mind as he met with Chiang. "This will be very useful twenty-five or fifty years hence," he wrote, speaking of China's alliance with the United States and Britain, "even though China cannot contribute much military or naval support for the moment."[3] Churchill was bored with the whole proceedings, describing the "Chinese story" as "lengthy, complicated, and minor."[4]

Roosevelt hosted a grand Thanksgiving dinner for selected American and British guests, Churchill included, on November 25. The president insisted on carving two turkeys himself, and as he performed the chore, Churchill kept watch over the president's own plate, which was empty. More and more meat fell off onto the plates of Roosevelt's guests. Churchill believed the president would be left with only bones to gnaw on. But Roosevelt was no novice at carving turkeys, and, to Churchill's relief, he saved just enough for himself. At last, Churchill wrote, "the two skeletons were removed" and the president ate "his own share."[5] After dinner, the guests listened to American big-band music, prompting Churchill to dance a foxtrot with Edwin "Pa" Watson, the president's secretary. Roosevelt, not surprisingly, found the spectacle hilarious. It was a memorable, relaxing evening in Cairo. "For a few hours," Churchill wrote, "we cast care aside."[6]

Then it was on to Tehran.

The president and Stalin met not long after Roosevelt arrived in the city. The president had received no shortage of advice about dealing with Stalin, but nearly all of his advisors agreed that the Soviet leader was a formidable figure: well-informed, intelligent, brusque, and ruthless. Like Ronald Reagan, another American politician who would form an historic partnership with a Soviet leader, FDR was convinced that the force of personality could overcome the policy and ideological differences that separated the two leaders and nations. As Roosevelt saw it, Stalin "could not be so very different from other people," according to Harry Hopkins.[7] Roosevelt did not lack for confidence in his ability to manage, and manipulate, other human beings.

The initial meetings among the leaders, their translators, and staff, focused on the postwar settlement in Germany. Stalin suggested that once the war was over the Allies ought to shoot fifty thousand German officers on the spot. Roosevelt smiled and said that perhaps the number ought to be a thousand fewer. Churchill, however, refused to partake in the gallows humor, and righteously rejected any suggestion that the Allies engage in such reprisals.

Discussions then moved to Poland and Eastern Europe. FDR explained privately to Stalin that while he could accept the Soviet proposal to adjust Poland's eastern border, he could not do so publicly, because he might run again in 1944. Roosevelt's further political ambitions were becoming more urgent in the United States as another presidential election loomed and no end to the war was in sight. Having already broken the two-term precedent, Roosevelt did not have tradition as an obstacle to another term. Still, he claimed that he did not wish to run again, although he conceded, as he did to Stalin, that he might feel obliged to do so.

The discussions turned sharper when talk focused on the impending cross-Channel operation, something the Russians had been demanding for years. Stalin wanted to know when it would take place. Churchill parried the question, returning again to the prizes he believed were awaiting the Allies in the Mediterranean. The president and his aides were stunned, because they believed Churchill and the British were committed to an invasion in May. Stalin, impatient with Churchill's diversionary talk, asked Roosevelt for the name of the invasion's commander. Roosevelt replied, truthfully, that a commander had not yet been named. Stalin snapped: "Then nothing will come of these operations. One man must be responsible and one man must make decisions."[8]

Roosevelt, in fact, had given the idea some thought, and while he had not reached a decision, he was inclined to give the command—the greatest of the war—to General George Marshall. But still, with the invasion only months away, he had made no announcement. Stalin was right: the invasion needed a commander. Roosevelt would have to decide soon.

The final night of the conference, November 30, 1943, was spent amid good cheer, with the disagreements of the previous day seemingly put aside. It was Winston Churchill's sixty-ninth birthday, and the three leaders made effusive toasts to each other and to the cause that united them. If Stalin seemed happier than he was the day before, when he made it clear that he was unhappy with the progress towards a cross-Channel invasion, he had reason. Stalin knew exactly what Roosevelt was saying behind closed doors because he had bugged Roosevelt's room. What's more, he was delighted to realize that Roosevelt was naïve enough not to consider the possibility that the Russians were listening to his conversations, so he spoke candidly. And what he said pleased the Soviet leader—he was heard telling aides that he sympathized with Stalin and would not, despite the advice of military aides, come down harder on him in discussions of the postwar settlement, as Churchill preferred.

The conference broke up on December 2, and Roosevelt flew back to Cairo for another conference with Churchill. Few great decisions were made in Tehran, but the three leaders of the Allied cause at least had a better sense of each other and their intentions. For Roosevelt, however, the conference served to remind him that he needed to make a difficult decision—fast. Operation Overlord required a Supreme Commander. Marshall was said to want the job, and Roosevelt himself admitted—to Dwight Eisenhower, during his visit to North Africa—that Marshall deserved the momentous assignment.

But FDR relied heavily on Marshall's advice. The general was an invaluable member of Roosevelt's inner circle, a man in whom he and Congress had great faith. Sending him across the Atlantic to command Overlord would remove him from the White House and from Roosevelt's side.

After returning to Cairo, Roosevelt invited Marshall to lunch on December 5 and asked him what he wished to do—stay in Washington, or go to Britain to assume command of Overlord. Ever the dutiful soldier, Marshall said his wishes should not matter.

With that cue, Roosevelt told Marshall that Dwight Eisenhower was his choice to command Overlord. "I feel I could not sleep at night with you out of the country," he explained.[9] When Roosevelt saw Eisenhower two days later, on December 7, he said, "Well, Ike, you'd better start packing."[10]

Roosevelt returned to Washington on December 17. He was, by all accounts, far more robust and relaxed than might have been expected after a long and strenuous three weeks of travel. He decided to spend the Christmas holidays at home in Hyde Park for the first time since becoming president. The old house was filled with grandchildren who could barely contain themselves as the great feast day approached.

During the afternoon of Christmas Eve, the president excused himself from the merriment and family chaos to deliver a fireside chat, from his own fireside in Hyde Park. In an atmosphere far more intimate that the broadcast room in the White House, Roosevelt spoke to the American people about his conferences in Cairo and Tehran, places many Americans would have a hard time finding on a map. He talked about his meetings with great world leaders, and the plans they were beginning to make for the postwar world. And he broke some news: he announced that General Eisenhower would command the invasion that everybody knew was coming. The secret was where, and when. But there was no "if" anymore. The Allies were coming.

Roosevelt began his chat by explaining why he chose the afternoon to speak to Americans, rather than the evening. "In fixing the time for this broadcast," he explained, "we took into consideration that at this moment here in the United States, and in the Caribbean and on the Northeast Coast of South America, it is afternoon. In Alaska and in Hawaii and the mid-Pacific, it is still morning. In Iceland, in Great Britain, in North Africa, in Italy and the Middle East, it is now evening. In the Southwest Pacific, in Australia, in China and Burma and India, it is already Christmas Day. So we can correctly say that at this moment, in those far eastern parts where Americans are fighting, today is tomorrow." He sought to remind his audience that American fighting men were operating on a grand scale, so grand, indeed, that for some, today was tomorrow.

While he wished to speak specifically about his trip abroad and about the decision he made about Operation Overlord, he could hardly resist an acknowledgment of the Christmas season. The holiday, he said, brought Americans "close to our homes, our families, our friends." The Christmas spirit of "peace on earth, goodwill toward men" was "unquenchable."

"During the past years of international gangsterism and brutal aggression in Europe and in Asia, our Christmas celebrations have been darkened with apprehension for the future," he conceded. "We have said, 'Merry Christmas—a Happy New Year,' but we have known in our hearts that the clouds which have hung over our world have prevented us from saying it with full sincerity and conviction." Now, however, the sun was breaking through the clouds, and while surely storms were lurking over the horizon, Americans could look forward to the dawn of peace, of a new world order, of an end to brutality.

That peace, that new world order, was among the topics under discussion in Cairo and Tehran, he said. Churchill, Chiang, and Roosevelt agreed that the people of Asia would have the right "to build up their own forms of self-government without molestation. Essential to all peace and security in the Pacific and in the rest of the world is the permanent elimination of the Empire of Japan as a potential force of aggression." In other words, Roosevelt once again made it clear that he would not settle for a negotiated peace. Japan in its current form, like Nazi Germany, had to be destroyed in order to build a lasting peace. General Marshall, he said, had recently conferred with top commanders in the Pacific theater, "conferences which will spell plenty of bad news for the Japs in the not too far distant future."

Roosevelt then switched to the European theater, telling Americans about his appointment of Eisenhower to "lead the combined attack" on Nazi Germany. That attack would help speed the postwar settlement for which Stalin, Churchill, and Roosevelt began planning in Tehran. The leaders, Roosevelt said, "were united in determination that Germany must be stripped of her military might and be given no opportunity within the foreseeable future to regain that might." The Allies "have no intention to enslave the German people. We wish them to have a normal chance to develop, in peace, as useful and respectable members of the European family. But we most certainly emphasize that word 'respectable'—for we intend to rid them once and for all of Nazism and Prussian militarism and the fantastic and disastrous notion that they constitute the 'Master Race.'" As with his mention of Japan earlier in the chat, Roosevelt reiterated his position that there would be no parlay with Nazis; they would be eliminated before reconciliation could begin.

The concept of an American leader meeting with the dictator of a brutal communist regime was not without controversy, even in the wartime setting. Roosevelt addressed those concerns, telling his audience: "To use an American and somewhat ungrammatical colloquialism, I may say that I 'got along fine' with Marshal Stalin. He is a man who combines a tremendous, relentless determination with a stalwart good humor. I believe he is truly representative of the heart and soul of Russia; and I believe that we are going to get along very well with him and the Russian people—very well indeed." Those were brave words in 1943. While there was great support for the Russian people in their struggle with Hitler, Americans schooled on anticommunism remained wary of such intimate contact between the U.S. president and the Soviet dictator.

The president promised Americans, many of them old enough to remember the bitter disappointments that followed World War—the treaties that did not lead to peace, the failures of the League of Nations to outlaw aggression—that the coming peace would be different. That would require engagement in the world, not withdrawal. Roosevelt was surprisingly harsh about this point.

"There have always been cheerful idiots in this country who believed that there would be no more war for us, if everybody in America would only return into their homes and lock their front doors behind them," he said. "Assuming that their motives were of the highest, events have shown how unwilling they were to face the facts."

On this Christmas Eve 1943, America had no choice but to face facts, he said. Otherwise, future holidays would once again be clouded by heartbreak and anxiety.

For Franklin Roosevelt, such a future was unthinkable.

As American casualties mounted, Roosevelt lashed out at those who, in his view, sought to profit from the war.

"An Unusually Bellicose Speech"

State of the Union Address

January 11, 1944

TRACK 26

A WARTIME ELECTION, THE FIRST SUCH PRESIDENTIAL CAMPAIGN SINCE THE CIVIL War, loomed as the nation paused to celebrate the holiday season in late December 1943. The atmosphere at Hyde Park was not entirely celebratory. Although the president was pleased with the outcome of his meeting in Tehran with Stalin and Churchill, he returned to a nation that seemed to him overconfident, selfish, and blind to the challenges that lay ahead. Roosevelt realized that victories in the Mediterranean would mean little if the forthcoming invasion of France failed. Terrible sacrifices lay ahead.

Roosevelt knew something of those sacrifices—during his tour of the Mediterranean theater, he saw the human cost of war during visits to military installations and hospitals, in the faces and scars of young doughboys. He wondered if his fellow citizens appreciated how much effort would be needed, indeed, how much had been expended already, in the fight against Germany and Japan. "One of the best things that could happen would be to have a few German bombs fall here to wake us up," he said during a Cabinet meeting.[1]

Critics in Congress and the press were becoming increasingly vocal, no doubt in anticipation of the coming campaign. Roosevelt's return to Washington prompted a clipped and cheerless response from Republican representative Hamilton Fish, who shared FDR's Hudson Valley, New York, roots if not his politics. Fish demanded to know if Roosevelt made any commitments to Stalin about the future of Poland, Latvia, and Lithuania. While his Democratic colleagues heaped praise on Roosevelt for his statesmanship, Fish insisted, "We want to know and we have the right to know about all commitments, and until we do I hope we will reserve judgment on this matter."[2]

In the face of growing criticism of the president, Harold Ickes, FDR's fiery interior secretary, let his temper get the better of him when he accused anti-Roosevelt newspaper publishers, including William Randolph Hearst, of preferring a German victory to one led by Roosevelt and Stalin. Adding to increased political tensions was a renewed outbreak of racial tension in Washington. Southern Democrats worked successfully to kill an education-spending bill, usually a political crowd-pleaser, after Republicans included language banning racial discrimination in public schools. Roosevelt did not intervene in the dispute.

In the president's view, Washington was conducting business as usual, based on the assumption that after the military successes of 1943, the war was done and the enemy defeated. Civilians, spared the destruction, displacement, and mass casualties that plagued Europe and Asia, seemed far too eager to place their individual concerns ahead of the nation's greater good. Two days after Christmas, Roosevelt took over the nation's railroads by fiat when three unions threatened a nationwide strike on December 30. "I cannot wait until the last moment to take action to see that the supplies to our fighting men are not interrupted," he said. "The major military offensives now planned must not be delayed by the interruption of vital transportation facilities. If any employees of the railroads now strike, they will be striking against the Government of the United States."[3] Roosevelt argued that his power as commander in chief gave him authority to seize the railroads. The unions never did go on strike and quickly settled on a new contract, allowing Roosevelt to return the railroads to their owners in mid-January.

Organized labor, of course, was a vital part of the great coalition Roosevelt put together through the 1930s, and no president had ever been as friendly to working people. But the war came first. Roosevelt said as much, and more, to a reporter after a press conference on December 17, the day he returned to the White House after his long overseas trip. After greeting aides and members of Congress, Roosevelt sat for his first session with reporters since November 9. Wearing a gray tweed suit, his long cigarette holder in hand, Roosevelt bantered with reporters about Stalin and Churchill as Eleanor and other family members looked on. As the session was breaking up, Roosevelt offhandedly told a reporter from the *Cleveland Press*, Dilworth Lupton, that he was tired of hearing about the New Deal because the New Deal didn't exist anymore. The war took priority.

Few presidents have been more adept with reporters than Franklin Roosevelt, but on this occasion, the press got the better of him. His obituary for the New Deal created an unwelcome political firestorm. *Time* magazine asserted that FDR was moving "to the right," a view that some of Roosevelt's own supporters shared.[4] A young congressman from Texas, Lyndon Johnson, thought voters might reject him in a primary in 1944 because of his continued support for a president who seemed to be moving to the right on domestic issues and away from the social-welfare policies that were at the heart of the New Deal. Old allies like Ickes worried about the moderating influence of Harry Hopkins and James Byrnes on FDR's newfound conservatism. Roosevelt, however, argued that the war changed everything, and those who insisted on yesterday's prescriptions simply didn't understand that 1943 was not 1933.

FDR assembled the press corps again on December 28, a day after he seized the railroads. Not surprisingly, he was asked about the reported death of the New Deal. He put on his best easygoing manner. "Oh, I supposed somebody would ask that," he said with a rhetorical wave of the hand. "I will have to be terribly careful in the future how I talk to people after these press conferences."[5]

Roosevelt then gave a long, deliberate, and obviously well-prepared answer in which he offered reporters a lesson in recent history, reminding them that in 1933, when he was sworn into office for the first time, "there was an awfully sick patient called the United States of America...And they sent for the doctor." The doctor prescribed remedies "to cure the patient internally," but now, Roosevelt complained, the ailments were different and yet people were demanding the very same cure.

"The people who are peddling all this talk about 'New Deal' today, they are not telling about why the patient had to have remedies," Roosevelt told reporters. It was a remarkable turn of phrase, with FDR referring to his own program in an almost sarcastic tone. But Roosevelt had a less-than-reverential view of the remedies of the past. "Old Dr. New Deal...knew a great deal about internal medicine, but nothing about surgery. So he got his partner, who was an orthopedic surgeon, Dr. Win-the-War, to take care of this fellow who had been in this bad accident. And the result is that the patient is back on his feet...He isn't wholly well yet, and he won't be until he wins the war."

Roosevelt went on to cite some of Dr. New Deal's greatest successes—federal deposit insurance, slum clearance, Social Security, unemployment insurance, the Works Progress Administration, the Tennessee Valley Authority. Dr. New Deal, he suggested, was not necessarily in retirement, but merely on holiday. While the war would continue to take priority, "it seems pretty clear that we must plan for, and help to bring about, an expanded economy which will result in more security, in more employment...in more education, in more health, in better housing...so that the conditions of 1932 and the beginning of 1933 won't come back again."

Roosevelt finished his long monologue by asking if the press now had a "sufficiently simple" story to write. His coining of the phrases "Dr. New Deal" and "Dr. Win-the-War" would become part of the nation's political vocabulary for the remainder of the conflict, but something else Roosevelt said stirred the reporters' interest. FDR's glimpse into the future, his vision of a postwar America that would offer "more"—jobs, housing, education, security—suggested that he had no plans to retire from the presidency. A reporter asked, "Does that all add up to a fourth-term declaration?" The room burst into laughter. The fourth-term question was very much on the minds of politicians and the press in late 1943. FDR remained as cagey and elusive as ever.

"Oh, now, we are not talking about things like that now," he said over the reporters' laughs. "You are getting picayune. That's a grand word to use..." Most politicians and reporters considered the fourth-term question settled—after shattering the two-term precedent in 1940, Roosevelt surely would not step down now, in the middle of a world war. Getting Roosevelt to admit as much, however, would prove as elusive as ever.

The good nature and brio he displayed during his end-of-the-year meetings with the press and Congress belied his private frustration with public and private attitudes towards the war and with a growing manpower crisis. With Americans seemingly convinced that the great battles to come would be no more than mop-up operations, they were less inclined to sacrifice and more inclined to make a fast buck on war contracts. Critics were quicker than before to score political points for the sake of partisan advantage. And there was within his own administration a rising tension between advocates of Dr. New Deal and spokesmen for Dr. Win-the-War.

Roosevelt was due to give his annual State of the Union message in January. In a contentious mood, he instructed speechwriters Robert Sherwood and Samuel Rosenman to prepare a message that would include a sweeping new domestic agenda for postwar America, and a startling wartime proposal to allow conscription of workers from private industry into war-related jobs.

The notion of conscripting a labor force in addition to an armed force was not new. It was discussed in the early years of the war, and, in fact, had been put into place in most of the other nations at war. As Rosenman went to work on the speech, he consulted two memos from Secretary of War Henry Stimson recommending civilian conscription in early 1943. Rosenman and several other aides, including Hopkins, Bernard Baruch, and James Byrnes, studied the proposal through the summer of 1943, but Roosevelt changed direction when he perceived that Congress would not support such a drastic measure. He changed his mind again, however, upon his return from the Mediterranean in December 1943. He told Rosenman and Sherwood to include a provision for a national service act in the State of the Union message. "I have made up my mind on it," he said, "and I don't want to argue about it any more with anybody." He told his speechwriters to work on the conscription portion of the address in secret. A befuddled Rosenman suggested that he at least tell aides like Byrnes, who, as chairman of the War Mobilization Board, was responsible for manpower issues. "I don't want you to tell it to anybody," Roosevelt said.[6]

The conscription proposal was treated as a separate text, to be dropped into the full speech at the last minute. Sherwood and Rosenman code-named the conscription proposal "Project Q 38," poking fun at FDR's demand for secrecy. All drafts of the language relating to conscription were typed not by the office staff, but by Grace Tully, the president's longtime assistant. Well into the process, Rosenman still wondered if Roosevelt might change his mind once again. After reading the third of what would be eight drafts of the speech, Roosevelt indicated where he thought the conscription passage should be inserted, although he added, "if you decide to use it."[7]

For all of the intrigue over civilian conscription, FDR's State of the Union message in 1944 would be remembered for another, equally controversial proposal, a program Roosevelt called a "second bill of rights." It was an ambitious list of economic and social welfare goals that expanded on the postwar vision he offered reporters during his Dr. New Deal press conference in late December. The president's insistence that government had a role to play in ensuring a right to housing, health care, and education made the 1944 State of the Union message "the most radical speech" of Roosevelt's life, according to historian James McGregor Burns.[8] Rosenman described it as an "unusually bellicose speech."[9]

Roosevelt came down with the flu just before he was scheduled to deliver the message to Congress. He worked with Sherwood and Rosenman on the final draft from his sickbed before deciding that he would simply send the message to Congress rather than deliver it in person. (Presidents from Thomas Jefferson to William Howard Taft routinely sent their annual message to Congress; Woodrow Wilson revived the practice of going to Capitol Hill to address Congress personally.) Congress received the message on January 11, and it was not until then that Baruch, Byrnes, and other top aides learned of its contents. Byrnes burst into the president's office and resigned on the spot, although Roosevelt talked him into staying at the helm of the War Mobilization Board. Both Baruch and Byrnes believed that Rosenman should have consulted them about civilian conscription, even though Roosevelt ordered complete secrecy.

Later that evening, Roosevelt read the message to a live radio audience. He feared that the speech would simply be buried in the nation's newspapers and would remain unread in the halls of Congress if the public didn't hear it firsthand. He had invested too much time and effort to allow the speech to die of neglect.

After explaining that his illness prevented him from reading the speech to Congress, he reprised the Tehran conference and other war-related news before launching into an attack on complacency and business as usual. A "noisy minority," he said, "maintains an uproar...There are pests who swarm the lobbies of Congress and the cocktail bars of Washington...who have come to look upon the war primarily as a chance to make profits for themselves at the expense of their neighbors—profits in money or profits in terms of political or social preferment." The populist rhetoric recalled the language of Roosevelt's 1936 reelection campaign with its withering contempt for self-interested elites in business and politics.

But Roosevelt's message was not intended as a mere polemic. Rather, it was an outline of his legislative agenda. The tone was strident at times, but the purpose was pragmatic, to begin a debate about the country's economic future and its ongoing manpower shortage.

He launched into his top-secret proposal for a "national service law, which, for the duration of the war, will prevent strikes, and, with certain appropriate exceptions, will make available for war production or any other essential services every able-bodied adult in this whole nation." National service, he argued, was the "most democratic way to wage a war...There are millions of American men and women who are not in this war at all. That is not because they do not want to be in it. But they want to know where they can best do their share. National service provides that direction."

That was Dr. Win-the-War speaking. But after his pitch for civilian conscription, FDR gave voice to that other medical practitioner, Dr. New Deal. He was not, after all, in permanent retirement. He simply was on the sidelines, awaiting an appropriate moment to begin his practice again.

Roosevelt declared that "true individual freedom cannot exist without economic security and independence." To achieve that goal, he listed the provisions of a new Bill of Rights, which would include the right to "a useful and remunerative job," "the right to earn enough to provide adequate food and clothing and recreation," "the right of every family to a decent home," "the right to adequate medical care," and "the right to a good education." Those rights, he said, "spell security. And after this war is won we must be prepared to move forward, in the implementation of these rights, to new goals of human happiness and well-being."

Roosevelt did not explain how government would guarantee these new rights, but implementation was not his point. In enumerating an economic bill of rights, Roosevelt sought to reassert a place for activist government in the postwar economy and to build on the remedies offered so long ago by his old friend, Dr. New Deal.

Impressed with Dwight Eisenhower's leadership and tact, Roosevelt appointed him as commander in chief of the Allied invasion of France. FDR passed over his chief military aide, George Marshall, saying that he needed Marshall by his side.

CHAPTER 27

A Prayer on D-Day

Fireside Chat

June 6, 1944

TRACK 27

There were many D days during World War II. The designation refers to the day on which a planned assault takes place, and its usage can be traced back to World War I. All of the major Allied operations—the landings in North Africa, the invasion of Sicily, the assault on the beaches of Anzio—had a D day of their own.

In American memory, however, there is only one D-Day: June 6, 1944, the morning on which U.S., British, and Canadian forces landed on the sands of northern France to begin a campaign of liberation in Western Europe.

The invasion of France was the largest, most complicated, and riskiest Anglo-American operation of the war. In the view of U.S. military planners, it marked the beginning of the main event, a full-scale assault on Adolf Hitler's Fortress Europe. The engagements in the Mediterranean—North Africa, Sicily, and even Italy—were, for some top U.S. generals, important but peripheral battles. The war, in their opinion, would be won not by moving up the Italian boot, but by assailing the German army in France and pushing it east, relentlessly, until it gave up the fight.

For the British, particularly for Prime Minister Winston Churchill,

D-Day was the culmination of a debate over strategy that began as soon as the United States entered the war. American war planners began discussing a cross-Channel invasion within weeks of the Japanese attack on Pearl Harbor. On January 22, 1942, a then-obscure U.S. general named Dwight Eisenhower wrote: "We've got to go to Europe and fight...we've got to begin slugging with air at West Europe, to be followed by a land attack as soon as possible."[1] Eisenhower, who was assigned to the Army War Plans Division, began drafting plans for an Anglo-American assault on northern France in the summer of 1942, although the timetable was soon changed to April 1943. Roosevelt saw the plan and was so enthusiastic he dispatched Harry Hopkins and General George C. Marshall to London to brief Churchill in person.

Churchill and his key advisors had another strategy in mind, one that would avoid a direct confrontation with the main German army in the west. Their strategy focused on the Mediterranean, where targets presumably were softer. Hovering over the War Cabinet were the ghosts of the Great War—the insane charges against German machine gun emplacements, the hopeless Australian assault on the fortified beachhead of Gallipoli.

The British, however, did not speak candidly about their misgivings about a cross-Channel invasion. Churchill dispatched a letter to Roosevelt in which he talked about an "agreed programme" of "activity on the Continent" leading to a "march forward into Europe together in a noble brotherhood of arms..."[2] The vague language disguised British opposition to the plan which Marshall and Hopkins outlined. The two Americans returned to Washington believing that the British agreed to a cross-Channel invasion as soon as possible. In fact, as British general Sir Hastings Ismay later wrote, "we were absolutely opposed to it."[3]

On August 19, 1942, a force of six thousand Allied troops, most of them Canadian, crossed the Channel for a planned raid on the coastal town of Dieppe. The raid was designed as a dry run for a full-scale invasion, and it was a disaster. Among the five thousand Canadian troops who formed the core of the raid, the casualty rate was 75 percent. Two thousand Allied troops were taken prisoner. From the British perspective, Dieppe was an object lesson in the risks of a cross-Channel invasion.

Even before Dieppe, the Americans acquiesced in a British plan to invade North Africa. Ensuing Allied victories led to the subsequent invasion of Sicily and then of Italy. Churchill described the strategy as closing the ring, enveloping Germany with a sweep through the Mediterranean and then north through Italy and the Balkans, with the Soviets moving in from the east. For U.S. military planners, however, the British strategy was so much nibbling around the edges. Finally, during the Tehran conference, the Allies agreed that a cross-Channel invasion would take place no later than June 1, 1944. The campaign in Italy, which had turned into a difficult slog through rugged terrain, would be transformed into a sideshow—a bloody sideshow, but a secondary theater all the same.

There was no question that an American would serve as commander of the invasion force, even though the operation would be carried out in partnership with British and Canadian forces. The vast resources of men and materiel from the United States meant that America was the dominant partner in the transatlantic relationship, to the chagrin of the British military establishment, which was used to policing and defending a global empire. The British army in 1944 consisted of a little less than 3 million troops. The U.S. army had nearly 6 million soldiers, and more on the way.

Through the winter and spring of 1944, preparations for the invasion stepped up as soldiers by the hundreds of thousands prepared for the greatest amphibious assault in military history. The Allies chose Normandy, a hundred miles across the English Channel from southern England, for their landings, rather than Pas de Calais, the seemingly obvious target because it was only twenty-five miles from Dover, where the Channel is much narrower. The landing beaches were divided into five sectors, code-named Gold, Sword, Juno, Utah, and Omaha. U.S. troops were responsible for Utah and Omaha; the British and Canadians would land on the other three zones.

The Germans knew an invasion was coming, and so Hitler ordered Field Marshal Erwin Rommel to take personal control of coastal defenses facing the English Channel. "If they attack in the west," Hitler said of the Anglo-Americans in 1943, "that attack will decide the war."[4] The German strategy was simple: force the invaders back into the sea. Rommel oversaw the installation of hundreds of thousands of obstacles on the beaches of northern France. Barbed wire was strung, mines were placed, and possible drop zones for paratroopers were flooded to prevent an assault behind the main line of defense. The defenses that the Dieppe raiders faced in late 1942 were now even stronger.

But where, and when, would the invasion come? The Germans could only guess. Calais seemed likely not only because of its proximity to the English coast, but because the Germans picked up radio transmissions and other activity generated by the First U.S. Army Group, based on eastern England across from Calais. With great fanfare, General George S. Patton had been named commander of the massive force. The Germans had no idea that they fell for an elaborate ruse: there was no First U.S. Army Group. The radio transmissions they intercepted were fake. The tanks and other materiel they spotted from the air were made out of wood. Patton, in fact, would play no role in the initial assault. The First U.S. Army Group was just one of many deceptions designed to keep the Germans from responding decisively when the invasion was launched. If they hesitated, if they were unsure whether the invasion was the real thing or a diversion, if they were confused and disorganized, fewer Allied solders would be sacrificed on the sands of Normandy.

As D-Day approached, the familiar sight of men and machines in the English countryside gave way to empty, quiet landscapes as soldiers and their equipment began boarding transport ships. Final briefings were held for the pilots assigned to soften up targets along the coast, for paratroopers who would be dropped behind the lines in the predawn hours to wreak havoc with the enemy's communications, and with the infantry who would have to take the fortified beaches and move inland before the Germans could mount an effective counterattack.

On the weekend before the assault, Roosevelt retreated to the Virginia home of his friend and advisor, Edwin "Pa" Watson. The invasion was scheduled for Monday, June 5. Although ebullient in public, Roosevelt was not immune to tension and anxiety. Aides noticed that he seemed on edge that weekend, just as other top Allied political and military leaders were. British General Alan Brooke wrote, on the eve of the invasion, "I am very uneasy about the whole operation. At the best, it will come very far short of the expectations of the bulk of the people...At its worst, it may well be the most ghastly disaster of the whole war."[5]

The weather in the Channel forced Eisenhower to postpone the invasion for twenty-four hours. Roosevelt returned to Washington on June 5 and spoke to the nation about the Allied march into Rome a day earlier. "The first of the Axis capitals is now in our hands," he said. "One up and two to go." He saw the fall of Rome as a symbolic, as well as strategic, victory. The city was in the hands of troops "determined that in the future no one city and no one race will be able to control the whole of the world."

Even as he spoke, in the darkness of the French night three thousand miles away, bombs and paratroopers were falling from the sky, and tens of thousands of infantrymen were praying, sweating, and vomiting aboard thousands of transport ships in the middle of the English Channel. They crossed undetected, their presence revealed only when the curtain of night rose to reveal the largest armada ever assembled. Navy guns commenced firing at 5:30 a.m. and then, after a heavy but ultimately ineffective bombardment, they became silent. The infantry hit the beach at about 6:30 a.m. French time.

The focus of concern all morning was Omaha Beach, where wave after wave of U.S. troops was stalled on the beach, exposed to deadly German fire. Omaha's defenders fought brilliantly, nearly forcing the Americans back to the sea. Had they succeeded, the entire invasion would have been endangered, for the Allied beachhead would be divided by the German stronghold above Omaha Beach.

Once the Americans reached the high ground above Omaha, the day was won. Thousands of reinforcements and fresh waves of tanks, trucks, and other materiel landed on the secured beaches and moved inland by nightfall. All told, some 156,000 Allied troops landed in France that day. About 10,000 Allied troops were killed or wounded, including about 2,000 on Omaha Beach. German figures are unknown.

That night, as exhausted soldiers sought some small measure of refuge from the day's fighting, President Roosevelt delivered his second radio address in as many days. Unlike the previous night's monologue about the fall of Rome and its significance, the fireside chat of June 6, 1944, was short, somber, and profound. Roosevelt decided not to converse with his fellow citizens, but to offer a prayer for the troops in France and for their families. In doing so, FDR outlined the moral imperative of the battle and of the war itself.

Americans at home had been listening to radio reports during the afternoon as word of the invasion made its way across the Atlantic. Newspapers printed extra editions with sketchy reports about the fighting. Roosevelt offered no new details, save to say that the invasion had "come to pass with success thus far." With that, he read the prayer he composed, and asked the nation to join him in an appeal to the Almighty.

"Our sons, pride of our nation, this day have set upon a mighty endeavor, a struggle to preserve our Republic, our religion, and our civilization, and to set free a suffering humanity...Lead them straight and true. Give strength to their arms, stoutness to their hearts, steadfastness in their faith. They will need Thy blessings. Their road will be long and hard...They will be sore tried, by night and day, without rest—until the victory is won. The darkness will be rent by noise and flame. Men's souls will be shaken with the violences of war."

Unlike Winston Churchill, whose stirring speeches tended to focus on valor, defiance, and glory, Roosevelt's D-Day prayer acknowledged the reality of war and its horrors. However worthy the cause, however necessary the battle, war produced noise and flame, and tested the souls of men. War produced multiple "violences"—the violence of physical devastation, and the violence committed against the human spirit.

Roosevelt noted that the American G.I.'s in France were not professional warriors, but men "lately drawn from the ways of peace. They fight not for the lust of conquest. They fight to end conquest. They fight to liberate. They fight to let justice arise, and tolerance and goodwill among all Thy people. They yearn but for the end of battle, for their return to the haven of home."

In a paragraph, Roosevelt defined the American narrative of World War II as a war forced upon the United States and its Allies, a war fought to liberate, not to oppress. Entire nations awaited the Allied promise of liberation. And so did millions of people living beyond the immediate reach of Allied soldiers—Europe's Jews. Transported to concentration camps in eastern Germany and Poland, Jews were being slaughtered on a barbaric, unprecedented scale. Although critics of Allied strategy have suggested the news of the ongoing Holocaust was suppressed during the war, American Jews like Rabbi Stephen Wise and journalists like Edward R. Murrow called attention to the genocide as it was taking place. The Allied invasion of France would come too late for millions, but was the beginning of liberation for those who would survive the horror and bear witness to it in the decades to come.

As he continued his D-Day prayer, Roosevelt turned his attention to soldiers who would not live to see victory, who would never again see their loved ones. "Some will never return," he said. "Embrace these, Father, and receive them, Thy heroic servants, into Thy kingdom...Give us strength, too—strength in our daily tasks, to redouble the contributions we make in the physical and the material support of our armed forces." FDR used his prayer to remind his listeners that the men and women in uniform were but a part of the war effort. His listeners, seated around radios in their homes, were part of the effort as well.

The prayer took six minutes to read. After Roosevelt finished, Americans kept their radios tuned to reports of Allied progress thousands of miles away, reminded through Roosevelt's words of the sacrifices and hard work that lay ahead.

Fala, a Scotch terrier, was the nation's most-famous house pet. For a brief time in 1944, Fala became a campaign issue as his devoted friend and master, Franklin Roosevelt, ran for a fourth term.

CHAPTER 28

Fala

Campaign Speech

September 23, 1944

TRACK 28

THE 1944 PRESIDENTIAL CAMPAIGN WAS THE FIRST WARTIME ELECTION HELD SINCE the Civil War, not counting the nation's numerous undeclared wars against Native Americans, Filipino insurgents, and others. The Republicans nominated forty-two-year-old Thomas E. Dewey, the governor of New York, as their candidate, and he tried to stir up public weariness not with the war, but with the sixty-two-year-old man who was in charge of it. Dewey promised to deliver the nation from the exhausted old men who had been in charge for so long.

Unlike 1864, when the incumbent commander in chief, Abraham Lincoln, was challenged by an antiwar candidate (ironically, George McClellan, onetime commander of the Army of the Potomac), Roosevelt did not find himself on the defensive about the war's outcome. The year brought victory after victory as the Allies swept across France and continued to advance towards the Japanese home islands. Dewey was in the difficult position of running against a candidate who was prosecuting a successful war. So he sought to position himself as a young, energetic leader, in contrast to the man who had been in the White House longer than any of his predecessors, and who now was asking for another four-year term.

In many ways, Dewey was not wrong in suggesting that Roosevelt was too tired to finish out the war. Many Democrats were extremely worried about the president's health. His foremost political advisor, Edward Flynn, was shocked when he visited the White House in June 1944. Although he left no physical description of the president's appearance, he came away from the meeting convinced that Roosevelt—his longtime friend—should not run for a fourth term. He asked Eleanor Roosevelt to do what she could to get her husband to retire. "I felt that he would never survive the term."[1]

Roosevelt, of course, was not about to stand down, but his insistence on moving forward with a reelection campaign led Flynn and other Democratic insiders to consider the choice of a running mate. Henry Wallace was the incumbent vice president, and while Flynn, a former chairman of the Democratic National Committee, liked him, many other local party officials did not. He was considered too liberal, too unreliable, too idealistic for the party professionals. With Roosevelt absent from the convention in Chicago, Flynn and other party leaders maneuvered to dump Wallace from the ticket. Roosevelt resisted the dump-Wallace movement at first, insisting that the vice president's international experience was critical as the war drew to a close. Eventually, through, he decided to reserve his energy for the campaign rather than expend it on a seemingly hopeless fight on Wallace's behalf. On the eve of the Democratic convention, Roosevelt seemed to support Supreme Court Justice William O. Douglas, a liberal favorite. But then he wavered again, signaling support for Truman during a meeting with party elders in Washington. The mixed signals continued at the convention as FDR tried to placate Wallace and another vice presidential aspirant, former U.S. Senator James Byrnes of South Carolina. Roosevelt decided to go with Harry Truman because, in the end, he seemed the least controversial choice. Truman's Missouri roots figured to help FDR among white Southerners, and his connections to the Pendergast machine in Kansas City made him acceptable to the party's urban leaders.

The selection of a vice president was even more urgent than many Democrats realized. Roosevelt became ill in California in mid-July while on his way to Hawaii and a meeting with General Douglas MacArthur. FDR's son, James, was with him in a railroad car when he suddenly suffered severe chest pains that made breathing difficult. "Jimmy, I don't know if I can make it," Roosevelt said.[2] After a few minutes, the president felt better. No doctor was ever called.

The president continued his trip and met as scheduled with MacArthur. Accompanying him, as was often the case, was the nation's First Dog, Fala, a Scotch terrier. A family friend gave Fala to the president as a Christmas gift in 1940.

Fala's real name, so to speak, was Murray the Outlaw of Falahill. Roosevelt donned that moniker on him in tribute to a Roosevelt ancestor named John Murray of Falahill, a Scotsman. But to the nation, and to the president, the little Scottie was known simply as Fala.

Fala was easily the nation's most famous house pet. He was photographed at the president's side, he was seen in newsreels, and he met dignitaries foreign and domestic when they visited either the White House or Hyde Park. He even costarred with the president in a documentary about life in the White House during the war years.

Roosevelt delighted in Fala's company during the long trip from California to Hawaii, where meetings with MacArthur and Admiral Chester Nimitz produced a blueprint for the rest of the Pacific war. Roosevelt left Hawaii and sailed to Alaska in early August before delivering a nationally broadcast speech at a navy yard in Bremerton, Washington. The speech was a disaster. The president struggled to maintain his balance as he stood behind a lectern on the deck of a destroyer. He seemed to lose his place as he turned the pages while keeping a firm grip on the lectern. Even as he struggled through the speech, he began suffering terrible chest pains.

At a time when the president was facing an energetic challenge from a young candidate who seemed willing to use age as an issue, Roosevelt's performance in Bremerton distressed his supporters. "His campaigning days are over," the *Washington Post* asserted.[3] Sensing that Roosevelt may be vulnerable, Republicans began to press an aggressive campaign, one that somehow managed to make an issue of the nation's First Dog. Republicans spread a rumor that Fala had been accidentally left behind in Alaska, on the Aleutian Islands, during the president's visit in August. Roosevelt, according to this account, ordered a navy destroyer to sail back to Alaska to pick up the unfortunate dog. Critics hoped the story would serve as a symbol of Roosevelt's arrogance and of his spendthrift habits, although dog owners around the country might well have wondered why Republicans were put off by the president's affection for his pet. The story achieved wide circulation, infuriating the president.

Roosevelt spent little time on the campaign trail in the summer of 1944. In mid-September, he journeyed to Quebec to meet once again with Winston Churchill. Like so many of the president's staff, Churchill was discouraged by the president's appearance: he seemed thin and tired. The Prime Minister's personal doctor, Lord Moran, wondered if Roosevelt's judgment and energy were impaired. He feared the worst, later noting that "men at his time of life do not go thin all of a sudden just for nothing."[4]

Postwar planning took on a special urgency at Quebec as the Americans and British discussed the occupation of Germany, which clearly would unfold in a matter of months. After the conference broke up, Roosevelt and Churchill had a series of meetings in Hyde Park, during which the president discussed America's ongoing work on building an atomic bomb. Churchill left Hyde Park on September 19, 1944, several days before the president was due to deliver his first overtly political speech of the campaign season. Roosevelt was worried about the speech, for Quebec and Churchill left him tired and cranky at a time when he had to be on top of his game. The address, to be delivered on September 23 in front of a friendly audience of Teamsters, would be broadcast live on radio. The nation would be listening to hear if he still had what it took to lead America through the war's final stages and into a new era of peace.

The president and his aides worked hard over the next few days on the Teamsters speech. He continued to tinker with it even after he arrived at the Statler Hotel in Washington for the Teamsters' dinner. He decided to remain seated for the speech rather than risk losing his balance while standing at a podium, his legs locked into position with heavy braces. The president's daughter, Anna Roosevelt, and speechwriter Sam Rosenman were seated together amid the teamster union officials and their rank-and-file members. Anna had seen a draft of the speech and knew the political risks involved. "Do you think Pa will put it over?" she asked Rosenman. "It's the kind of speech which depends almost entirely on delivery, no matter how good the writing. If the delivery isn't just right, it'll be an awful flop."[5] Rosenman tried to reassure Anna, but he, too, was worried about how the president would perform.

Their anxieties were understandable. The man at the head table clearly was thinner and grayer than ever before. The circles under his eyes were becoming pronounced. The jaunty confidence, so much of it pure performance, seemed to be gone.

But when the time came for the president to speak, it was as though the voice of the old Roosevelt—the sunny Roosevelt, the playful Roosevelt, the warrior Roosevelt—took possession of the president's tired body. Those in the room heard not the voice of a tired old man, but of a man fully engaged, fully aware of his circumstances, and fully cognizant of the stakes involved in this thirty-minute talk.

He began with humor, a clever tactic when facing an opponent like Dewey, not known for his sense of humor or self-deprecating wit. After waiting out a six-minute ovation, Roosevelt began as if in a conversation with old friends. "Well, here we are together again—after four years—and what years they have been!" he said. "You know, I am actually four years older, which is a fact that seems to annoy some people." One of the people FDR had in mind, of course, was young Dewey.

He then launched into a playfully sarcastic attack on Republicans who said they supported various Roosevelt-era reforms like Social Security and the National Labor Relations Act—reforms that had the enthusiastic support of unions like the Teamsters. Many such Republicans, he said, "would not even recognize these progressive laws if they met them in broad daylight. The whole purpose of Republican oratory these days seems to be to switch labels. The object is to persuade the American people that the Democratic Party was responsible for the 1929 crash and the Depression, and that the Republican Party was responsible for all social progress under the New Deal."

Even in wartime, even with full employment and the promise of postwar prosperity, Roosevelt was not shy about playing on memories of the Depression and on his response to it. It was a winning formula, one

Democrats would continue to use until the 1960s. Liberal Republicans, he said, could not expect voters to believe that they supported the New Deal's new social order. "We have all seen many marvelous stunts in the circus but no performing elephant could turn a hand-spring without falling flat on his back," he said. From her seat in the audience Anna Roosevelt could relax. Her father was at the top of his game, inspiring laughter and applause at the expense of the unmentioned Dewey and his fellow Republicans. His delivery was impeccable, his voice was strong, his timing pitch-perfect. Few would have predicted such an outcome minutes before Roosevelt began speaking.

What made the speech memorable, however, were not Roosevelt's energetic, sarcastic jabs at Dewey and the Republican Party platform. While the president achieved his goal of showing the nation that he still was vital enough for the job, it was his defense of his dog that captured the nation's heart and which reestablished Roosevelt as the grand old master of American politics. After reciting, with practiced impatience, the litany of attacks made on him, he turned to the rumors about the lost-dog rescue that wasn't.

"These Republican leaders have not been content with attacks on me, or my wife, or on my sons," he said, his voice rising in mock—or was it genuine?—annoyance. "No, not content with that, they now include my little dog, Fala." He paused, like a comedian, for laughter. "Well, of course, I don't resent attacks, and my family doesn't resent attacks,"—another comedic pause—"but Fala does resent them." Once again, the Teamsters burst into sustained laughter. They were thoroughly enjoying themselves, and so was the thin, gray man at the head table. He turned to the matter of his dog's ethnicity, which, according to stereotype, would incline him to take offense at wasteful spending. Presidents could get away with ethnic humor in 1944.

"You know, Fala is Scotch, and being a Scottie, as soon as he learned that the Republican fiction writers in Congress and out had concocted a story that I had left him behind on the Aleutian Islands and had sent a destroyer back to find him—at a cost to the taxpayers of two or three, or eight or twenty million dollars—his Scotch soul was furious. He has not been the same dog since."

The campaign of 1944 was never the same since. With his witty, well-delivered defense of his beloved pet, Franklin Roosevelt told millions of Americans that he still had the magic they remembered. He turned serious after his listeners had their fill of laughter, reminding them that the nation still faced months of hard fighting, which would be followed by the challenge of establishing a lasting peace.

After the Fala speech, Roosevelt never again had to face charges that he was too old and tired for the job of finishing the war and winning the peace. On Election Day 1944, the Roosevelt-Truman ticket won 432 votes in the Electoral College, capturing 54 percent of the popular vote to Dewey's 99 electoral votes and 45 percent of the vote.

The country prepared for four more years of the man who had led them since 1932.

With victory approaching, Winston Churchill, Franklin Roosevelt, and Joseph Stalin met at Yalta to make plans for a post-war settlement. Roosevelt's health problems were evident in his gaunt appearance.

CHAPTER 29

"We Cannot Live Alone"

Fourth Inaugural Address

January 20, 1945

TRACK 29

Victory was in the winter air as Franklin Roosevelt prepared to take the oath of office as president for the fourth time. On the western front, a desperate German counterattack in the Ardennes—known to history as the Battle of the Bulge—in December failed in the face of determined Allied resistance. A final Allied thrust across the Rhine River and into the German heartland was now just a question of timing.

To the east, the Red Army continued its inexorable march through Poland towards Berlin. In the Pacific theater, an American naval victory at the Battle of Leyte Gulf in the fall cost the Japanese four aircraft carriers, three battleships, and nearly two dozen other vessels. Winston Churchill considered Leyte Gulf one of the great American victories of the war, although it was overshadowed by Allied victories in France. The Battle of Leyte Gulf crippled the Japanese navy and allowed the Americans to step up their campaign to retake the Philippines. By early January, U.S. land forces were closing in on Manila, the Filipino capital.

With millions of Americans on the front lines and many more millions praying each night for the safety of their loved ones so far from home, Franklin Roosevelt decided to keep his fourth inauguration as simple as possible. When a reporter asked if the ceremonies would include the usual parade of the armed services, Roosevelt said no. After all, he said, there was nobody left at home to march. American troops were in Europe and Asia, engaged in the final battles of a catastrophic but ultimately necessary world war. There would be no parade.

Nor would there be the usual elaborate ceremony on the east side of the Capitol building. Roosevelt believed such a ceremony was both inappropriate and too costly during a time of war. Instead, he directed that the ceremony take place at the White House, on the south porch, with only a few thousand people in attendance.

In keeping with the event's simplicity, Roosevelt planned to deliver a short inaugural address—the first explicitly wartime inaugural since Abraham Lincoln's in 1865. Like Lincoln, Roosevelt had the luxury of looking ahead to peace and reconciliation, rather than dwelling on the need for sacrifice and fortitude. So, even though he wished to keep his speech short and to the point, he found time to work with speechwriters Archibald MacLeish, Robert Sherwood, and Sam Rosenman on several drafts. On January 6, he sent the writers a memo entitled, "Some thoughts for inaugural address."[1] In the memo, the president recalled the advice he was given by a schoolmaster and mentor at Groton, Endicott Peabody, many years earlier. Roosevelt remembered the teacher's warning, "Things in life will not always run smoothly. Sometimes we will be rising towards the heights—then all will seem to reverse itself and start downward." It was important to remember, Peabody told Roosevelt, that "the trend of civilization itself is forever upward." The speechwriters included the entire passage from Roosevelt's memo. The president's expression of optimism, indeed, his affirmation in the progress of civilization, seemed necessary and appropriate after years of war and the deaths of millions.

Although Roosevelt had gathered himself for the climactic stage of his reelection campaign, his health and appearance continued to deteriorate. He seemed even thinner in January than he did in the fall, when Churchill and his doctor were so shocked by Roosevelt's frailty. Outgoing vice president Henry Wallace found that Roosevelt had a hard time keeping his focus on policy matters. "His mind isn't very clear anymore," Wallace wrote.[2]

Inauguration Day 1945 was cold and gray. The capital was covered in snow and sleet, making Roosevelt's decision to hold a simple inauguration all the more welcome. The president, his family, and his aides attended a religious service in the White House before moving out to the south porch for the official swearing-in. Despite the cold weather, the president refused to wear an overcoat or a hat. But he did wear his heavy leg braces so that he could walk to the podium, while leaning on the arm of his son James before taking the oath of office. He continued to stand as he delivered his speech.

The eight thousand people gathered to witness the occasion saw a pale, thin man in a dark business suit, a man who clearly had grown ill and weak in service to his country. His voice retained its distinctive, patrician accent, but lacked the vigor of past inaugurals. Woodrow Wilson's widow, Edith, could not help but see in Roosevelt's gaunt face an image of her disabled, dying husband. "He looks exactly as my husband did when he went into his decline," Mrs. Wilson told Labor Secretary Frances Perkins.[3] Perkins, who has served FDR from Day One of his presidency, was well aware of the president's dreadful appearance. A day earlier, during the last Cabinet meeting of Roosevelt's third term, Perkins noted that the president "looked like an invalid who had been allowed to see guests for the first time and the guests had stayed too long."[4]

The president spoke for less than five minutes. It was the second-shortest inaugural address in American history—only George Washington's second inaugural was shorter. He began with an acknowledgment that he would be brief, saying that he was sure his listeners would understand why there would be a minimum of fanfare and celebration. As he noted, Americans and their allies were "passing through a period of supreme test," a test of their courage, their resolve, and their wisdom as the war ended its climactic stage. But the tests would not disappear with the coming of victory, now inevitable, and peace. Most Americans in 1945 had living memories of the failures that followed World War I. The war to end all wars had led to even more bloodshed. This time, Roosevelt said, the United States would work for "a just and honorable peace, a durable peace…

"We shall strive for perfection. We shall not achieve it immediately—

but we still shall strive. We may make mistakes—but they must never be mistakes such result from faintness of heart or abandonment of moral principle." He then recalled the words of his mentor Peabody—his warning that life was not without unexpected struggle, but in the end, the forces of progress were bound to prevail.

He then turned to the lessons the United States could draw from the war, lessons that were lost on a previous generation of Americans. "We have learned that we cannot live alone, at peace; that our own well-being is dependent on the well-being of other nations far away." Roosevelt remained wary that American isolationism was not dead but merely in hiding, waiting in the shadows for the war's end.

The president sought a preemptive strike against conservatives who might be preparing to reargue the debate over the League of Nations from a generation earlier. He summoned the memory of the great New England philosopher Ralph Waldo Emerson to make his case against American retreat from the world. "We have learned the simple truth, as Emerson said, that, 'The only way to have a friend is to be one.' We can gain no lasting peace if we approach it with suspicion and mistrust or with fear. We can gain it only if we proceed with the understanding, the confidence, and the courage which flow from convictions."

He closed with a prayer that God would allow Americans to "see our way clearly—to see the way that leads to a better life for ourselves and for all our fellow men."

Roosevelt's immediate listeners—the thousands dressed in warm coats, hats, scarves, and gloves outside the White House porch—saluted the president with muffled applause as he finished. "It was deeply moving to watch him standing there in the cold winter air, without overcoat or hat, delivering these simple words," Rosenman wrote. "Oblivious of the people in front of him or the people all over the world who were listening to him, he seemed to me to be offering a prayer. It was a prayer...that all the peoples of the world, and their leaders, be endowed with the patience and faith that could abolish war."[5]

Roosevelt made his way back to the warmth of the White House and almost immediately felt ill. He asked his son James to pour him a whiskey. "You'd better make it straight," he said. The whiskey, warm and potent, seemed to fortify Roosevelt. He made his way to a reception without letting on how poorly he felt after his speech.

Two days later, the president set sail from Virginia for a journey that would take him to Yalta and one last wartime conference with Winston Churchill and Joseph Stalin.

End of a journey: Franklin Roosevelt's body is transported to a grave in Hyde Park.

CHAPTER 30

Final Words

Speech to Congress

March 1, 1945

TRACK 30

With the war in Europe winding down and victory inevitable, the issue of a postwar settlement moved from abstraction to imminent reality. On January 22, 1945, Franklin Roosevelt crossed the Atlantic Ocean one more time to meet with Winston Churchill and Joseph Stalin to discuss the new world order that peace would bring.

Before the so-called Big Three met at Yalta on the Black Sea, Roosevelt and Churchill met separately on the island of Malta in the Mediterranean. The crossing from Virginia to Malta took about two weeks, during which the president celebrated his 63rd birthday—on January 30—with a celebratory dinner aboard the USS *Quincy*. The sea voyage seemed to invigorate Roosevelt. He studiously avoided the thick briefing books that were piled up in his quarters. Instead, he stayed in bed for several days while nursing a cold, and then, once he felt better, insisted on joining his fellow passengers on the destroyer's deck for games and sunshine. Secretary of State Edward Stettinius noted that Roosevelt looked "rested and calm."[1] The president spent ten hours a day resting during the voyage, leading him to wonder why he seemed to need so much sleep.

Awaiting him on Malta was Winston Churchill, who was anything but calm. He was concerned about the next leg of the journey—the trip to Yalta would entail travel over primitive roads—and about the final stages of the war in Europe. The British were pressing the Americans to support their idea of a quick, narrow thrust into Germany led by Field Marshal Bernard Montgomery, the mercurial English warrior. The Americans, however, continued to support Dwight Eisenhower's vision of a broad, massive push across the Rhine and into Germany's industrial heartland.

Churchill also was less than pleased by Roosevelt's reaction to a British armed intervention in Greece in late December, after the Athens government collapsed in the face of a communist-led insurgency. The American press harshly criticized the British intervention, seeing it as an attempt to reestablish the old imperial framework on weaker nations rather than a show of support for Greek's democrats, as Churchill framed the issue. Advisors told Roosevelt that many newspapers in the Midwest—the stronghold of old isolationist sentiment—were voicing concerns about Britain's intentions once the war ended. Roosevelt's dream of an American commitment to collective security could be jeopardized if Americans concluded that another world war had been fought in vain, that the same old power arrangements would be restored with the coming of peace.

Churchill, for his part, deeply resented American criticism. A story in the *New York Times* reported that Roosevelt had warned the British of a new wave of American "disillusionment" if the nation concluded that the war was "just another struggle between rival imperialisms."[2] The British concluded that the *Times* report was a deliberately planned leak from the Roosevelt White House designed to embarrass them. Years later, the American criticism still rankled the Prime Minister. In his memoirs of the war, Churchill condemned the "vehement attacks to which His Majesty's Government, and I in particular at its head, were subjected."[3]

If Churchill and the British hoped to discuss some of these issues in their presummit meeting with Roosevelt at Malta, they were sorely disappointed. The president avoided contentious issues during a dinner with Churchill aboard the *Quincy*. The dispute over the final Anglo-American drive into Germany had been resolved before Roosevelt even arrived, as U.S. General George Marshall made it clear that he supported Eisenhower's concept of a broad assault across the Rhine. So dinner between the two leaders was "pleasant" but "no business" was discussed, in the words of Churchill's foreign minister, Anthony Eden.[4]

From Malta, Roosevelt, Churchill, and their parties flew to the Crimea, a seven-hour journey that began before dawn on February 3. A series of planes was required to ferry fourteen hundred officials to an airport in Saki, which was about eight hours by car from Yalta. Roosevelt's plane, dubbed the Sacred Cow, landed some time after Churchill's arrival. The president's appearance shocked the Prime Minister. In the hours since their pleasant dinner broke up, Roosevelt suddenly seemed "frail and ill." Perhaps the long journey from Virginia was only beginning to show its effects, or perhaps the sleepless flight from Malta left the president exhausted. Whatever the cause, Churchill's physician, Lord Moran, knew he was looking at a very sick man. "He has all the symptoms of hardening of the arteries on the brain in an advanced stage," Moran wrote after observing Roosevelt for several days.[5] He concluded that the president had "only a few months to live."

The Yalta conference has inspired decades of controversy and scholarly argument for decades. As the wartime alliance broke down and the Soviet Union and United States settled into a protracted cold war, American conservatives blamed Roosevelt's performance at Yalta for the Russian occupation of Eastern Europe, especially Poland. Critics charged that Roosevelt refused to confront Stalin over his territorial ambitions despite Winston Churchill's warnings of Soviet expansionism.

Other scholars point out that Roosevelt had few cards to play when the conversation at Yalta turned to Poland. The Red Army was in firm control of the country and the Soviets already had installed a communist government.[6] Forward units of the Red Army were just forty miles east of Berlin, preparing for a final assault on the German capital. The Anglo-Americans, on the other hand, still had not crossed the Rhine. The U.S. ambassador to Moscow,

Averell Harriman, noted that removing the Soviets from Poland would have required "a great deal more leverage than Roosevelt and Churchill in fact possessed."[7] The president settled on a vague statement that called for the establishment of provisional governments "broadly representative of all democratic elements in the population," leading to "free elections of governments responsive to the will of the people."[8]

The language was designed to be flexible, because Stalin continued to insist that a friendly Poland was a "question...of life and death" for the Soviets.[9] Roosevelt was more concerned about avoiding a public difference of opinion over Poland. He withdrew a demand that Allied ambassadors observe and report on the progress of free elections in Poland. In addition, he offered to support an expansion of the pro-Soviet Polish provisional government, rather than insist on the legitimacy of the pro-Western Polish government in exile. The Soviets agreed to join the war against Japan, no small gesture at a time when the Japanese were resorting to suicidal attacks in the Pacific. They also agreed on Roosevelt's plans to begin organizing a United Nations organization, starting with a multinational conference in San Francisco. Roosevelt was not entirely happy with the result, but he insisted that "it's the best I can do for Poland at this time."[10]

The conference broke up on February 11. It was an abrupt ending for such a momentous meeting, but Roosevelt had an appointment in Egypt with three monarchs—King Ibn Saud of Saudi Arabia, Egypt's King Farouk, and Haile Selassie, the emperor of Ethiopia. Churchill asked Roosevelt to remain at Yalta to continue their talks with Stalin, but FDR departed as scheduled. Roosevelt biographer Frank Freidel observed that Churchill may have been less concerned with continuing the talks with Stalin and more concerned about thwarting U.S. influence in the Middle East and east Africa.[11]

The Prime Minister joined the president in Alexandria, Egypt, after first visiting Athens. They had lunch together on February 15, giving Roosevelt a chance to tell Churchill about America's development of atomic weaponry. FDR told Churchill that the bomb would likely be tested later in the year, most likely in September. Roosevelt, Churchill thought, looked "frail."[12]

"I felt that he had a slender contact with life," Churchill later wrote. Pictures taken of the president during his long journey show him slack-jawed and thin, with dark circles under his eyes.

The president returned to America aboard the *Quincy*, his journey marked by personal sadness and irritation. Harry Hopkins, his health precarious as always, decided not to accompany his boss on the long sea voyage. He decided to fly home instead. Roosevelt, according to biographer Frank Freidel, felt that Hopkins had abandoned him, preferring "to escape the boredom" of the ship for the speed of an airplane.[13] Then, in mid-voyage, the president's longtime aide, Edwin "Pa" Watson, died. The president was upset and depressed, staring out at the sea for hours at a time. His aides, Freidel wrote, believed the president was thinking about his own mortality as he sat quietly on the ship's deck.

He roused himself enough to begin working on a summary of the Yalta conference that he planned to deliver to Congress. On March 1, 1945, less than two days after his return, Franklin Roosevelt appeared in the House of Representatives in an old wheelchair, the first time he ever gave in to his disability in such a public setting. He was wheeled down the chamber's center aisle as members of Congress let out a roar of approval. FDR's relations with Congress were not what they once were—Capitol Hill was a far less friendly place in 1945 than it was in 1935. Nevertheless, even Roosevelt's critics could not help but admire the man's courage and determination.

The applause died down as Roosevelt was brought to the front of the chamber and positioned to face his audience and the small forest of microphones spread in front of him. As a worldwide radio audience listened, Roosevelt broke precedent by acknowledging his disability, explaining to his immediate audience that he wished to remain seated while he spoke. "I hope you will pardon me for this unusual posture of sitting down during the presentation," he said, "but I know that you will realize that it makes it a lot easier for me not to have to carry about ten pounds of steel around the bottom of my legs." The chamber exploded in cheers again.

While the skin under his eyes was dark and his face was almost painfully thin, some in the audience, including Labor Secretary Frances

Perkins, thought the president looked relatively healthy. Perkins noted that his "eyes were bright" and that his "delivery and appearance were those of a man in good health."[14]

The president spoke for an hour. When he was finished, the representatives and senators saluted him with another vigorous round of applause. Roosevelt once again summoned that magical smile, acknowledging cheers that were meant not for his immediate message but for his courage in the face of so many obstacles, for his refusal to give into fear, for his assertion, even in the darkest of times, that the nation's best days lay in the future.

When the cheering stopped, Franklin Roosevelt went back to work, for there still was a war to win. The nation's enemies were reeling, but not without the ability to inflict pain and suffering in thousands of American homes. Before long, the president's doctor complained that Roosevelt was working too hard, and Roosevelt himself noticed that he couldn't taste his meals. His energy level again seemed low—during a trip to Hyde Park, the president put his wife in charge of making their pre-dinner cocktails. The president always took special delight in presiding over his beloved "children's hour," coaxing aides to take another "little sippy" of some demonic concoction. Delegating the task to Eleanor was a sure sign that all was not well.

The president traveled south, to his retreat in Warm Springs, Georgia, in late March. The news from Europe was heartening, although not unexpected. The Third U.S. Army occupied Frankfurt on March 29, while other Allied forces fanned north, west, and south to envelop German defenses east of the Elbe River. Meanwhile, the Russians were engaged in a brutal but unstoppable march towards the German capital. In the Pacific, an incredibly brutal battle for a volcanic speck of rock called Iwo Jima ended in an American victory, further clearing the way for a seemingly inevitable invasion of Japan.

Through early April, visitors to Warm Springs came away with diametrically opposite impressions of the president's health. Lucy Mercer Rutherfurd, his once and current lover, arrived in early April, improving Roosevelt's spirits. His appetite returned, he was animated at the dinner table, and his wonderful voice seemed stronger than it had been after his long journey home from Yalta. But when Treasury Secretary Henry Morgenthau saw the president for dinner on April 11, he was dismayed as he watched his boss attempt to pour cocktails. The president's hands shook so badly that he knocked over glasses. He had a hard time remembering the names of other guests. And he looked exhausted.

The president had a fairly light schedule the following day, April 12. In the morning, he worked on some correspondence while sitting in a leather chair. An artist, Elizabeth Shoumatoff, was in the room, working on a portrait of the president. Just after one o'clock in the afternoon, Roosevelt complained that he had a "terrific headache." It was, in fact, a cerebral hemorrhage. He lost consciousness, and was pronounced dead at three thirty.

With victory so close, with his dream of a United Nations nearing fruition, with the country he led for so long on the verge of conquering the forces of hatred and fear, Franklin Roosevelt was gone. Americans grieved for the man who buoyed their spirits during the hardest of times, the man who explained complex issues in simple language, the man who was raised amid affluence but who knew how to speak to working men and women.

Franklin Roosevelt was only sixty-three years old when he died, but he was an old sixty-three, an exhausted and spent sixty-three. Having rejected the sedentary life his mother envisioned for him when he was stricken with polio, he plunged into politics with a zest and enthusiasm that inspired unprecedented loyalty from millions of Americans who believed that he understood their fears, and their hopes.

He built a political coalition that dominated politics for more than a generation, a coalition whose power was invoked long after it began to fracture and fade. But even after the New Deal coalition was consigned to history, Franklin Roosevelt's words, courage, and determination remained a treasured part of the nation's folk memory. Franklin Roosevelt found the language to inspire the nation at a time of unprecedented despair and tremendous anxiety. He spoke to the nation's ideals when they were called into question, stood up for democracy when dictators were on the march, and comforted the wounded, the grieving, and the voiceless when nobody else would.

He remains one of the nation's most beloved presidents, and for good reason. For twelve years, he had a conversation with the American public, not only as a president, but as a friend.

Notes

Introduction

[1] Jean Edward Smith, *FDR*, 23.

[2] Frank Freidel, *Franklin D. Roosevelt: A Rendezvous with Destiny*, 8.

[3] Smith, *FDR*, 98.

[4] Ibid., 197.

[5] Freidel, *Franklin D. Roosevelt*, 44.

Part I

Chapter 1

[1] Papers of Edward Flynn, FDR Library, Box 20, Folder 1.

[2] Slayton, *Empire Statesman*, 366.

[3] Ibid., 368.

[4] Ibid., 366.

[5] Edward J. Flynn, *You're the Boss*, 115.

[6] Freidel, *Franklin D. Roosevelt*, 70.

[7] Ibid., 73.

Chapter 2

[1] William E. Leuchtenburg, *Franklin D. Roosevelt and the New Deal*, 39.

[2] Ibid., 39.

[3] Freidel, *Franklin D. Roosevelt*, 91.

[4] Samuel I. Rosenman, *Working With Roosevelt*, 92.

Chapter 3

[1] Freidel, *Franklin D. Roosevelt*, 94.

[2] Leuchtenburg, *Franklin D. Roosevelt and the New Deal*, 45.

[3] Freidel, *Franklin D. Roosevelt*, 96.

[4] Leuchtenburg, *Franklin D. Roosevelt and the New Deal*, 45.

[5] Ibid., 51.

[6] Lawrence W. Levine and Cornelia Levine, *The People and the President: America's Extraordinary Conversation with FDR*, 64–65.

[7] Ibid., 62.

Chapter 4

[1] Leuchtenburg, *Franklin D. Roosevelt and the New Deal*, 118.

[2] T. H. Watkins, *The Hungry Years*, 178.

[3] Leuchtenburg, *Franklin D. Roosevelt and the New Deal*, 124.

[4] Ibid., 122.

[5] Ibid., 90.

[6] Freidel, *Franklin D. Roosevelt*, 123; Herbert Hoover, *The Challenge to Liberty*, 193.

[7] Leuchtenburg, *Franklin D. Roosevelt and the New Deal*, 99.

Chapter 5

[1] Levine and Levine, *The People and the President*, 128.

[2] Ibid., 128.

[3] Leuchtenburg, *Franklin D. Roosevelt and the New Deal*, 124.

[4] Watkins, *The Hungry Years*, 259.

[5] Smith, *FDR*, 353.

[6] Levine and Levine, *The People and the President*, 129.

[7] Leuchtenburg, *Franklin D. Roosevelt and the New Deal*, 149.

[8] Smith, *FDR*, 354.

[9] Leuchtenburg, *Franklin D. Roosevelt and the New Deal*, 133.

[10] Ibid., 131.

Chapter 6

[1] Freidel, *Franklin D. Roosevelt*, 163.

[2] Ibid., 164.

[3] Smith, *FDR*, 359.

[4] Ibid., 362.

[5] Ibid., 360.

[6] Slayton, *Empire Statesman*, 389.

[7] Smith, *FDR*, 363.

[8] Rosenman, *Working With Roosevelt*, 98.

[9] Ibid., 99.

[10] Smith, *FDR*, 366–67.

Chapter 7

[1] Smith, *FDR*, 370.

[2] Rosenman, *Working With Roosevelt*, 133.

[3] Smith, *FDR*, 371.

[4] Rosenman, *Working With Roosevelt*, 133.

[5] Ibid., 133.

Part II

Chapter 8

[1] Rosenman, *Working With Roosevelt*, 142.

[2] Ibid., 143.

[3] Alan Brinkley, *The End of Reform*, 15.

[4] Leuchtenburg, *Franklin D. Roosevelt and the New Deal*, 194.

[5] Ibid., 232.

[6] Rosenman, *Working With Roosevelt*, 143.

[7] Ibid., 143.

Chapter 9

[1] Freidel, *Franklin D. Roosevelt*, 227.

[2] Smith, *FDR*, 381.

[3] Rosenman, *Working With Roosevelt*, 147.

[4] Ibid., 148.

[5] Ibid., 150.

[6] Ibid., 154.

[7] Leuchtenburg, *Franklin D. Roosevelt and the New Deal*, 234.

[8] Smith, *FDR*, 383.

[9] Rosenman, *Working With Roosevelt*, 157.

[10] Smith, *FDR*, 384.

Chapter 10

[1] Smith, *FDR*, 176.

[2] Ibid., 418.

[3] Ibid., 420.

Chapter 11

[1] Smith, *FDR*, 396; Conrad Black, *Franklin Delano Roosevelt: Champion of Freedom*, 430.

[2] Levine and Levine, *The People and the President*, 221.
[3] Ibid., 222.
[4] Ibid., 221.
[5] Alan Brinkley, *The End of Reform*, 25.
[6] Ibid., 26.
[7] Ibid., 28.
[8] Smith, *FDR*, 398.
[9] Rosenman, *Working With Roosevelt*, 173.
[10] Ibid.,174.
[11] Robert Dallek, *Franklin D. Roosevelt and American Foreign Policy*, 163.

Chapter 12
[1] Freidel, *Franklin D. Roosevelt*, 276.
[2] Ibid., 283.
[3] Rosenman, *Working With Roosevelt*, 176.

Chapter 13
[1] Smith, *FDR*, 422.
[2] Freidel, *Franklin D. Roosevelt*, 293.
[3] Smith, *FDR*, 432-33.
[4] Ibid., 429.
[5] Ibid., 434.
[6] Freidel, *Franklin D. Roosevelt*, 317.
[7] Ibid., 321.
[8] Ibid., 321.

Chapter 14
[1] Smith, *FDR*, 439.
[2] Ibid., 437.
[3] Freidel, *Franklin D. Roosevelt*, 323.
[4] Leuchtenburg, *Franklin D. Roosevelt and the New Deal*, 298.
[5] Smith, *FDR*, 441.
[6] www.winstonchurchill.org.
[7] Smith, *FDR*, 449.

Chapter 15

[1] Smith, *FDR*, 442.

[2] Flynn, *You're the Boss*, 170.

[3] Rosenman, *Working With Roosevelt*, 210.

[4] Ibid., 215.

Chapter 16

[1] James MacGregor Burns, *Roosevelt: The Soldier of Freedom*, 12.

[2] Dallek, *Franklin D. Roosevelt and American Foreign Policy*, 254.

[3] Ibid., 254.

[4] Burns, *Roosevelt: The Soldier of Freedom*, 13.

[5] Smith, *FDR*, 483.

[6] Robert Sherwood, *Roosevelt and Hopkins*. 225.

[7] Burns, *Roosevelt: The Soldier of Freedom*, 26.

[8] Ibid., 26.

[9] Rosenman, *Working With Roosevelt*, 261.

[10] Ibid., 262.

Part III

Chapter 17

[1] Levine and Levine, *The People and the President*, 340.

[2] Burns, *Roosevelt: The Soldier of Freedom*, 42.

[3] Rosenman, *Working With Roosevelt*, 264.

[4] Ibid., 264.

[5] Ibid., 263.

[6] Smith, *FDR*, 487.

[7] Rosenman, *Working With Roosevelt*, 264.

Chapter 18

[1] Robert Remini and Terry Golway, *Fellow Citizens: The Penguin Book of U.S. Presidential Inaugural Speeches*, 350.

[2] Smith, *FDR*, 489.

[3] FDR to Churchill, Feb. 9, 1941, www.winstonchurchill.org.

[4] www.winstonchurchill.org.

[5] Smith, *FDR*, 490.

[6] Levine and Levine, *The People and the President*, 342.
[7] Rosenman, *Working With Roosevelt*, 272.

Chapter 19
[1] Winston S. Churchill, *Memoirs of the Second World War*, 414.
[2] Smith, *FDR*, 492.
[3] Levine and Levine, *The People and the President*, 344.
[4] Ibid., 346.
[5] Churchill, *Memoirs of the Second World War*, 416.
[6] Smith, *FDR*, 502.
[7] Churchill, *Memoirs of the Second World War*, 491–92.
[8] Ibid., 492.

Chapter 20
[1] Freidel, *Franklin D. Roosevelt*, 377.
[2] Ibid., 379.
[3] Smith, *FDR*, 514.
[4] Ibid., 515.
[5] Ibid., 537.

Chapter 21
[1] Smith, *FDR*, 541.
[2] www.churchill-society-london.org.uk.
[3] Smith, *FDR*, 548.
[4] Rosenman, *Working With Roosevelt*, 329.
[5] Ibid., 330.
[6] Ibid., 330.
[7] Ibid., 3–4.

Chapter 22
[1] Douglas Brinkley, ed. *A Grateful Nation Remembers*, 231.
[2] Freidel, *Franklin D. Roosevelt*, 436.
[3] Rosenman, 358.

Chapter 23
[1] Freidel, *Franklin D. Roosevelt*, 456.

[2] Dallek, *Franklin D. Roosevelt and American Foreign Policy*, 364.
[3] Freidel, *Franklin D. Roosevelt*, 457.
[4] Dallek, *Franklin D. Roosevelt and American Foreign Policy*, 364.
[5] Rosenman, *Working With Roosevelt*, 364.
[6] Smith, *FDR*, 561.

Chapter 24
[1] Burns, *Roosevelt: The Soldier of Freedom*, 300–301.
[2] Ibid., 336.

Chapter 25
[1] Burns, *Roosevelt: The Soldier of Freedom*, 403.
[2] Smith, *FDR*, 586.
[3] Freidel, *Franklin D. Roosevelt*, 478.
[4] Smith, *FDR*, 587.
[5] Winston Churchill, *The Second World War: Closing the Ring*, 341.
[6] Smith, *FDR*, 587.
[7] Ibid., 588.
[8] Ibid., 593.
[9] Burns, *Roosevelt: The Soldier of Freedom*, 415.
[10] Ibid., 416.

Chapter 26
[1] Freidel, *Franklin D. Roosevelt*, 496.
[2] *New York Times*, December 18, 1943.
[3] www.presidency.ucsb.edu.
[4] *Time*, January 3, 1944.
[5] www.presidency.ucsb.edu.
[6] Rosenman, *Working With Roosevelt*, 422.
[7] Ibid, 423.
[8] Burns, *Roosevelt: The Soldier of Freedom*, 424.
[9] Rosenman, *Working With Roosevelt*, 427.

Chapter 27
[1] Robert Beitzell, *The Uneasy Alliance: America, Britain, and Russia, 1941–1943*, 33.

[2] Francis L. Loewenheim, Harold D. Langley, and Manfred Jonas, eds., *Roosevelt and Churchill: Their Secret Wartime Correspondence*, 208.
[3] Ibid., 208.
[4] Max Hastings, *Overlord*, 58.
[5] Ibid., 19.

Chapter 28
[1] Flynn, *You're the Boss*, 198.
[2] Smith, *FDR*, 620.
[3] Ibid., 623.
[4] Freidel, *Franklin D. Roosevelt*, 552.
[5] Rosenman, *Working With Roosevelt*, 478.

Chapter 29
[1] Rosenman, *Working With Roosevelt*, 317.
[2] Freidel, *Franklin D. Roosevelt*, 573.
[3] Smith, *FDR*, 628.
[4] Ibid., 628.
[5] Rosenman, *Working With Roosevelt*, 517.

Chapter 30
[1] Freidel, *Franklin D. Roosevelt*, 579.
[2] Dallek, *Franklin D. Roosevelt and American Foreign Policy*, 505.
[3] Churchill, *Memoirs of the Second World War*, 904.
[4] Freidel, *Franklin D. Roosevelt*, 580.
[5] Ibid., 581.
[6] Smith, *FDR*, 631.
[7] Ibid., 631.
[8] Freidel, *Franklin D. Roosevelt*, 589.
[9] Dallek, *Franklin D. Roosevelt and American Foreign Policy*, 513.
[10] Ibid., 515.
[11] Freidel, *Franklin D. Roosevelt*, 593.
[12] Churchill, *Memoirs of the Second World War*, 928.
[13] Freidel, *Franklin D. Roosevelt*, 595.
[14] Smith, *FDR*, 633.

Bibliography

Beitzell, Robert. *The Uneasy Alliance: America, Britain, and Russia, 1941–1943*. New York: Knopf, 1972.

Black, Conrad. *Franklin Delano Roosevelt: Champion of Freedom*. New York: Public Affairs, 2003.

Brinkley, Alan. *The End of Reform: New Deal Liberalism in Recession and War*. New York: Vintage Books, 1996.

Brinkley, Douglas, ed. *The World War II Memorial: A Grateful Nation Remembers*. Washington, DC: Smithsonian Books, 2005.

Burns, James MacGregor. *Roosevelt: The Soldier of Freedom*. New York: Harcourt Brace Jovanovich, 1970.

Churchill, Winston S. *Memoirs of the Second World War*. New York: Bonanza Books, 1978.

———. *The Second World War: Closing the Ring*. Boston: Houghton and Mifflin, 1951.

Dallek, Robert. *Franklin D. Roosevelt and American Foreign Policy, 1932–1945*. New York: Oxford University Press, 1995.

Davis, Kenneth S. *FDR: The Beckoning of Destiny, 1882–1928*. New York: G. P. Putnam's Sons, 1972.

Flynn, Edward J. *You're the Boss: The Practice of American Politics*. New York: Collier Books, 1962.

Freidel, Frank. *Franklin D. Roosevelt: A Rendezvous with Destiny*. Boston: Little, Brown, 1990.

Hastings, Max. *Overlord: D-Day and the Battle for Normandy*. New York: Simon & Schuster, 1983.

Hoover, Herbert. *The Challenge to Liberty*. New York: Charles Scribner's Sons, 1934.

Kimball, Warren F. *The Juggler*. Princeton, NJ: Princeton University Press, 1991.

Leuchtenburg, William E. *Franklin D. Roosevelt and the New Deal: 1932–1940*. New York: Harper & Row, 1963.

Levine, Lawrence W. and Cornelia Levine. *The People and the President: America's Extraordinary Conversation with FDR*. Boston: Beacon Press, 2002.

Loewenheim, Francis L, Harold D. Langley, and Manfred Jonas, eds. *Roosevelt and Churchill: Their Secret Wartime Correspondence*. New York: E. P. Dutton, 1975.

Remini, Robert and Terry Golway. *Fellow Citizens: The Penguin Book of U.S. Presidential Inaugural Addresses*. New York: Penguin Books, 2008.

Rosenman, Samuel I. *Working with Roosevelt*. New York: Harper & Brothers, 1952.

Sherwood, Robert. *Roosevelt and Hopkins: An Intimate History*. New York: Harper and Brothers, 1948.

Slayton, Robert. *Empire Statesman: The Rise and Redemption of Al Smith*. New York: Free Press, 2001.

Smith, Jean Edward. *FDR*. New York: Random House, 2007.

Watkins, T. H. *The Hungry Years: America in an Age of Crisis, 1929–1939*. New York: Henry Holt and Company, 1999.

Index

1920s, 73–74, 102, 109

A

Africa, 179, 205, 221–224
African Americans, 53, 122, 175. *see also* civil rights
Agricultural Adjustment Act, 39
Agricultural Adjustment Administration (AAA), 43, 59
agricultural prices, 38–39, 217, 218
air power, 139, 204, 226
air raids
    on England, 155–156
    on Japan, 213–241
alcohol, 37–38
Allen, Fred, 216
America, postwar, 233, 250, 254
America First Committee, 169
American Institute of Public Opinion, 109
American Legion, 234
American Liberty League, 46, 62, 72
anti-lynching legislation, 175
anti-Semitism, 70
appeasement, 131–133
arms embargo, 138
arms production, plans for, 206
"arsenal of democracy," 159–162
Asquith, Herbert, 84
Atlantic, Battle of, 185, 188
Atlantic Charter, 188–189
atomic bomb, 282

B

Bankhead, William, 95–96, 130, 149
banks
    closing of, 28–29
    crisis in, 27
    Emergency Banking Act, 29
    fireside chat regarding, 30–32
    new regulation of, 29
Baruch, Bernard, 38, 251, 252
Battle of the Atlantic, 185, 188
Battle of the Bulge, 273
Black, Conrad, 109
Black, Hugo, 120
Borah, William, 137
"brain trust," 28
Brandeis, Louis, 60, 94, 95
Bremerton, Washington, 267
Brinkley, Alan, 111
Britain. *see also* Churchill, Winston; World War II
    concern of about events in Europe, 102
    concerns about postwar intentions of, 280
    declaration of war on Germany, 134
    and defense of U.S., 173
    financial situation of, 156–159 (*see also* Lend-Lease)
    Germany's attacks on, 155–156
    Roosevelt's attempts to help, 133
    U.S. support for, 156–157
Brooke, Alan, 261
budget, federal, 36–37, 45, 111
"Building of the Ship" (Longfellow), 178–179
Bullitt, William, 133
Burns, James McGregor, 169, 224, 252
business, Roosevelt's relationship with, 59, 71
Byrnes, James, 109, 148, 249, 251, 252, 266

C

Cabinet, shakeup in, 147
Camp, Lawrence, 126
campaign speech (September 23, 1944), 269–271
Camp David, 217
Canada, 192
capitalism
    blamed for economic crisis, 32
    relationship with government, 47–48
Cardozo, Benjamin, 60
Cermak, Anton, 23
Chamberlain, Neville, 132
Chiang Kai-shek, 237, 239–240
Chicago, Illinois, speech in, 104–107
Chicago Tribune, 104

child labor, 120
China, 101, 104, 196. *see also* Chiang Kai-shek
Christmas (1943), 243–244
Churchill, Winston
  address to Congress, 205
  address to House of Commons, 140–141
  attempts to emphasize threat of Hitler, 106
  letter to Roosevelt, 156
  meetings with Roosevelt, 188–189, 237, 239–242, 268, 279
  plans for invasion of France, 258
  resentment of American criticism, 280
  Roosevelt's letter to, 178–179
  visit to White House, 205
civilian conscription, 251–253
Civilian Conservation Corps (CCC), 35, 38
civil rights, 53, 248
Civil Works Administration (CWA), 44–45, 54
Cleveland, Grover, 3
coal, 230–231
Cohen, Ben, 71, 150, 170, 171
college, for veterans, 232
Collier's magazine, 146
Committee to Defend America by Aiding the Allies, 170
Comstock, William, 28
Congress
  Roosevelt's relationship with, 37–38
  special session (1933), 36
  speech to (March 1, 1945), 284
conscription of civilian workers, 251–253
conservatism, Roosevelt's, 52, 53, 249
Conservative Party (Great Britain), 84
Constitution, U.S., 86–87, 97
Continental Army, 209, 211
Copperheads, 124
Coral Sea, Battle of, 214
Corcoran, Thomas, 64, 71, 113–114, 121, 122, 123, 126
Coughlin, Charles, 47, 61, 70, 72, 121
Crimson, 3, 5, 83
Crosby, Bing, 215
cross-Channel invasion, 238, 241–242, 244, 257–263
Cuba, 192
Cummings, Homer, 91, 92, 95
Curley, James Michael, 20
Czechoslovakia, 131, 132

D

Dallek, Robert, 222
Darlan, Jean, 222
Davis, John W., 62, 72
"Day of Infamy" speech, 200–201
D-Day, 257–263
defense, U.S.
  aid to Britain as, 161, 173
  need for, 192–193
  need to build up, 138
  need to prepare for, 172
Delano, Sara, 1, 2, 4, 6, 7, 190
Delano (family), 2
democracy
  defense of, 170–171
  need to preserve, 115
  pessimistic views of, 177–178
  Roosevelt as supporter of, 72
  and social justice, 174
  war for survival of, 66
Democratic National Convention (1924), 7–8
Democratic National Convention (1932), 9–10, 18–22
Democratic National Convention (1936), 64–66
Democratic National Convention (1940), 148–152
Democrats. *see also* Democratic National Conventions
  Copperheads, 124
  midterm elections (1934), 49, 51
  opposition to Roosevelt's reelection, 62
  presidential losses, 18
  Roosevelt's attempts to purge, 122–126
Denmark, 186
Dewey, Thomas E., 265–266
dictator, Roosevelt accused of being, 75, 121
Dieppe, France, 258
dog, Roosevelt's, 267–268, 269–271
Doolittle, James, 213–214
Douglas, William O., 266
"Dr. New Deal," 250
"Dr. Win-the-War," 250
Dunkirk evacuation, 140

E

economic stimulus package, 113
economy
  in 1930, 9
  Americans' views of, 109–110
  apparent recovery of, 109, 111–112
  crisis in banking system, 27
  government intervention in, 41, 216
  improvement in, 84
  Roosevelt Recession, 112–116
  setbacks to recovery, 112–113
  worsening of, 23
Eden, Anthony, 281
Eisenhower, Dwight, 223, 242–243, 258, 261, 280
El Alamein, 223
elections, presidential. *see* Democratic National Conventions; presidential campaigns/elections
Emergency Banking Act, 29
Emergency Relief Appropriation Act, 53. *see also* Works Progress Administration
Emerson, Ralph Waldo, 276
The End of Reform (Brinkley), 111
England. *see* Britain
Ethiopia, 129
executive branch, plans to reorganize, 119–120, 121

F

Fair Labor Standards Act, 120–121, 123
Fala, rumor about, 267–268
Fala speech, 269–271
Farley, James, 9, 18, 19, 20, 70, 145
farm prices, 38–39, 217, 218
fascism, Roosevelt's determination to eradicate, 232–234
Fay, James, 126
fear, as America's greatest enemy, 10
"fear itself" speech, 23–25
Federal Emergency Relief Administration (FERA), 44
Finland, 137, 138
fireside chats
  April 14, 1938, 113–116
  April 28, 1935, 56–57
  beginning of, 30
  December 24, 1943, 243–245
  December 29, 1940, 159–162
  February 23, 1942, 208–211
  July 28, 1943, 232–234
  June 6, 1944, 262–263
  June 24, 1938, 123–126
  March 9, 1937, 96–99
  March 12, 1933, 30–32
  May 7, 1933, 39–41
  responses to, 41
  September 3, 1939, 134–135
  September 7, 1942, 216–219
  September 11, 1941, 191–193
  September 30, 1934, 47–49
First U.S. Army Group, 260
fiscal policy, Roosevelt's, 36–37
Fish, Hamilton, 248
Flynn, Edward J., 9, 17, 19, 20, 21, 123, 126, 146, 266
four freedoms, 171–175, 233
fourth term
  campaign, 265–271
  concerns about, 266
  inaugural address, 275–277
  Inauguration Day, 274–275
  questions about, 250–251
  Roosevelt's desire for, 241
  vice presidential candidate for, 266–267
France. *see also* World War II
  Allied invasion of, 238, 241–242, 244, 257–263
  American ideas for frontal assault on, 223–224
  concern about events in Europe, 102
  declaration of war on Germany, 134
  Roosevelt's attempts to help, 133
  Roosevelt's view of, 102
  Vichy government, 221–222
Frankfurter, Felix, 60, 150, 160, 222
freedom of the seas, 156
freedoms, four, 171–172, 174–175, 233
Freidel, Frank, 28, 37, 196, 282, 283

G

Gable, Clark, 159
Garner, John, 10, 110, 145, 147
General Motors, 110
geography, 207–208, 210
George, Walter, 126
George V, 84

George VI, 133
Germany. *see also* World War II
  annexation of Austria, 130
  attack on Norway, 140
  declaration of war on U. S., 203–204
  invasion of Poland, 133
  rise of Hitler in, 36–37
  strategy for cross-Channel invasion, 260
  violation of Treaty of Versailles, 103
G.I. Bill of Rights, 232, 233–234
Gillette, Guy M., 122
Gish, Lillian, 169
gold standard, 28, 38
government
  morality in, 88
  new powers of, 39–41
  plans to reorganize executive branch, 119–120, 121
  plans to restructure Supreme Court, 87, 91–99
  relationship with capitalism, 47–48
  Roosevelt's view of role of, 39–41
Grant, Ulysses, 91
Great Britain. *see* Britain
Great Depression, 9. *see also* economy
Great War, 101, 102, 103
Greece, British intervention in, 280
Greenland, 186
Greer, U.S.S. 190–191
Grew, Joseph, 198
Groton, 3

H

Hall, Anna, 4
Harding, Warren, 6
Harriman, Averell, 282
Harvard University, Roosevelt's career at, 3–4
health insurance, national, 55
Hearst, William Randolph, 248
Heflin, Tom, 120
Hickok, Lorena, 44
High, Stanley, 62, 63, 64, 71
Hill, Lister, 120
Hitler, Adolf. *see also* Germany
  appointed chancellor, 101
  rise of, 36–37
  Roosevelt on, 182
  war experiences of, 103
Holocaust. *see also* Jews
  coverage of, 263
  Roosevelt's actions during, 192
home front, war effort on, 215–217
home purchases, 232
Hoover, Herbert, 9, 28, 46
Hoover, J. Edgar, 207
Hopkins, Harry, 44–45, 51, 53, 54, 110, 112, 113, 157, 159, 171, 178, 190, 208, 241, 258, 283
House, Edward, 52
House of Commons, 84
House of Lords, 84
Howe, Louis, 6, 7, 9, 18, 19, 62–63
Hughes, Charles Evans, 95
Hull, Cordell, 131, 145, 146, 147, 148, 192, 197
Hundred Days, 35–41
The Hungry Years (Watkins), 44

I

Ickes, Harold, 53–54, 112, 171, 186, 197, 198, 229, 248, 249
inaugural address (1941), 177
inaugural address (January, 1945), 275–277
inaugural address (January 20, 1937), 85–88
inaugural address (March 4, 1933), 23–25
Inauguration Day (1937), 86
Indochina, 196, 198
inflation
  concerns about, 111
  during World War II, 216–219
Iowa, U.S.S., 237, 239
Irish-Americans, 179
Irish Catholics, 9, 19, 20, 21
Ismay, Hastings, 258
isolationism
  accused of aiding Nazis, 160
  neutrality acts, 104 (*see also* neutrality)
  organized, 169–170
  Roosevelt on, 105–106
  Roosevelt's drift away from, 133
  Roosevelt's opposition to, 102, 210
  Roosevelt's view of, 142
  support for, 104, 129–130, 137, 139
Italy, 129, 143, 203–204, 232, 238–239, 261. *see also* Mussolini, Benito; World War II
Iwo Jima, 284

J

Japan. *see also* World War II
- aggression of, 195–196
- air raid on, 213–214
- attack on Pearl Harbor, 199
- attack on U.S. ships in China, 107
- invasion of Indochina, 196, 198
- negotiations with, 199
- Pacific offensive, 204, 214
- relations with U.S., 195
- Roosevelt's attempts to negotiate with, 197
- view of war, 104
- war with China, 101, 104, 196

Japanese Americans, internment of, 207
Jazz Age, 73–74, 102, 109
Jews
- anti-Semitism in U.S., 70
- Nazi campaign against, 132
- reluctance to defend, 191–192
- slaughter of, 263

jobs
- Civil Works Administration, 44–45
- desire for, 44
- Emergency Relief Appropriation Act, 53

Johnson, Hugh, 46, 47
Johnson, Lyndon, 249
journalists, Roosevelt's relationship with, 181
judges, federal, 93. *see also* Supreme Court

K

Knox, Frank, 147, 157, 186, 199, 200, 215
Konoye, Fumimaro, 199
Kristallnacht, 132

L

labor, 48, 59, 110, 230–231, 248–249. *see also* Wagner Act
La Follette, Robert, Jr., 133, 137
Landon, Alf, 63, 70, 75, 130
League of Nations, 102
legislation, signing of, 238
LeHand, Missy, 113–114
Lehman, Herbert, 71
Lemke, William, 63
Lend-Lease
- debate over, 179–180
- presentation to Congress, 170
- and protection of shipping, 185–187, 192–193
- public's reaction to, 159
- Roosevelt's conception of, 158–159
- speech on, 160–162
- support for, 180

Leuchtenburg, William E., 27, 43, 85, 139
Levine, Cornelia, 109, 187
Levine, Lawrence, 109, 187
Lewis, John L., 230–231
Leyte Gulf, Battle of, 273
Liberal Party, 84
Liberty League, 46, 62, 72
Libya, 179
Lilienthal, David, 230
Lincoln, Abraham, 265
Lindbergh, Anne Murrow, 177
Lindbergh, Charles, 169
Lippman, Walter, 222
Lombard, Carole, 159
loneliness, 178
Long, Huey, 21, 46, 61
Longfellow, Henry Wadsworth, 178
Ludlow, Louis, 130
Lupton, Dilworth, 249

M

MacArthur, Douglas, 22, 204, 211, 267
MacLeish, Archibald, 150, 274
Madison Square Garden, speech at, 72–75
maps, 207–208, 210
Markham, Edwin, 64
Marshall, George C., 223, 224, 241, 242, 244, 258, 281
McCormick, John, 179
McKinley, William, 4
McReynolds, James, 91
Mercer, Lucy, 6, 284
Meyer, Agnes, 28
Midway, Battle of, 214
military, U.S. *see also* defense, U.S.
- air power, 139
- need to build up, 138

minimum wage, 98, 120, 123
mobilization, 215
Moley, Raymond, 9, 32, 39, 64
Monnet, Jean, 159

Montgomery, Bernard, 280
Moore, Harry, 55
morality and government, 88
Morgenthau, Henry, 54, 111, 113, 157, 186, 217, 222, 285
Moses, Robert, 8
Moskowitz, Belle, 8
Munich conference, 132
Murphy, Charles Francis, 5, 21
Murrow, Edward R., 263
Mussolini, Benito, 104, 129–130, 141, 143, 232. *see also* Italy

N

Nation, 20, 96, 111
National Association for the Advancement of Colored People (NAACP), 230
national emergency, declaration of, 187
National Industrial Relations Act, 60
National Labor Relations Act, 59, 98, 110
National Recovery Administration (NRA), 43, 46, 47–48
National Union for Social Justice, 47
Navy Department, Roosevelt's service in, 5–6
Nazis
 Roosevelt accused of associating with, 222
 Roosevelt on, 182
 Roosevelt's condemnations of, 192
neutrality, 104, 143, 190–191. *see also* isolationism
Neutrality Act of 1939, 138, 199
New Deal
 African American support for, 175
 criticism of, 56
 endorsement of, 120
 hopes for in second term, 83
 opposition to, 46–47, 62, 120
 Roosevelt on opposition to, 74
 Roosevelt's defense of, 65, 86
 and Supreme Court, 60
 and wartime priorities, 249–251
New Republic, 83
newspapers, 207–208, 248
New York
 Roosevelt as governor of, 22
 Roosevelt nominated as governor of, 8–9
New York Times, 280
Nimitz, Chester, 214, 267
Nomura, Kichosaburo, 197
North Africa, 179, 205, 221–224
Norway, 140

O

O'Connor, John J., 120, 121, 126
Office of Economic Stabilization, 219
Office of Price Administration, 215
oil embargo, 198
Omaha Beach, 261
Operation Overlord, 238, 242. *see also* France, Allied invasion of
Oran, 239
overtime, 120

P

Paine, Thomas, 211
Panay, U.S.S., 107, 129, 130
parity, 217, 218
Patton, George S., 260
pay-envelope campaign, 70, 74–75
Peabody, Endicott, 3, 4, 274
Pearl Harbor
 attack on, 199
 "Day of Infamy" speech, 200–201
 Europe's reaction to, 203–204
Pepper, Claude, 121
Perkins, Frances, 9, 55, 275, 283–284
Philippines, 211
philosophy, 125
phony war, 137–138, 139
Poland, 133, 241, 281–282
polio, Roosevelt's contraction of, 7
Powers, John James, 214–215, 218, 219
pragmatism, 40
prayer, on D-Day, 262–263
presidency, transformation of, 35–36
presidential campaign/election (1932), 9–10, 18
presidential campaign/election (1936), 62–64, 69–75
presidential campaign/election (1940), 145–152
presidential campaign/election (1944), 265–271
primary challenges, 123, 125, 126
Progressives, 88

Prohibition, 37–38
public works, 45
Public Works Administration (PWA), 43, 112, 113

Q

quarantine speech, 104–107

R

radio, Roosevelt's use of, 29–30. *see also* fireside chats
railroads, 248
rationing, 215
Reed, Stanley, 92
reformer, Roosevelt as, 5
regulation
  of banks, 29
  Securities Exchange Commission, 45
relief, 44, 52
Republican National Convention (1940), 147
Republicans
  in 1936 campaign, 70
  in 1940 election, 147
  in midterm elections (1934), 49, 51
Revolution, American, 65, 142, 211
Richberg, Donald, 92
Rickenbacker, Eddie, 169
riots, race, 230
Roaring Twenties, 73–74, 102, 109
Roberts, Owen J., 98
Robinson, Joseph, 98–99
Rockwell, Norman, 175
Rogers, Will, 17
roll of honor, 72
Rommel, Erwin, 223, 224
Roosevelt, Anna, 268–269
Roosevelt, Eleanor, 4, 6, 7, 24, 146, 149, 175
Roosevelt, Elliot, 4
Roosevelt, Franklin D., Jr., 141
Roosevelt, Franklin Delano
  as assistant secretary of navy, 5–6
  children of, 4
  contraction of polio, 7
  death of, 285
  early life of, 2–4
  early political career of, 5
  education of, 3–4
  elected president (*see* fourth term; presidential campaigns/elections; third term)
  first appearance after polio, 7–8
  health of, 7, 266–267, 268, 274–275, 284–285
  marriage of, 4, 6
  parents of, 1
  presidential ambitions of, 17
  rehabilitation of after polio, 7
Roosevelt, James, 1, 2, 3
Roosevelt, Sara Delano, 1, 2, 4, 6, 7, 190
Roosevelt, Theodore, 3, 4, 41, 88
Roosevelt (family), prosperity of, 1–2
Roosevelt Longworth, Alice, 4, 169
Roosevelt Recession, 112–116
Rosenman, Samuel, 23, 24, 30, 62, 63, 64, 70, 71, 75, 83, 85, 92–93, 95, 107, 113–114, 122, 146–148, 150, 159, 170, 171, 180, 190, 200, 207, 208, 217, 222, 237–238, 251, 252, 268–269, 274, 276
rubber, 215
Russia. *see* Soviet Union

S

Saturday Evening Post, 175
Schechter decision, 60
Seabury, Samuel, 21
Second Hundred Days, 60–61
Securities Exchange Act of 1934, 45
Securities Exchange Commission, 45
security, national. *see* defense, U.S.
segregation, 53, 175
Shangri-La, 217, 221
"Share our Wealth," 46
Sherwood, Robert, 159, 170, 171, 172, 200, 208, 251, 274
shipping, 185, 190
Short, Dewey, 120
Shoumatoff, Elizabeth, 285
Sloan, Alfred, 57
Smith, Alfred E., 5, 7–8, 9, 19–20, 41, 46, 62, 72, 139
Smith, Ellison, 126
Smith, Howard, 126
Smith, Jean Edward, 64, 69, 109, 141
social insurance, 54
social justice, 171, 174. *see also* civil rights; four freedoms

Social Security, 45, 54–55, 56–57, 70, 74–75, 98
Social Security Act of 1935, 54–55, 98
South, Roosevelt's criticism of, 122
Southern Democrats, 120–121, 122–126, 130, 248
Soviet Union. *see also* Stalin, Joseph
    concerns about postwar intentions of, 281
    invasion of Finland, 137, 138
    siege of Stalingrad, 224
    support for, 188
Spain, 101
speeches
    in Bremerton, Washington, 267
    campaign speech (September 23, 1944), 269–271
    in Charlottesville, Virginia, 141–143
    in Chicago, Illinois, 104–107
    "Day of Infamy" speech, 200–201
    at Democratic National Convention (1936), 64–66
    at Democratic National Convention (1940), 150–152
    Fala speech, 269–271
    "fear itself" speech, 23–25
    fireside chat (April 14, 1938), 113–116
    fireside chat (April 28, 1935), 56–57
    fireside chat (December 24, 1943), 243–245
    fireside chat (December 29, 1940), 159–162
    fireside chat (February 23, 1942), 208–211
    fireside chat (July 28, 1943), 232–234
    fireside chat (June 6, 1944), 262–263
    fireside chat (June 24, 1938), 123–126
    fireside chat (March 9, 1937), 96–99
    fireside chat (March 12, 1933), 30–32
    fireside chat (May 7, 1933), 39–41
    fireside chat (September 3, 1939), 134–135
    fireside chat (September 7, 1942), 216–219
    fireside chat (September 11, 1941), 191–193
    fireside chat (September 30, 1934), 47–49
    inaugural address (1941), 177
    inaugural address (January, 1945), 275–277
    inaugural address (January 20, 1937), 85–88
    inaugural address (March 4, 1933), 23–25
    in Madison Square Garden (October 31, 1936), 72–75
    quarantine speech, 104–107
    Roosevelt's writing of, 85
    speech to Congress (March 1, 1945), 284
    speech to White House Correspondents Association, 181–183
    stab-in-the-back speech, 141–143
    State of the Union Address (1936), 61–62
    State of the Union Address (1942), 206
    State of the Union Address (January 6, 1941), 172–174
    State of the Union Address (January 7, 1943), 225–227
    State of the Union Address (January 11, 1944), 251–254
spending, government, 36–37, 110–111
St. Louis, SS, 191–192
stab-in-the-back speech, 141–143
Stalin, Joseph, 188, 237, 239–242, 279
Stalingrad, 224
State of the Union Address (1936), 61–62
State of the Union Address (January 6, 1941), 172–174
State of the Union Address (January 7, 1943), 225–227
State of the Union Address (January 11, 1944), 251–254
State of the Union Address (January 1942), 206
Stettinius, Edward, 279
Stimson, Henry, 147, 186, 199, 251
Stone, Harlan, 94
strikes, 48, 110, 230–231, 248
successors to Roosevelt, possible, 147
Sudentenland, 131
Summers, Hatton, 96
Supreme Court, U.S.
    as barrier to change, 84
    criticism of, 85

and dinner at White House, 93–95
on National Industrial Relations Act, 60
plans to restructure, 87, 91–99
upholding of New Deal legislation, 98
surrender, unconditional, 227

T
Tabor, Walter C., 41
Tammany Hall, 5, 9
taxes, during World War II, 216–217, 219
teachers, 45
Tehran, conference in, 240–242
Tennessee Valley Authority, 35, 38, 230
term, fourth. *see* fourth term
term, third. *see* third term
third term
acceptance speech, 150–152
inauguration, 177
Roosevelt's consideration of, 139–140
Roosevelt's desire for, 148
Roosevelt's lack of comment on, 146
Thomas, Norman, 20
Thoreau, Henry David, 24
tires, 215
Tojo, Hideki, 196, 199
Tokyo, Japan, 213
Townsend, Francis Everett, 63
trains, Roosevelt's enjoyment of, 69
Treaty of Versailles, 103
Truman, Harry S, 266
Tugwell, Rexford, 53
Twentieth Amendment, 86
Tydings, Millard, 126, 139

U
unemployment, 43–44. *see also* relief
unemployment insurance, 57
Union Party, 63, 70
unions. *see* labor
United Mine Workers, 230–231
United States, postwar, 233, 250, 254
U.S.S.R. *see* Soviet Union

V
veterans
American Legion, 234
G.I. Bill of Rights, 232, 233–234
march on National Mall, 22, 36
vice presidency
nominee for (1940), 148–150
nominee for (1944), 266–267
Roosevelt nominated for, 6
Victor Emmanuel III, 232
Virginia, University of, 141

W
Wagner, Robert, 5, 21, 71, 121
Wagner Act, 59, 98, 110
Walker, James, 9, 20, 22
Wallace, Henry, 38, 145, 148, 149, 229, 274–275
Walsh, Frank, 21
war
Hitler's experiences of, 103
and mechanization, 142
modern weapons of, 101, 209
power to declare, 130
Roosevelt's view of, 102, 103, 105
war effort, 215–217
War Industries Board, 47
War Mobilization Board, 252
Warm Springs, Georgia, 284
warplanes, production of, 132
war powers, 217
war production
plans for, 206
and profit, 251, 253
warplanes, 132
War Production Board, 215, 216
Warren, Lindsay, 96
Washington, George, 208, 209
Watkins, T. H., 44
Watson, Edwin, 149, 240, 260, 283
The Wave of the Future (Lindbergh), 177
Wearin, Otha, 122
Wheeler, Burton, 98, 180
White, Stanford, 2
White, William Allen, 138, 170
White House Correspondents Association, speech to, 181–183
Wilcox, J. Mark, 121
Willkie, Wendell, 147, 151, 169, 178–179, 180
Wilson, Edith, 275
Wilson, Hugh, 132
Wilson, Woodrow, 5, 18, 59, 88, 102
Wise, Stephen, 263

Wood, Robert, 169
Woodin, William, 111
work. *see* jobs
workers, conscription of, 251–253
Works Progress Administration (WPA), 54, 57, 112, 113
workweek, 120
World War I, 101, 102, 103
World War II. *see also* Britain; France; Germany; Italy; Japan
  air power in, 226
  arguments over U.S.'s role in, 139
  concerns about Britain's postwar intentions, 280
  concerns about Soviet Union's postwar intentions, 281
  D-Day, 257–263
  Dunkirk evacuation, 140
  expansion of Asian conflict, 196–197, 198
  France, Allied invasion of, 238, 241–242, 244, 257–263
  internment of Japanese Americans, 207
  opposition to U.S. entry into, 186 (*see also* isolationism; neutrality)
  phony war, 137–138, 139
  postwar planning, 268
  Roosevelt's attempts to avert, 131–132
  Roosevelt's attempts to stay out of, 134–135
  Roosevelt's understanding of threat of, 137–138
  and Roosevelt's vision for postwar America, 233, 250, 254
  support for American entry into, 170
  U.S. declaration of war, 201
  U.S. entry into, 204
  U.S.'s need to take stance on, 152
  Yalta conference, 281–282

Y

Yalta conference, 281–282
Yamamoto, Isoroku, 197–198, 214

Z

Zangara, Guiseppe, 23

Credits

Photos have been obtained with the kind assistance of the Franklin D. Roosevelt Presidential Library and Museum (located in Hyde Park, NY), the National Archives, and the Library of Congress. All photos are in the public domain.

The full version of most of the speeches selected can be accessed through the University of Virginia's Miller Center of Public Affairs website, http://www.millercenter.org.

Audio segments have been edited for time and content. In the interest of clarity and accuracy, all edits within each speech are made apparent by the fading out of the audio, then the fading in of the next segment. While we have attempted to achieve the best possible quality on this archival material, some audio quality is the result of source limitations. Audio denoising by Christian Pawola at Music & Sound Company, DeKalb, Illinois.

For a wealth of information about Franklin Roosevelt, visit the website of the Franklin D. Roosevelt Presidential Library and Museum at http://www.fdrlibrary.marist.edu.

About Sourcebooks MediaFusion

Launched with the 1998 *New York Times* bestseller *We Interrupt This Broadcast* and formally founded in 2000, Sourcebooks MediaFusion is the nation's leading publisher of mixed-media books. This revolutionary imprint is dedicated to creating original content—be it audio, video, CD-ROM, or Web—that is fully integrated with the books we create. The result, we hope, is a new, richer, eye-opening, thrilling experience with books for our readers. Our experiential books have become both bestsellers and classics in their subjects, including poetry (*Poetry Speaks Expanded*), children's books (*Hip Hop Speaks to Children*), history (*Ronald Reagan's America*), sports (*Harry Caray: Voice of the Fans*), the plays of William Shakespeare, and more. See what's new from us at www.sourcebooks.com.

Acknowledgments

This is my third book for Sourcebooks and its executive editor, Hillel Black. The relationship gets even better with age. My thanks to Hillel for his sharp eye and wisdom. Thanks, also, to Jennifer Crosby, Stephen O'Rear, Kelly Bale, and Heather Moore.

The staff at the Franklin D. Roosevelt Library in Hyde Park, NY, particularly Bob Clark, could not have been more helpful. They went out of their way to assist me in this project.

As always, my thanks to John Wright, Eileen Duggan, and Kate and Conor Golway.

About the Author

© William Tomlin

Terry Golway is curator of the John Kean Center for American History at Kean University in Union, New Jersey. This is his third book on presidential speeches, along with *Ronald Reagan's America* and *Let Every Nation Know*. He is also the author of *Washington's General*, a biography of Nathanael Greene, and writes for the *New York Times*, *American Heritage*, and the *New York Observer*. He lives in Maplewood, New Jersey.